London's Grand Guignol
and the Theatre of Horror

A companion to *Grand-Guignol—The French Theatre of Horror*

"When Jos... evy staged the world première of *The Old Women* by the 'Prince Terror' André de Lorde in 1921 as part of the fourth series of (d Guignol at the Little Theatre, he commissioned Aubrey Ha: ond to create a publicity poster in a Beardsley style. So harrowin, as Hammond's poster that it was banned by London Underground. Hammond also produced a publicity postcard for the theatre, a ca oon drawing of a horrified audience, literally running screaming from the auditorium. As with the original Théâtre du Grand-Guig ol in Paris, stories circulated of audience members fainting or ing physically sick before the on-stage horrors they witnessed. L ndon's Grand Guignol was a sensation and audiences ventured there at their own risk to share in the thrills and chills on offer."

from the first chapter of
London's Grand Guignol and the Theatre of Horror

Richard J. Ha d and **Michael Wilson** are Professors of Drama, both at the Cardiff School of Creative and Cultural Industries at the University of Glamorgan. Together they have delivered workshops on Grand Guignol, and presented Grand Guignol performances at universities, international conferences and at the Edinburgh Fringe Festival.

Also by Richard J. Hand and Michael Wilson: *Grand-Guignol— The French Theatre of Horror* (University of Exeter Press, 2002)

Exeter Performance Studies

Series editors: Peter Thomson, Professor of Drama at the University of Exeter; Graham Ley, Professor of Drama and Theory at the University of Exeter; Steve Nicholson, Reader in Twentieth-Century Drama at the University of Sheffield.

From Mimesis to Interculturalism: Readings of Theatrical Theory Before and After 'Modernism'
Graham Ley (1999)

British Theatre and the Red Peril: The Portrayal of Communism 1917–1945
Steve Nicholson (1999)

On Actors and Acting
Peter Thomson (2000)

Grand-Guignol: The French Theatre of Horror
Richard J. Hand and Michael Wilson (2002)

The Censorship of British Drama 1900–1968: Volume One 1900–1932
Steve Nicholson (2003)

The Censorship of British Drama 1900–1968: Volume Two 1933–1952
Steve Nicholson (2005)

Freedom's Pioneer: John McGrath's Work in Theatre, Film and Television
edited by David Bradby and Susanna Capon (2005)

John McGrath: Plays for England
selected and introduced by Nadine Holdsworth (2005)

Theatre Workshop: Joan Littlewood and the Making of Modern British Theatre
Robert Leach (2006)

Making Theatre in Northern Ireland: Through and Beyond the Troubles
Tom Maguire (2006)

"In Comes I": Performance, Memory and Landscape
Mike Pearson (2006)

London's Grand Guignol
and the Theatre of Horror

Richard J. Hand
and
Michael Wilson

UNIVERSITY
of
EXETER
PRESS

First published in 2007 by
University of Exeter Press
Reed Hall, Streatham Drive
Exeter EX4 4QR
UK
www.exeterpress.co.uk
Printed digitally since 2011

British Library Cataloguing in Publication Data
A catalogue record for this book is available
from the British Library.

Paperback ISBN 978 0 85989 792 1
Hardback ISBN 978 0 85989 789 1

Typeset in Sabon, 10 on 12
by Carnegie Book Production, Lancaster
Printed by Edwards Brothers
in Plymouth(UK) and Chicago(USA)

To Shara, Danya and Jimahl (RJH)

To Phillip, Gemma and Hannah (MW)

The Grand Guignol Annual Review
1921

Frontispiece: Aubrey Hammond: London's Grand Guignol, 1921

1

Contents

Illustrations

Acknowledgements

The authors would like to express their gratitude to the following individuals and organisations who have offered support of one sort or another during the preparation of this book:

The British Academy and the Society for Theatre Research for their generous financial support.

University of Exeter Press: Simon Baker and all the team; Peter Thomson, Graham Ley and Steve Nicholson for painstakingly reviewing early drafts of the manuscript.

University of Glamorgan: Colleagues in the Department of Drama and Music for their interest in and support of this continuing project; students from the Division of Drama who have persisted in asking searching questions and helped bring some of this research work to life in the drama studio.

Libraries: Staff at the British Library (St. Pancras and Colindale) and the National Library of Wales for their help in tracking down our obscure requests.

Plays: Alan Brodie Representation and the Noël Coward Estate for permission to reprint *The Better Half*; Samuel French Ltd for permission to reprint *The Nutcracker Suite*; David Higham Associates for permission to reprint *The Sisters' Tragedy*.

San Francisco: Russell Blackwood and Thrillpeddlers; Brad Rosenstein and the San Francisco Performing Arts Library and Museum, all for hospitality and unfailingly good-humoured conversations.

Mick Eaton for his enthusiasm and generosity especially in relation to Fred Paul's Grand Guignol films.

And, of course, to both our families for their unconditional love and support.

SECTION 1

1

A History of London's Grand Guignol

When José Levy staged the world première of *The Old Women* by the 'Prince of Terror' André de Lorde in 1921 as part of the fourth series of Grand Guignol[1] plays at the Little Theatre, he commissioned Aubrey Hammond to create a publicity poster in a Beardsley style, much as he had done for all of Levy's Grand Guignol seasons. So harrowing was Hammond's poster that it was banned by London Underground.

Hammond had also produced a publicity postcard for the theatre, a cartoon drawing of a horrified audience, literally running screaming from the auditorium. As with the original Théâtre du Grand Guignol in the rue Chaptal in Paris, the theatre that Levy was attempting to replicate in London, stories circulated of audience members fainting or being physically sick before the on-stage horrors they witnessed. London's Grand Guignol was a sensation and audiences ventured there at their own risk to share in the thrills and chills on offer.

And yet also, as with the Parisian Grand Guignol, many of those stories were exaggerated for their own ends, to create the myth of a theatre heavily charged with eroticism and where the blood flowed freely. In reality, London's Grand Guignol was a much more genteel, indeed British affair, checked on the one hand by the Lord Chamberlain, the public censor, and on the other hand by the tastes of the London theatre-going public. Sex was suggested, rather than explicit, and where disembowellings and throat-slittings were nightly events on the stage of the Parisian Grand Guignol, at the Little Theatre a poisoning or a strangulation was generally preferable.

Levy's project was a genuine success and, as tame as some of the plays may seem today, they were disturbing enough to their audience to scandalize certain sections of the press and to severely test the limits and the patience

---

[1]   In our previous book, *Grand-Guignol: French Theatre of Horror* (University of Exeter Press, 2002), we favoured the hyphenated form, after advice from Professor Claude Schumacher, as both hyphenated and non-hyphenated forms were used in France. London's Grand Guignol – the subject of this present study – was, however, only ever referred to in its non-hyphenated form.

of the Lord Chamberlain. What Levy had on his side were some of the finest actors on the English stage at the time, in the shape of Sybil Thorndike and Lewis Casson, and a team of extremely able writers, such as Eliot Crawshay-Williams, Sewell Collins, H.F. Maltby and Noël Coward. In addition he had the *Zeitgeist* on his side, a post-war public that was eager for thrills and excitement – the artificial, high theatricality of on-stage horror, rather than the devastating reality of the horror that had so recently taken place on the battlefields. In 1920 Levy's dream of a Grand Guignol theatre with its own company based in the centre of London, was an idea whose time had come.

The Political Context of Post-War Britain

When the sound of the guns ceased and the dust settled over the bloody fields of northern France in late 1918, a Europe was revealed that had changed so fundamentally, and was continuing to change, that the optimistic days of the warm summer of 1914 must have seemed an age away. In Russia the Czar had been overthrown and the fledgling Soviet Union established by the Bolsheviks under the leadership of Vladimir Lenin. In the defeated Germany, stripped of its colonies and vast sections of its territories at home, Kaiser Wilhelm II had abdicated and been sent into exile while the country, economically devastated, descended into anarchy and revolution. The centuries-old Austro-Hungarian Empire was disassembled and the United States of America, for the first time, became a major player and powerbroker on the stage of European politics.

In Britain too the changes were no less significant. Whilst on the surface little may have seemed to be different – broadly speaking society was 'made up of people whose habits and assumptions had been formed in the late-Victorian and Edwardian era' (Stevenson, 1984, 17) – many of those assumptions were being challenged and overturned. Principally the notion of Great Britain as the greatest of all imperial powers, which had been 'almost part of the Edwardian psyche' (Stevenson, 1984, 48) was beginning to be questioned and the gradual, but inevitable, disintegration of the British Empire, which concluded in the years after the Second World War, had already begun with moves towards the settlement of the Irish question through partition. The historian E.H. Carr talks of the Great War signalling the end of a 'golden age of continuously expanding territories and markets, of a world policed by the self-assured and not too onerous British hegemony [...] and that what was right could not be morally wrong' (quoted in Barker, 2000, 7).

Whilst at its heart Britain remained a society that was strictly and clearly defined by its distinction between the social classes, the spirit of reform, if not revolution, was in the air. As Clive Barker says, the 'aristocracy fragmented and declined, the middle classes trembled at close scrutiny and the working classes were exultant (but still oppressed)' (Barker, 2000, 6). Trade Union membership, which had already been on the increase in the years leading up to the outbreak of war, had mushroomed from 2.5 million in 1910 to 8.3 million by 1920, 1.25 million of whom were women (Clarke, 2004, 97; Stevenson, 1984, 195). The theatre too began to organize itself with the formation of the Actors' Association in 1919 (the same year as the first British Theatre Conference in Stratford), which ultimately led to the formation of the British Actors' Equity Association (Equity) ten years later. An ambitious programme of social housing building and slum clearance had begun with the passing of the Addison Act by Lloyd George's post-war Government in 1919, which 'established housing as a national responsibility and proved the forerunner of later legislation' (Stevenson, 1984, 222). Although the council house building programme to create 'homes for heroes' was soon to become a victim of the cutbacks, as the economy hit serious difficulties and 'social reform became a dispensable luxury which the country could no longer afford', by the time the central government subsidies were withdrawn 170,000 council houses had already been built (Clarke, 2004, 108).

It was, though, the issue of unemployment, above all others, that dominated the political landscape in Britain during the years immediately following the armistice, as the numbers of those out of work gradually grew to more than two million by the end of 1921 (Stevenson, 1984, 266). The opening years of the 1920s were characterized by a series of demonstrations and hunger marches (most notably the Jarrow March), which often ended in violent confrontations with the police:

> The first big demonstration occurred in October 1920, when crowds
> of unemployed men, converging on Whitehall to support a deputation
> of Labour mayors seeking to see Lloyd George, were charged upon by
> the police, mounted and on foot, and beaten about by police batons.
> (Mowat, 1955, 126)

In addition one must also not forget the impact of the trauma of the war, which had cost the lives of millions, on the national psyche. The notorious 'Pals' regiments, whereby soldiers from the same towns and villages were sent out to fight shoulder to shoulder, had led to the young male populations of some communities (in particular rural villages) being practically wiped out. It was, as Peter Clarke points out, not simply 'the demographic but the human impact of the losses that burned so deep'. Never before had a war resulted in such horrific casualties and not only the numbers of dead, but also the stories of the traumatized survivors were a constant reminder of 'the lost generation' which became 'an emotional and psychological reality which made a lifelong impact on its surviving members' (Clarke, 2004, 81).

A Selective Overview of British Theatre During the War and in the Post-War Period[2]

The years leading up to the First World War had seen in British theatre the continuation of realist drama. The plays produced in this period include works of broad social consciousness in realist mode such as John Galsworthy's *Strife* (1909) and *Justice* (1910), Harley Granville Barker's *The Madras House* (1910) and Stanley Houghton's *Hindle Wakes* (1912). Similarly realist and yet often with a more precise political consciousness, George Bernard Shaw continued to be a prolific playwright with, among numerous other works, *Androcles and the Lion* (1912), *Overruled* (1912), *Pygmalion* (1913) and *Misalliance* (1914). The arrival of the war would slow the seemingly indefatigable Shaw and it was not until *Heartbreak House* (1919) – appropriately enough a Chekhovian reflection on the world that had come to an end in 1914 – that the stage would see a new work by the playwright. Although 'serious' drama may have stepped back from the limelight during the war years, the theatre in London continued with a focused and urgent purpose: the war effort. For example, in November 1914, Harley Granville Barker – an important actor much associated with Shaw's work as well as a significant playwright in his own right – produced selected scenes from Thomas Hardy's epic Napoleonic war play *The Dynasts* at the Kingsway Theatre which were, in Hardy's words, 'staged mainly for patriotic and practical object[ive]s' (Hardy, 1985, 65). As well as jingoistic productions, there was also a perceived need for collective entertainment and escapism: the rallying or sentimental songs in music hall flourished as did its recipe of comic diversion. Elsewhere on the popular stage, examples of frivolous and escapist musical theatre thrived, such as J. Harry Benrimo and George C. Hazleton's *The Yellow Jacket* – a hugely successful American musical 'in the Chinese manner' – which was written in 1912 and was continuing to do the international rounds as late as 1922.

In the immediate aftermath to the war, despite the soul-searching retrospection of the aforementioned *Heartbreak House*, there was still a continuation of pre-war melodrama. Marie Löhr appeared as the Duke of Reichstadt in the première of Louis N. Parker's translation of Edmond Rostand's *L'Aiglon* (1900) at the Globe Theatre in November 1918 with a revival the following summer. The role had been made legendary by Sarah Bernhardt in the original French production. Bernhardt and her French company were, of course, well known to London audiences especially in the early years of the twentieth century, as was Eleanora Duse, 'Italy's Sarah

---

2   What follows is a general overview to provide a sense of the theatrical context out of which London's Grand Guignol emerges. For a more comprehensive survey of British theatre at this time, the reader would be advised to refer to Barker and Gale (2000).

Bernhardt'. Duse and Bernhardt's appearances in touring productions of the late nineteenth-century melodramas of playwrights such as Rostand and Victorien Sardou were an important example of the British audience's experience of European drama in the pre-war period. Löhr's appearance in *L'Aiglon* in 1918 and 1919 and in an adaptation of Sardou's *Fedora* (1882) at the Globe Theatre in 1920–21, as well as Ethel Irving's performance in Sardou's *La Tosca* (1887) at the Aldwych Theatre in 1920, demonstrate how some British theatre still actively drew on a pre-war melodramatic aesthetic. In addition, it is worth mentioning that the London audience was also very familiar with European opera: this is especially clear when one considers that Puccini's *Tosca* (1900) – an adaptation of Sardou's play – had been staged in London in some twenty-five productions between 1900 and 1919, including five productions during 1918–19 alone. With this in mind, it is clear how radical Levy's 'Continental' form of Grand Guignol was: the fact that the experiment was a popular success is not just more impressive but accountable. The ground-breaking experiment of the London Grand Guignol reveals that, despite the hangovers of melodrama, times were rapidly changing.

Given the horrors of the war and the resulting trauma, one might reasonably expect that a distaste for horror and the macabre would find expression in the cultural tastes of the 1920s, especially in France which had witnessed so much of the worst trench warfare and had become the graveyard of so many young men. Nevertheless this was a period that became a golden age for one of Paris's most celebrated and unique tourist attractions: the Grand Guignol, Montmartre's theatre of horror and eroticism. All through the 1920s the Grand Guignol, supported by a strong team of writers, directors, technicians and actors, went from strength to strength.

In Britain too theatre audiences were demanding their share of thrills. This was the age when the hugely successful Bulldog Drummond and the plays of Edgar Wallace were about to be launched on the theatre-going public. So what at first glance might seem to have been rather unfavourable circumstances for launching a Grand Guignol experiment in London, was in fact very much in tune with the mood of the times.

The traditional scholarly view of British theatre in the inter-war period in general is that it was a period of stagnation. Whilst Europe was witnessing the experiments of Brecht, Piscator, Meyerhold, Artaud and the Dadaists, Eugene O' Neill was staging his expressionist experiments in America and Ireland had Sean O'Casey causing controversy and even riots at the Abbey Theatre in Dublin, Britain had the comparatively conventional playwriting of Noël Coward, Somerset Maugham, J.B. Priestley and Terence Rattigan. This view of a theatre that was frivolous and inconsequential has begun to be revised more recently, as new scholarship reveals it to have been more complex and sophisticated than previously assumed (see Barker and Gale, 2000).

Even contemporary writers, critics and men of the theatre began to despair over the state of the theatre in Britain. Writing in 1935, the Italian scholar Camillo Pellizzi claimed that since the First World War

> Half the theatres in London are permanently given over to musical comedy, variety and revue, in fact, to spectacles which have nothing to do with Art with a capital A. [...] [T]he present day is characterized by the fact that even the best geniuses of the theatre dedicate themselves to this form of production, or to constructing a type of spectacle which has a fundamental lack of *seriousness*. (Pellizzi, 1935, 288)

The critic J.C. Trewin is almost a lone voice in defending the theatre of the 1920s as merely reflecting 'this age of relaxed conventions' (Trewin, 1958, 9), but even he had to admit that it 'was not yet a time for experiment' (24), as everyone seemed to be caught up in 'the gay froth of existence' (32). William Poel blamed the sorry state of the British theatre on its being governed by the commercial interests of City investors, rather than those who knew about theatre:

> The play-producing centre for the British Empire is London, and the men who control the output walk the pavement of Threadneedle Street.
>   All the methods by which the theatres thrive on the continent are ignored by London managers because they are interested only in one class of play, the one which is likely to appeal to the undiscriminating in all parts of the English-speaking world. (Poel, 1920, 10)

Its fiercest critic was probably the critic, playwright and former manager of the Abbey Theatre in Dublin, St. John Ervine. Ervine was on the one hand an arch conservative and bigot, whilst also at times advocating pacifism, and being a radical exponent of theatrical democracy. In a series of lectures delivered at the University of Liverpool in 1923, Ervine admitted that the 'English theatre is, at the moment under a cloud' (Ervine, 1924, 15), but declared, in contradiction to Poel, that it was still in a better state than the 'intellectually and spiritually bankrupt' French theatre (113) and the 'largely neurotic' theatre of the German Expressionists (36).

For Ervine, the state of the British Theatre was a reflection of a society that was enfeebled, physically, morally and spiritually, by the ravages of war and that this is reflected in the frivolity of the age:

> We are an exhausted people, sick from a great effusion of blood, and we will not create a great drama or a great anything else until we have recovered our health. (Ervine, 1924, 123)

Ervine also asserts:

> When a nation is strongest, physically and spiritually, its people delight most in tragedy. When a nation is weakest, physically and spiritually, its people will not listen to tragedy, but demand what is called light entertainment: comic plays, spectacle pieces, trivial shows. (Ervine, 1920, 96–97)

But in spite of these cries of despair, in many ways British theatre remained in a healthy state during the 1920s, at least in terms of audience numbers, in spite of the unabated growth in popularity of motion pictures. The number of actors in the profession increased at a rate of around twenty per cent per year (Barker, 2000, 17) and in a theatre 'which allowed for an almost purely profit-making agenda' (8–9) there even became a shortage of theatres in London, as speculators fought to establish themselves in the West End. The theatre was a place where big money could be – and was – made.

The Rise of the Thriller

One of the most popular of dramatic forms to emerge during the twenties was the thriller play which achieved a certain respectability through the involvement of one of the last great actor-managers (a breed that became increasingly rare during the twenties),[3] Sir Gerald du Maurier (son of George, the author of the hugely successful novel *Trilby*, and father of novelist Daphne). Du Maurier made his name as a respectable actor-manager at Wyndham's Theatre in London in the years before the war, his most popular role being that of Raffles the gentleman-thief. Du Maurier no doubt saw himself as the true inheritor of the Irving tradition, taking on both serious and popular roles with equal relish and was himself rewarded with a knighthood in 1922. It was with the creation of Bulldog Drummond, a character who became central to the whole thriller genre, in 1921 that he made arguably his greatest contribution to the popular theatre of the 1920s. The play was an adaptation of H.C. McNeile's enormously successful 1920 novel and it is interesting that du Maurier caused a huge and genre defining impact, not by turning, as Levy did, to European popular theatre but to the dramatisation of British popular fiction. As James Harding says:

---

[3]   St. John Ervine cites the decline of the actor-manager as being one of the reasons for declining standards in the theatre generally in the 1920s, stating that 'before the outbreak of the War, the actor-managers were flourishing, and the theatre was in a very healthy state. At the end of the War, the actor-managerial system was wrecked, and the actor-managers were in their graves.' (Ervine, 1933, 147–48)

> With *Bull-Dog Drummond*, [Du Maurier] plunged right into the
> spirit of the 1920s and caught the essence of an age that already
> had recognizable characteristics. Here were crude thrills, spectacular
> villainy, titillating horror and sadism unashamed. (Harding, 1989,
> 112)

In his essay on the inter-war thriller, John Stokes argues that the genre grew
naturally out of the aftermath of the war, as one of the consequences of
slaughter on such a grand scale was the realization that, under a certain set
of circumstances, everybody was capable of extreme acts of brutality – what
Stokes calls 'the post-war idea of the murderer as Everyman' (Stokes, 2000,
57). The fascination with stage violence, Stokes claims, is a recurring feature
of post-war drama and is part of a coming to terms with the collective
trauma of the war:

> Contrasts and comparisons among individual acts of aggression and
> the enormity of war crimes, as well as between the self-interest of
> the thug and the high-minded patriotism of the soldier, are made
> continually in the drama of the 1920s. (Stokes, 2000, 47–48)

The portrayal of criminal violence on the stage distinguishes it from the
patriotic violence of war and therefore reminds us of our collective guilt
and responsibility, whilst simultaneously absolving us of it. The Bulldog
Drummond plays, in particular, would seem to support such a view, as in
his transformation from upper-class criminal (Raffles) to upper-class crime-
solver (Bulldog Drummond). Du Maurier's character may still not shirk
from (and indeed is driven by) violence, it is a violence that 'is still expressed
within an atmosphere of camaraderie where male values are held to have
been betrayed rather than undermined by the war' (Stokes, 2000, 46).

Camillo Pellizzi, on the other hand, claims that whilst the popularity of
thrillers was unique to the 1920s, the form itself was, in fact, nothing new,
but rather offered 'contemporary versions of theatrical devices which have
existed ever since the drama began' (Pellizzi, 1935, 280). Instead Pellizzi
explains, rather unconvincingly, the phenomenon as something inherent to
the Anglo-Saxon psyche:

> In the damp and capricious climate of England, the thrill is a need
> which is universally felt, and is hence an institution – many things
> which some people complain of (with a certain degree of truth) in
> the moral attitude and inconsistent humour of the English can be
> explained by the necessity of reacting with the nerves against the
> heaviness and boredom of the environment. (Pellizzi, 1935, 278)

In addition, Pellizzi argues that the popularity of the thriller was also due to the public having no other pressing concerns which they required their dramatists to deal with, a claim which, given the high rates of unemployment, the General Strike of 1926, hyper-inflation and the rise of Fascism in parts of Europe, and the Wall Street Crash in 1928 (to name but a few issues), hardly seems credible.

Given the profusion of thrillers on the British stage in the 1920s, it would be easy to include Grand Guignol as part of this same genre, but it would be a mistake to do so. Certainly the forms are closely related in many ways and both were in tune with the 1920s, prospering with the fashion for thrills, but whilst the thriller spawned a whole series of sub-genres, the Grand Guignol was not one of them. The similarities and differences between the two forms are considered in more detail in the final chapter of this book. In the meantime, London's Grand Guignol has a unique story to tell.

José Levy and the Establishment of London's Grand Guignol

Little is known of the early life of José Levy, the founder of London's Grand Guignol. Since his death in 1936, at the age of fifty-two, he has

Figure 1. José G. Levy

sunk into relative theatrical obscurity. During his lifetime he became a leading producer, impresario and translator of French drama. A confirmed Francophile, in March 1934 Levy received the order of Chevalier of the Legion of Honour for services to French Dramatic Art in England. Yet no biography exists of him and now he is merely remembered in a passing reference or footnote in the memoirs of the more famous actors with whom he once associated.

Levy was born in Portsmouth on 29 June 1884 and was educated at Portsmouth Grammar School and L'école de Commerce in Lausanne, Switzerland, which suggests a strictly middle-class upbringing and a fluency in French from an early age. We cannot be sure when Levy first encountered the Grand Guignol, but it is likely that he would have visited Paris as a young man and, given that the Théâtre du Grand Guignol in Montmartre had quickly become established as a popular tourist venue under the directorship of Max Maurey during the first years of the twentieth century, it is very probable that by the time the Parisian company toured to London in 1908, Levy would already have been familiar with the genre.

The Parisian Grand Guignol's 1908 tour had a mixed reception and Mel Gordon's claim that the tour was a 'financial disaster' (Gordon, 1988, 35) sounds very feasible given the general antipathy towards French drama in England and the limited audience that there would have been for French language theatre. Many of those who went must have gone out of curiosity. The actor and stalwart of the English theatre establishment Max Beerbohm, for example, was not impressed:

> Horror for horror's sake offends me. I do not say that I always shun it; merely that I am rightly ashamed of yielding to it [...] It does seem to me a matter for congratulation that native equivalents for such plays as *L'Angoisse* could not possibly become popular in London. (quoted in Trewin, 1958, 20)

Nevertheless, the young Levy certainly was impressed. Whether he was already working in the theatre by 1908 we cannot be sure, but four years later he was certainly established in the business.

On 23 August 1912 the Lord Chamberlain's Office issued a licence to Levy for a play entitled *Seven Blind Men* to be staged at the Palladium from 20 September. The play, described as 'a sketch of the Grand Guignol type' (reader's report, 23 August 1912), was an adaptation and translation by Levy of *L'Atelier d'Aveugles* by Lucien Descaves. The action takes place in the brush-making workshop of an institution for the blind, where a number of men, unhappy with their working conditions, stage a protest. The head of the institution locks the men in the workshop whilst he goes to fetch the police. Unfortunately, whilst he is away, the blind men become convinced that the building is on fire and they are driven mad in their attempts to

Figure 2. Seven Blind Men, 1921 (note the heavy make-up used on Lewis Casson (third from right))

escape. One person hurls himself through the window to his death, whilst another stabs a fellow inmate in the ensuing chaos.

In comparison to many French Grand Guignol plays of this period, this is a relatively mild and inoffensive piece (presumably Levy chose it for that reason in order to get it past the censor), but its licence was only granted with a certain degree of reluctance on the part of the Lord Chamberlain's Office. In his report, Charles H.E. Brookfield found it '[a] depressing little piece in wh no detail that might harrow is omitted', but concluded that 'I suppose it must be passed' (reader's report, 23 August 1912). *Seven Blind Men*[4] may well have been Levy's first professional experiment with the Grand Guignol, but he remained sufficiently enthusiastic about staging the plays in London and convinced that there was an audience for such a theatre. Only two months later, in November 1912, Levy obtained a further licence for a production at the Palladium of *The Medium*, an English adaptation of *L'Angoisse* by Mme de Vylars and Pierre Mille, the very play to which Beerbohm had taken exception when the Parisian company had visited London in 1908.

In 1915 the Coronet Theatre, under the management of H. Rowlands,

---

[4]   Emendations on the typescript in the Lord Chamberlain's archives in the British Library suggest that Levy at some point contemplated changing the title to *Blind Terror*, but then had second thoughts and reverted to *Seven Blind Men*. Quite probably he was concerned that the revised title might adversely tip the balance with the Lord Chamberlain.

staged 'Mr. Collin Messer's French Season', a series of French language plays in which Grand Guignol drama played a significant role. Levy was engaged as the producer of this part of the programme and he duly submitted applications for licences for *Cent Lignes Emues* by Charles Torquet, *La Veillée* by Jean Remy, *L'Horrible Expérience* by André de Lorde and *Le Baiser dans la nuit* by Maurice Level. Levy might have been forgiven for, hoping for a more enthusiastic response from the Lord Chamberlain than he had received for *Seven Blind Men*, given that these plays were to be performed in their original language, but he was to be sorely disappointed. Only three were granted licences and then only on the proviso that certain conditions were met.

George Street felt that he could only recommend a licence for *Le Baiser dans la nuit*, which centres around an acid attack (see Hand and Wilson, 2002, 180–94), on condition that the curtain fell before the climactic vitriol attack and that the victim's screams were not heard and the perpetrator's face (which has also been previously scarred by acid) was not seen. Although Lord Sandhurst and Sir Douglas Dawson, respectively the Lord Chamberlain and comptroller at the time, felt that to demand such an edit was beyond their remit, the licence was still granted for the play only on condition that 'the Management will be careful to avoid detail which might revolt their audience' (letter to Coronet Theatre from Dawson, 10 June 1915).

In spite of their reluctance to 'edit' *Le Baiser dans la nuit*, the Lord Chamberlain was more interventionist when it came to granting the licence for *La Veillée*, which was allowed only as long as 'the business of screams heard "off" when the children's throats are supposed to be cut, shall be omitted' (reader's report, 1915). Likewise *Cent Lignes Emues* was only licensed after a minor proviso has been agreed to. *L'Horrible Expérience* was less fortunate and this was flatly refused a licence on the grounds that 'the play was too dreadful and horrible for public presentation' (George Street's reader's report, 1915) since 'the stage seems [...] no place for surgical operations' (Ernest Bendall's [5] reader's report, 1915).

All this took place within the context of the Lord Chamberlain's licensing on average 700 plays per year between 1910 and 1922 and only refusing licences for about four per year (Johnston, 1990, 76–77), a significant number of which would turn out to be Grand Guignol plays submitted by Levy for the Little Theatre between 1920 and 1922. In hindsight this unusually high level of antipathy towards Levy's applications for Grand Guignol plays, especially coming on the back of the less than enthusiastic response he had received for *Seven Blind Men*, might have been an omen for the trouble that lay in store with the censor for London's Grand Guignol, but perhaps Levy felt encouraged by what he saw as a new precedent. During

---

5   Ernest Bendall was Joint Examiner of Plays with George Street from 1914–20.

their discussions concerning the licensing of *Le Baiser dans la nuit*, Dawson wrote to Street expressing the opinion that 'It all depends on whether grand guignol horrors are admissible in London, & if free from indecency I don't see where we can object' (memorandum, 8 June 1915). Arguably Levy could have felt that with the licensing of these three plays, in spite of the difficulties, the Rubicon had been crossed and that the future licensing of Grand Guignol plays would prove less controversial.

By 1920 the First World War was over and the news from Paris was that the Grand Guignol had not gone out of fashion following the real-life horrors of the battlefields of Northern France, as had been feared. Max Maurey had given up directorship of the Parisian theatre in 1915 for that very reason (see Pierron, 1995, 1383; Hand and Wilson, 2002, 16–17) and even as late as 1921 the critic Fernand Gregh was declaring that 'We have been shown too much in the small dark auditorium at the rue Chaptal, its walls dripping with artificial anguish and theatrical fear, and we have had our fill of it' (*Comoedia*, 24 April 1921). In fact, if anything the Grand Guignol was entering its Golden Age and Levy felt that the time had arrived for him to realize his dream of establishing a permanent Grand Guignol theatre in London, especially when two other vital pieces of the jigsaw fell into place.

The first of these was the recruitment of Sybil Thorndike, her husband Lewis Casson and her brother Russell Thorndike to the project. Casson was already well established and respected as an actor and director and Sybil Thorndike, 'the young emotional actress of Euripedes and Shakespeare (...) was regarded as one of the hopes of the British Theatre' (Trewin, 1958, 21). Not only were the Thorndike-Cassons able to bring artistic respectability to the project and draw audiences in their own right, but they were also able to attract other gifted actors and writers to the venture. In addition, Levy had a crucial piece of good luck when he was offered the lease of the Little Theatre.

Levy clearly recognized the importance of the venue and its location to the whole Grand Guignol experience in Paris and its consequential success (see Hand and Wilson, 2002, 26–32) and he knew that finding the right theatre in London was vital if the venture was to be a lasting success. The Little Theatre in John Adam Street was located in a small, atmospheric side street (like the Grand Guignol in Paris) between the Strand and the Embankment and whilst it did not carry with it the exoticism of the red-light district of Pigalle, it was away from the bright lights of 'theatreland'. More importantly, though, the Little Theatre had established for itself a reputation for confrontational and oppositional theatre. Established in 1910 by Gertrude Kingston, a suffragette and women's rights activist, the Little Theatre played home during the war years to experimental groups such as the Pioneer Players and the Abbey Theatre's Irish Players (Wheatley, 2002, 73). Its programmes were controversial; enough for the Little to be considered by some as 'the perfect reason to continue the official censorship of plays' (Wheatley, 2002, 73).

Additionally, Levy recognized the importance of intimacy to the success of the Grand Guignol. The Théâtre du Grand Guignol in Paris was the smallest theatre in Paris and, with a seating capacity of less than 300 and a stage of approximately seven by seven metres, it was tiny even by Montmartre standards. Jules Lemaître claimed that the 'stage was so small that only the most elementary scenic attempts were possible, and the audience was so close that illusion was an impossibility' (quoted in Homrighous, 1961, 4–5). The auditorium was arranged so as to ensure an intensely intimate experience with no member of the audience being very far from the stage.

Whilst perhaps not quite possessing the intimacy and the atmosphere of the theatre in the rue Chaptal, with its carved angels still intact from its former days as a Jansenist chapel, the Little Theatre was almost identical in dimensions to its Parisian counterpart. The stage was twenty-six feet wide and twenty-one feet deep and the auditorium had a seating capacity of 377 (Parker, 1924). As such, the Little Theatre was the smallest theatre in London, according to John Parker's *Who's Who in Theatre* (1924). Levy himself declared it was 'Small, comfortable, in a side street as a Guignol theatre should be – yet within one minute's walk of the Strand' (quoted in Devlin 1982, 129). With actors, writers and venue secured, the stage was literally set for Levy's bold experiment of establishing London's own Grand Guignol theatre. The curtain was finally raised at 8.00 p.m. on Wednesday 1 September 1920.

An Historical Overview of London's Grand Guignol

The story of London's Grand Guignol over the next two years is one in which the office of the Lord Chamberlain plays a very significant role and is, therefore, told in the later pages of this book. What is clear, though, is that the experiment was, broadly speaking, a commercial and critical success. Audiences flocked to see what was universally agreed to be the first-rate acting of the company and in return the audiences were repaid with an impressive level of productivity. Over less than two years eight series of plays were staged. In total forty-three plays were produced and many others written and refused a licence.

Yet it was not all plain sailing for Levy. The near-constant battling with the censor and the uncertainty this produced must have been exhausting for Levy and he was dogged by bouts of ill health. Had it not been for the tireless enthusiasm of the Thorndike-Cassons and, in particular, the willingness of Lewis Casson to take control when Levy was indisposed, the Grand Guignol in London would probably not have lasted as long as it did. After the staging of de Lorde's *The Old Women* in 1921 relations with the Lord Chamberlain became increasingly strained and, during the Spring of 1922, Levy was 'laid up with double pneumonia, peritonitis, and God knows what else' (private correspondence to Eliot Crawshay-Williams, 17 April 1922) which was followed by a period of convalescence abroad, leaving Casson to handle the tricky negotiations over the licences for the eighth series.

By the beginning of June 1922 the eighth series was in production and Levy was back at the helm. He was, however, in despondent mood. On 3 June he wrote to Crawshay-Williams:

> I am glad you liked the new series, but business is so bad everywhere that really one does not know what to do for the best and it is almost impossible to formulate any plans; one must be guided by circumstances. It is all very worrying, but these things have a way of straightening themselves out and one can only hope for the best. (letter to Eliot Crawshay-Williams, 3 June 1922)

Levy may have been hoping for the best, but things did not turn out that way. The Eighth Series ran for only twenty-nine performances, the shortest of any of the series, and it closed down on 24 June. A combination of business worries (the Grand Guignol was not Levy's only enterprise at the time) and pressure from the Lord Chamberlain finally took its toll and Levy decided not to re-open with a ninth season in the autumn. London's Grand Guignol had run for almost two years and in that time had enjoyed substantial critical and popular acclaim with performances of over forty different plays. Its opening season had included a play, *The Hand of Death*, from that old Grand Guignol master André de Lorde, and it was a play that was reprised for the final season, where it played alongside a comedy from one of the young rising stars of the British theatre – *The Better Half* by Noël Coward. In the meantime Sybil Thorndike and Lewis Casson moved on to even greater things and Levy continued to produce plays in London, occasionally including ones from the repertoire of the Grand Guignol.

2

Issues of Genre and Writing

Grand Guignol as French Drama

When José Levy launched the Grand Guignol at the Little Theatre, the British press fully endorsed the choice of venue with, for example, *The Times* describing the venue as 'certainly the most appropriate playhouse in the West End for the purpose' (2 September 1920). However, it was not simply a matter of an appropriate venue. Establishing a Grand Guignol theatre in London's West End was an ambitious project and a broad and efficacious repertoire of plays needed to be developed. When the *Stage* reviewed the opening night of London's Grand Guignol, it immediately drew attention to the regrettable fact that the enforcement of stage censorship in Britain would, by default, seriously compromise 'the real Grand Guignol play' (9 September 1920). The fact that 'our drama is controlled at St James's Palace' has profound implications for the new venture at the Little Theatre:

> At the best, (José Levy) can give us but partly Anglicised Grand Guignol: the Gallic cock must lose many of his best and gaudiest feathers in crossing the Channel. Happily, however, the Grand Guignol is not wholly concerned with the eternal relations, comical or otherwise, between man and woman. There is still its naked, undiluted horror for those who enjoy the real Parisian 'frisson'; and there is no sex in human gore. In this connection lovers of the gruesome and ghastly will rejoice – if they ever rejoice – in the knowledge that Mr Levy has secured an option on all the plays of André de Lorde, an author who is known in Paris as 'le Prince de la Terreur' – a very poet laureate of the charnel house ...

It is interesting that the *Stage*, one of the pre-eminent theatre journals, seems to associate the Grand Guignol first and foremost with its study of sexual relations in both the genres of comedy and more serious drama. Moreover, this indicates that the journal considers that it is the broadly 'erotic' aspect to the Grand Guignol that is going to give Levy trouble. Indeed, it seems that the fact that there is 'no sex in human gore' (although this is an argument which might be challenged as the Grand Guignol can be interpreted as very closely entwining horror and the erotic (see Hand and Wilson, 2002, 72–76)) is seen as Levy's lifeline with the de Lorde oeuvre being the most significant resource at his disposal.

To return to the *Stage* review, given that 'Grand Guignol' as a term soon became synonymous with the excesses of heightened horror, it is fascinating that its distinguishing and problematic feature is deemed to be its treatment of 'the eternal relations ... between man and woman'. The French Grand Guignol emerged from the tradition of Zola-inspired naturalism and, although it is a form not without violence, it is in its realistic display of human relations that it is most ground-breaking. When the *Stage* seems to suggest that the horrific and violent will not be problematic with the censor, one is reminded how important, broadly speaking, horror and terror had been in the previous generations of English culture. With regard to fiction, there are the Gothic precedents of Mary Shelley's *Frankenstein, or the Modern Prometheus* (1818), Robert Louis Stevenson's *The Strange Case of Dr Jekyll and Mr Hyde* (1886), and several of H.G. Wells's scientific romances notably *The Time Machine* (1895), *The Island of Doctor Moreau* (1896) and *The Invisible Man* (1897): works which may stray further into the extrapolation of rational science than the Grand Guignol ever would, but nonetheless depict archetypes of the 'mad scientists' who will bring their similarly terrifying and morally dubious experiments to the stages of the rue Chaptal and John Adam Street.

Neither was horror and terror alien to the British stage before the Grand Guignol. The Elizabethan and Jacobean stage abounded with acts of violence, and there is very little that the Grand Guignol displays, even in its most gruesome episodes, which had not been seen in Renaissance London, above all in the genre of revenge tragedy. The onstage blinding of Gloucester in *King Lear* – a violent episode which finds an unambiguous echo in *The Old Women* at the Grand Guignol – perhaps pales in comparison to the action of Thomas Middleton and Cyril Tourneur's *The Revenger's Tragedy* (1606) wherein the Duke has his lips burnt off with acidic poison, his tongue nailed down and eyelids torn off while he is forced to watch his wife's adultery before finally being stabbed to death. Indeed, it is significant that another violent and bloody play, John Ford's *'Tis Pity She's a Whore* (1623), would be a major influence on Antonin Artaud in his development of his theories of the Theatre of Cruelty. What is remarkable is that, possibly contrary to expectations, Artaud never mentions the Grand Guignol in his work.

Horror on the British stage continued in the nineteenth century when there were numerous melodramatic versions of *Frankenstein* and other Gothic works and a prolific number of heightened 'blood and thunder' or 'crime' melodramas such as George Dibdin Pitt's *The String of Pearls or*

The Fiend of Fleet Street (1847), the first Sweeney Todd melodrama, while some plays were based on fact, such as the numerous stage adaptations of the notorious 1828 Maria Marten murder case (popularly known as the 'Murder in the Red Barn'). A particularly striking example where fiction crossed over into reality is in the case of the American actor Richard Mansfield. Mansfield enjoyed his greatest stage success in Thomas Russell Sullivan's 1887 adaptation of *Dr Jekyll and Mr Hyde* which toured to London in 1888. However, Mansfield's red-blooded performance and transmutations were deemed so realistic that the actor was, as Andrew Smith informs us, 'marked out as a suspect for the [Jack the Ripper] murders' (Smith, 2004, 77) and the production was forced to terminate. However, despite these examples it is clear that what is most important to the devout Francophile Levy is the introduction of a French form to the English stage.

The Grand Guignol was quintessentially a French form, and more specifically Montmartrean, and whilst it adapted to local conditions as it was exported around the world,[1] it remained resolutely French in its approach to the portrayal of sex and violence in particular. Indeed critics of London's Grand Guignol often referred to its French provenance. Steve Nicholson reports, for example, that during a performance of the French farce *G. H. Q. Love* – Sewell Collins's adaptation of Pierre Rehm's *G. Q. G. d'amour* (1909) – performed at the Little Theatre in the autumn of 1920 as part of the opening season of Grand Guignol plays, 'One woman in the audience successfully disrupted a performance to complain about "the importation of French filth into our theatres"' (Nicholson, 2003, 208). St. John Ervine, who considered French theatre in general as 'intellectually and spiritually bankrupt' (1924, 113), complained about the 'lascivious French' who would be 'very indelicate about furniture, and would not only show a whole bed to the audience, but would make no bones about popping a lady into it' (1933, 123). With Ervine's attitude in mind, it is perhaps hardly surprising that *G. H. Q. Love*, set outside the toilets in a restaurant with rooms marked 'Messieurs' and 'Dames' visible on stage, caused such a scandal. It was known that Sir Douglas Dawson, the former comptroller at the Lord Chamberlain's Office, always liked 'to read questionable Plays, especially those of French origin' (unattributed memo, LCP 1920/3074).

Nevertheless, there was clearly an audience for French drama at the time, and there is evidence to suggest that 'plays in French are admittedly given a greater freedom than those in English' (LR 1921/9, reader's report on *Cupboard Love* by Eliot Crawshay-Williams, 13 December 1921), simply because they were French and the expectation was that a different moral standard would be applied. In other words, although George Street, the

---

[1]   Perhaps most famously, there were attempts to establish permanent Grand Guignol theatres in Italy and New York, and the French company embarked on a number of tours across Europe and North and South America.

Chief Examiner, regretted the reliance of London's Grand Guignol on French plays, writing in his report on *A Man in Mary's Room* by Gladys Unger, 'if the Little Theatre would only stick to such things by reputable English authors it would save us much trouble'[2] (reader's report, 5 October 1920), many plays were allowed 'on the grounds that no-one would go and see them without knowing what to expect' (Johnston, 1990, 76). In 1915, when a licence was requested for a French language production of Maurice Level's *Le Baiser dans la nuit* at the Coronet Theatre, Street's response was:

> Such a brutal and shocking horror would not be allowed in an English play. On the other hand it might be contended that the Grand Guignol audience should be allowed their thrill of exotic horror. (reader's report, 8 June 1915)

The censor was particularly lenient towards plays performed in the original French on the basis that only the educated middle-classes (who were presumably less corruptible) would be able to access them.

The rather ambivalent attitude towards French theatre by the London theatre-going public is exemplified by the following letter which appeared in the *Playgoer* in November 1916:

> I went to the theatre one evening with a man whom I knew to be highly educated and very broad-minded. The play dealt with so-called 'life' in Paris, as the costumes were as near 'nature' as the law allowed. My companion, judging from his continued applause and apparent interest, thoroughly enjoyed the performance. But as we left the theatre he said, in an answer to my casual question, 'Well, how did you like the show?' 'Oh, Why do they allow it? I can't uphold plays of that kind.' And he expected me to believe him. (quoted in Poel, 1920, 34)

Opinion amongst the critics was similarly divided with the *Daily Telegraph* claiming that 'this translation of the Grand Guignol to London has lost nothing of the torture chamber quality of the original' (2 September 1920), and the programmes were certainly true to the original French form in the use of the *douche écossaise*, a hot and cold shower of horror plays of increasing intensity alternating with comedies (see Hand and Wilson, 2002, 11), although cleaned up for the English audience. Indeed, the *Daily Chronicle*, reviewing the opening night of London's Grand Guignol,

---

[2] *A Man in Mary's Room* premièred in December 1920 as part of the Second Series of Grand Guignol plays at the Little Theatre. Gladys Unger was, in fact, an American writer.

concluded with some disappointment that 'Grand Guignol lovers must still go to Paris for the real thing' (2 September 1920).

Building a Repertoire for London's Grand Guignol

The importation of the French Grand Guignol onto the British stage required a certain Anglicisation and Levy achieved this through a careful balance between the translation and adaptation of French Grand Guignol plays and the nurturing of home-grown talent. In striving to recreate the same impulse and mood of the Paris Grand Guignol, Levy used numerous translations of some of its most successful standards, including several of de Lorde's key works. But it was not just de Lorde that Levy staged: in fact, although de Lorde may have been the single most performed playwright of any nationality at London's Grand Guignol with six plays staged over the eight seasons, there were, as a whole, even more horror plays translated and adapted from other French writers including Maurice Level, Pierre Veber, Robert Francheville and Lucien Descaves. Moreover, it is essential to note that the French repertoire did not furnish London only with its 'shockers': a significant batch of comedies – several adapted by Sewell Collins – made the journey across the Channel, including plays by Max Maurey and the 'double act' writers Pierre Chaine and Robert de Beauplan, and Léon Frapié and Georges Fabri.

José Levy ensured that his Grand Guignol theatre would make a major contribution to a form that had become much neglected in the English drama of the time: the short play. As Allardyce Nicoll clarifies, in the earliest years of the twentieth century one-act plays:

> ... were frequently to be seen in the theatres of the West End: by the close of the period, they had virtually disappeared in that area, save for the programmes presented by the Grand Guignol company and for the tiny sketches introduced into revues. (Nicoll, 1973, 124)

A night at the British Grand Guignol re-introduced the one-act play to the West End by offering an evening that would include an average of four to six plays. The Little Theatre thus became a champion for the shorter drama and the one-act play, a form that was characteristic of the French Grand Guignol, but less familiar to English audiences. As A.E. Wilson, writing in the *Star* claimed:

> The one-act play, like the short story, is an art form which hitherto has received less encouragement in England than it has in France, where it has been raised to a pitch of perfection that has found its finest expression at the famous Grand Guignol. (2 September 1920)

When Eliot Crawshay-Williams published his first volume of *Five Grand Guignol Plays*, after the discontinuation of the Grand Guignol at the Little Theatre, he particularly bemoaned the loss of a theatre that was committed to the one-act form:

> At any rate it is to be hoped, and, I trust, to be expected, that before long further experiments in establishing a theatre presenting programmes of one-act plays may be made in this country, and will succeed. If so, our drama will be enriched, and our sources of enjoyment extended. (Crawshay-Williams, 1924, 3)

As well as using new translations and adaptations of tried and tested French plays, Levy's Grand Guignol project also afforded important opportunities to home-grown playwriting talent, including Crawshay-Williams himself. The mixture of French adaptations and home-grown plays perhaps represents the Little Theatre's other *douche écossaise*: the mixture of French plays and new works. There were over forty plays in the eight series of the Grand Guignol at the Little Theatre; around a third of these were translations from the French repertoire but the majority were original plays by new English language writers.

The potential opportunities for English language playwrights were proclaimed from the start, not least in terms of promoting the venture before it had premièred. In July 1920, an article appeared in *The Times* which heralded Levy's forthcoming experiment in the following terms:

GRAND GUIGNOL FOR LONDON
A CHANCE FOR BRITISH PLAYWRIGHTS

The article reveals two interesting features in the build-up to the launch of this new theatre. First of all, it reveals that the Grand Guignol is a form with a popular familiarity to the British audience. José Levy and Joseph Benson, the 'lessees', are seen as attempting to launch a Grand Guignol which 'will be modelled in every way on the theatre in Paris which has achieved such remarkable popularity' (*The Times* 22 July 1920). However, despite being modelled on a quintessentially Parisian theatre, the enterprise is seen as a major opportunity for British playwrights. As the article elaborates:

> An option has already been obtained on some of the most thrilling of the French short plays, but every effort is to be made to persuade the British playwrights to devote their energies to this kind of work as well. All the plays will be presented in English, and it should be clearly understood that there is no intention whatever of merely producing gruesome plays. Any kind of work will be considered, whether it be farce, satire, comedy, or drama; the only stipulation being that there

shall be originality in the dialogue and in the method of treatment. Four or five plays will be produced in each programme, and efforts will be made to keep the comedy and tragedy carefully balanced, though Mr. Levy explains that when there is a thrill to be provided no attempt will be made to spare the feelings of the audience. If they are to be harrowed they will be harrowed on the approved Grand Guignol principle. It is intended to run each programme as long as the public support justifies it. A special feature will be made of the *foyer*, where music will be provided between the plays, and where there will be accommodation for any members of the audience who wish to sit out during any of the items in the programme which do not appeal to them.

For *The Times*, Grand Guignol is evidently synonymous with the 'gruesome', and yet Levy makes it clear that he is looking for a wide repertoire of short plays that cross a diverse range of genres. By the same token, it is clear that horror will be an essential part of the experience at the Little Theatre which will utilise 'the approved Grand Guignol principle' in its performance of horror. A key part in the Grand Guignol experience is, of course, the *douche écossaise*: the 'hot and cold shower' of horror and comedy. For Levy, this is not simply a question of alternating between tragedy and comedy, but a very careful balance between the two. Very interestingly, the article publicises Levy's safety zone: a foyer where music will provide entertainment between performances and will also serve as a place of refuge if the spectacle proves too thrilling or disturbing. This feature may well be a kind consideration for the sensibilities of the West End audience: more likely, it is a cunning device like the original Grand Guignol's use of a house doctor, whereby a seemingly beneficial security measure is in fact another strategy through which suspense can be manipulated and exacerbated.

In Mervyn McPherson's preface to *The Grand Guignol Annual Review 1921*, the author contends that a key purpose of the British Grand Guignol is to encourage:

> ... the great art, which disuse had almost lost us, of one-act playwriting: a movement to present sections of life as it is, gay sometimes, frequently sad, occasionally very horrible, but as it is, without the sugar coating, or saccharine centre of the so-called 'popular' play. (McPherson, 1921, 3)

The British Grand Guignol is thus presented as a radical challenge – in both its formal structure and its treatment of narrative and characterisation – to the conventional popular theatre of the time. The appeal was obviously significant: comparatively established writers such as H.F. Maltby and Eliot Crawshay-Williams were successfully drawn to write for Levy, and even erstwhile critics of the venture such as St John Ervine would eventually be lured by the irresistible challenge of London's Grand Guignol. In addition, emerging writers such as Gladys Unger, Richard Hughes and Noël Coward seized the opportunity of submitting one-act plays to Levy's theatre with the attractive possibility of their plays being produced and featuring well established and highly regarded actors such as the Thorndike-Cassons. The interest that was obviously sparked by Levy's enterprise is also evidenced by writers whose plays were unsuccessfully submitted to the Little Theatre such as Joseph Conrad whose play *Laughing Anne* was written specifically for London's Grand Guignol.[3]

The potential of the British Grand Guignol to open up opportunities for home-grown writing talent is exceedingly important to the theatrical reviewers of the time. Leslie Henson, in his theatre column for the *Weekly Dispatch* (5 September 1920), lavishes praise on Levy's enterprise inasmuch as he hopes that it may become 'permanent, as a home for clever one-act plays has long been needed'. Henson has a serious word of warning, however, declaring:

> The sooner English playwrights are discovered the better for the scheme, for the plan of translating a French play into English and setting English players to act characters which remain highly un-English is not always happy.

Henson goes on to single out the play that had obviously affronted him

---

[3]   In a letter to Thomas J. Wise (1 November 1920), Joseph Conrad stresses that he is writing his short play *Laughing Anne* 'with a view to the *Little Theatre*' (Wheatley, 2002, 65). This is during the English Grand Guignol's opening season, and before Conrad has even visited it. Conrad and his literary agent attended the Grand Guignol on Thursday 2 December 1920, and Conrad – always a reluctant theatregoer – was clearly inspired. He completed his experiment in Grand Guignol playwriting and submitted it to the Little Theatre. Conrad claims that Levy rejected *Laughing Anne* on the following grounds:

> But Mr Levy did not see his way to produce it – at which I was not surprised – the second Act being very difficult to stage with convincing effect. Too much darkness; too much shooting. (Partington, 2000, 179–80)

From this it would seem that Levy rejected the play on the grounds of its technical demands and not because of what John Galsworthy called the 'unbearable spectacle' of a man 'without hands' (a central character). The abstract quality of the final scene – 'shudderings grounded in dim light' which Galsworthy rather pompously declares Conrad should have 'avoided' (Galsworthy, 1924, vii) – may have made the play difficult to perform on the London stage in the early 1920s, but would not have troubled the German Expressionists, and would soon become less problematic, even in the English and American theatre. For a detailed analysis of *Laughing Anne*, see Hand, 2005, 87–125.

in this regard, reproving the 'sordid' *G. H. Q. Love* for its 'irritating characterisation'. Not all critics would agree, however. In reviewing the revised First Series programme, *Reynolds's Newspaper* (3 October 1920) praises the new addition – *The Medium* by Pierre Mille and C. de Vylars – by comparing it to the production of the same play (*L'Angoisse*) which the Parisian Grand Guignol company brought to London on their 1908 tour:

> Curiously, it is suited to our style of acting, and played even better in English than in its original French, for it was done in London some years back.

During the Grand Guignol's penultimate series, the *Observer* (April 2, 1922) is pleased 'to note that Mr José G. Levy is holding out the hand of encouragement to our native dramatists' with André de Lorde's early work *Au Téléphone* the only French play on offer (as *At the Telephone*).

Grand Guignol Comedy

Although synonymous with the extremes of *horror*, the Grand Guignol is also extremely dependent on *comedy*. In the French repertoire, comedy is found in farces with adulterous or morbid plotlines, such as the lascivious soirée in René Berton's *Après Coup! ... ou Tics* (1908) or the surgeon's gruesome attempts to recover his prized gold forceps from several of his patients in Élie de Bassan's *Les Opérations du Professeur Verdier* (1907). Less farcical but equally fast-paced comedies include Octave Mirbeau's *Les Amants* (1901), an acutely observed satire on gender and the rituals and etiquette of courtship.

Arguably, in Britain the Grand Guignol comedy enjoyed an increased level of diversity and even sophistication. Certainly there are farces, but these are – at least to contemporary sensibilities – gently risqué more than examples of outright vulgarity. Generally, innocent misunderstanding or dramatic irony is more likely to be to blame than the brazenly unfaithful or illicit *dramatis personae* who stalked the comedic stage across the Channel. When a play such as *Save the Mark*, adapted by Wilfred Harris from Marcel Nancey and Jean Manoussy's *La Ventouse* (performed at the Parisian Grand Guignol in 1916), was proposed it would prove far too salacious. This play – prospectively submitted for the First Season at the Little Theatre – was assessed by the Lord Chamberlain's Office in August 1920. In the play, Francine Chatenay, a lady with a '*pretty and good figure*' discovers a love bite on her neck caused by her lover Georges St Clair, '*a smart man about town*'. Harris's translation is generally very true to the original: for example, like so many British adaptations of original Grand Guignol works, the location of the play remains firmly in France. Regardless of locale and all the moral implications that could be construed there (i.e.

Figure 3. Sybil Thorndike, Russell Thorndike and Lewis Casson in *Oh, Hell!!!*,
1920

the play depicts French moralities and infidelities), the censor took exception
to the following passage, and in the manuscript it is firmly excised with the
blue pencil:

> FRANCINE: I dare not look my husband in the face!
> GEORGES   (*completely mystified*): But why?
> FRANCINE: Because he has only to look at me to know I have a lover!
> GEORGES   (*ironically*): Rubbish: is it written on your face?
> FRANCINE   (*tragically*): Worse than that! It's printed on my skin.
>   Look! (*She undoes cloak, disclosing elegant evening gown
>   decolettee, and in the centre of neck where a pendant would
>   rest – a bright red mark*)
> GEORGES   (*not grasping the situation*): What is it – a mosquito?
> FRANCINE: Yes – a horrid mosquito on four legs – called Georges!

Despite this and other piecemeal expurgations, the piece is ultimately
deemed to be too risqué for Britain and the play was completely banned.
Likewise, even a home-grown play like H.F. Maltby's farce *I Want to Go
Home* – in which a suspected adulterous husband proves his guilt while

inebriated (by mistaking his wife for his mistress) – felt the full weight of the Lord Chamberlain's wrath and was banned outright.

However, London's Grand Guignol also produced comedies which were consciously in a broader tradition of popular theatre, such as Reginald Arkell and Russell Thorndike's *The Tragedy of Mr Punch* which is emphatically and successfully pantomimic. The Little Theatre was also able to stage examples of self-parody. The 'revuette' *Oh, Hell!!!* – another work by Reginald Arkell and Russell Thorndike – is an enjoyably self-referential comic exploration of the Grand Guignol form with performers such as George Bealby and Dorothy Minto scripted to, as it were, play themselves and featuring a sustained pastiche of *The Hand of Death* – Bealby recreating his role but for comic ends – which deftly satirizes the Grand Guignol's use of science and suspense (see Appendix 3).

Looking at the British repertoire, the generic categorizations of horror and comedy are broadly apt, but there are many fine distinctions within these. *The Times* (16 December 1920) comes up with its own definitions when it comes to the horror dramas on offer in the second season of the repertoire. *Eight O'Clock* is regarded as *realistically creepy*: it is praised for avoiding any 'dramatic exaggeration' making the spectators feel that they 'had "been there" and were sick and sorry' that they had. The reviewer comments that the experience of such creepy realism is 'a rather strange sensation … after dinner, but just what the Grand Guignolians seem to like'. In stark contrast, *Private Room Number 6* is categorized as *romantically creepy*. The reviewer regards the story as one which is familiar and yet entirely unbelievable. This is not levelled as a criticism as it merely reflects the melodramatic (that is what is meant by the 'romantic') nature of the play. The play is predictable and implausible, but it is nonetheless these qualities which make the performance so very enjoyable (and, presumably, more conducive to digestion). The reviewer seems to take delight in the stereotype of the diabolical Russian general (played by George Bealby) 'caressing and occasionally biting' Sybil Thorndike's undercover Nihilist assassin. The reviewer concludes: 'Mr George Bealby was amusingly ogreish and Miss Sybil Thorndike amusingly intense and "fatal"'. This is a very revealing statement as it makes it clear that, for all the controversy of the Grand Guignol's horror plays and its onstage murders and sadistic brutality, they were seen from some quarters of its audience as delightfully amusing. The laughter in the Grand Guignol was not necessarily reserved for the comedies.

The fact that a horror play can evoke mirth without its being detrimental to the enjoyment of the play is an interesting point. As we have seen, it was partly the predictability of *Private Room Number 6* that caused this reaction. This has implications about Grand Guignol horror writing. It is an intense and concise style of writing where, although there may be a smattering of red herrings, shock moments and dramatic irony, the ultimate tragic conclusion and/or gruesome climax tends to be signposted from very early in the play. The economy of the form places a major demand on exposition: in short, the horror playwright in the Grand Guignol cannot waste any words. This is why Grand Guignol horror is often predictable. This, however, should not necessarily detract from the narrative and theatrical journey of the form: it is not necessarily *what will happen* but *how we get there* that matters. This is highlighted in another review of the same production:

> The only questions we ask are, How is she going to kill him, and how does she get away. Both are answered fairly satisfactorily. But the value of the piece lies solely in the opportunity it gives to Miss Sybil Thorndike and Mr George Bealby for fine melodramatic acting of the most full-blooded type. (un-sourced press cutting, Theatre Museum Archives)

This review relishes the acting while for *The Times* this journey is romantically creepy with many a laugh. From yet another perspective one can admire the dramatic structure and measured unfurling of dialogue that is established. For example, in June 1921, Sybil Thorndike defended the controversy that was being sparked by the notorious horror play *The Old Women* to the *Daily Express* in the following terms:

> It is a beautiful play, perfectly worked out. The only thing to which it can be adequately compared is the music of Mozart. The fear inspired by it in the audience should be more than counterbalanced by the perfection of the play.

Thorndike's argument is a remarkable one as it reclaims the Grand Guignol from being a theatre of controversy, full of shocks and provocations, and makes it a theatre of 'beautiful' plays, almost, perhaps, operatic in their attention to structure and balance. It is an argument that insists on a move away from an obsession with content: again, a rejection of 'what' in favour of 'how'.

Returning to *The Times*'s terms of the *realistically creepy* and the *romantically creepy* as a key, one can detect how horror in the London Grand Guignol repertoire pushed in almost opposite directions. The realism of *The Person Unknown*, *The Sisters' Tragedy* and *Eight O'Clock* – the latter play described by *Reynolds's Newspaper* (19 December 1920) as 'a quietly effective piece of writing … terrible but pitiful' – juxtaposed with the post-romantic and more thunderous melodramatic thrills of *Private Room Number 6* and, it must be said, most of the other de Lorde pieces. It works the same in comedy too – the farce and romp of Sewell Collins's adaptation of Léon Frapié and Georges Fabri's comedy of cannibalism *Shepherd's Pie* or Reginald Arkell and Russell Thorndike's overtly pantomimic *The Tragedy*

Figure 4. Victor Hicks cartoon in *The Stage* (11 August 1921)

of Mr Punch contrasting with the gentle satire of Gladys Unger's *A Man in Mary's Room* or the comedy of manners in Noël Coward's *The Better Half*. In his *Autobiography*, Noël Coward writes:

> In May (1922) a one-act comedy that I had written a year before was produced by the London Grand Guignol at the Little Theatre. It was called *The Better Half*, and was wittily played by Auriol Lee. In spite of this it was received with apathy; I think, possibly, because it was a satire and too flippant in atmosphere after the full-blooded horrors that had gone before it. (Coward, 1986, 115)

Despite his claims, *The Better Half* is, in fact, very much in keeping with some of the satirical offerings at the Little Theatre. Much more likely, the 'apathy' Coward detects was due to the fact that the London Grand Guignol had nearly run its course.

Figure 5. Jean de Bosschère's 'Impression' in the *Sketch* (2 November 1921)

Not only was the Grand Guignol home to a broad range of comedy: it elicited humorous responses to its offerings in the form of caricatures and cartoons in the press such as Victor Hicks's excellent cartoon in *The Stage* (July 1921) and the Belgian artist Jean de Bosschère's full page 'Impression' in the *Sketch* (2 November 1921). Another humorous example of Grand Guignol reception – and one which demonstrates how well known the Little Theatre repertoires had become – was in July 1921 when the Actor's Orphanage organized a fund-raising garden party which included a variety of performances and was afforded the patronage of the Prince of Wales. For the reviewer of the *Era* (6 July 1921), the highlight was a 'wonderfully funny' trilogy of plays produced by Gerald du Maurier entitled the 'Grand Giggle'. Du Maurier's satirical response to the British Grand Guignol included three plays written for the occasion, *The House Next Door* by J. Hastings Turner; *And Did He?* by Dion Clayton Calthrop and *The Bitter Truth* by Roland Pertwee (which starred Gerald du Maurier in the leading role). The *Era* review provides a summary of each play for the benefit of the reader which may indicate how familiar, by this time, was the formula of the Grand Guignol: enough for a reader to enjoy the account of these sketches. Indeed, these short plays do reveal a successful and wittily incisive understanding of the form.

The House Next Door was subtitled 'A Horrible Affair' and is the story of an adulterous couple who misunderstand a telegram and end in the same room at the Grand Hotel, Aberystwyth as the woman's cuckolded husband and meet a terrible fate. The final scene is described thus:

> *No action. Well-balanced picture of still life. – three corpses!*
> *Apparently two murders and one suicide.*

The salacious theme has all the potential of a Grand Guignol horror play, including a gruesome denouement (this is no Gladys Unger's *A Man in Mary's Room* irony: the protagonists are thoroughly guilty) but it is 'acted in delightfully comic fashion' which is evidently enough to make it a well-received comedy. In *And Did He?* a 'dissipated and garrulous' father is seen trying to persuade his three daughters to 'Go out and kill her!' The play – not altogether dissimilar in its depiction of a dysfunctional family to Richard Hughes's *The Sisters' Tragedy* which would be performed at the Little Theatre the following year – built up its suspense with the father himself setting out on his homicidal mission, only to have his daughters and the cook, gardener and eventually the police try to restrain him. The punch line is that the 'she' that he wants to kill is, in fact, a parrot. Although the play is rather puerile as comedy, the manipulation of suspense and escalation of threatened violence represent a convincing understanding and satire of the Grand Guignol style. If the first two plays satirize theme and style (and could be seen as satirical of French Grand Guignol as much as English), the final play *The Bitter Truth* explores the British Grand Guignol comedy. The simple plot involves an exploration of British class relations: a middle class wife demands that her husband reprimand one of the servants. In an audience with the servant, the parlour maid gradually turns the tables so that she ends up reprimanding the master who later boasts of his triumph to his wife. It is a simple piece but demonstrates that the Grand Giggle perceived such class relations and obsessions to be integral to the impetus of the comedy on display at London's Grand Guignol.

We have seen how the writing in the British Grand Guignol repertoire, just like the French original, crossed the broad genres of horror and comedy and spanned a wide range of approaches within these genres. The reliance upon a diverse but carefully balanced range of one-act plays strove to rediscover for a London audience a neglected form of dramatic writing. Some spectators, however, evidently found some plays in the repertoire to be offensive, just as some unquestionably found much of it to be predictable. In reviewing *Private Room Number 6*, for example, the *Sunday Express* (19 December 1920) declared that 'Miss Thorndike's passionate acting ... raised that otherwise crudely melodramatic piece to the level of tragedy'. Nearly a year later, *The Times* would take things even further. In its review of *Fear*, de Lorde's horror play set in a waxworks museum (*Figures de cire*, 1910), staged in the Fifth Season of London's Grand Guignol, *The Times* (13 October 1921) comments:

> Miss Thorndike's wan face, her penetrating voice, her skill in presenting a gradual *crescendo* of 'nerves', her general sense of style, lend these shockers an artistic dignity which they do not intrinsically possess. You feel that the actress is too good for the work, and yet so fine in it that you couldn't bear the thought of her absence.

For all the emphasis on its offering a ground-breaking repertoire of one-act plays from a range of established and emerging talents, for many people London's Grand Guignol was a venue where you went to see the *acting*.

3

Performers and Performing

The Grand Guignol Ensemble

One of the most defining characteristics of London's Grand Guignol was
the remarkable company of actors that José Levy was able to recruit to the
project. In this respect it was very different to the company that Camille
Choisy was working with in Paris at the time. That is not, of course,
to suggest that the French company was not remarkable in its own way
– by 1920 Paula Maxa, 'the Sarah Bernhardt of the impasse Chaptal', and
L. Paulais, 'the Mounet-Sully of the Grand Guignol', were both permanent
members of the company, along with more established pre-war Grand
Guignol actors. What is significant is that Levy decided to build London's
Grand Guignol around a *specific* company of actors and, moreover, actors
who were already well-established and successful in their careers.

Sybil Thorndike was nearly thirty-eight when the First Series opened at
the Little Theatre in September 1920 and, although she was seen as 'one
of the hopes of British Theatre', one of its rapidly rising stars, she already
had sixteen years of professional experience behind her. Much of that
time had been spent establishing herself and learning her craft, with three
years touring America playing mainly minor Shakesperean roles (although
eventually progressing to Viola, Ophelia and Rosalind) and the four years
of the war with the Old Vic Company, again playing Shakespeare and the
classics. By 1920 she had established herself not only as a Shakespearean
actress of impressive emotional intensity, but had also consolidated her
reputation with critically acclaimed performances as Hecuba in Euripides's
The Trojan Women in 1919 and early 1920, a production that had been
directed by her husband, Lewis Casson. Casson was seven years his wife's
senior, but had entered the theatre as a professional actor in 1904, the
same year as Sybil, after four years working semi-professionally (whilst still
engaged in the family business of organ-building), acting under the direction
of figures such as William Poel, Charles Fry and Harley Granville Barker.
By 1908 he had begun directing, as well as acting, often taking minor roles
in his own productions. Respected as an actor, it was as a director and

producer that he was most admired and by 1920 he had amassed a prolific number of credits to his name, in spite of spending the war years in the army.

It is not difficult to understand why Levy was so keen to have Thorndike and Casson on board from the very beginning – their association would immediately lend a degree of esteem to the project and, given the controversial nature of the whole enterprise, Levy could very well use the respectability that they would bring. In addition, their abilities were widely recognized, not least by Levy himself, who described Sybil Thorndike as 'the best emotional actress now appearing on the English stage' and Casson as 'the most consistently excellent producer I know' (quoted in Devlin, 1982, 129). It is at first glance less understandable what drew Thorndike and Casson to London's Grand Guignol. Levy was by now a reputable man of the theatre, but he was hardly a leading figure in the theatrical establishment. It is difficult to see what was in it for them. Their participation was not an obvious way to advance either of their careers and would at best be 'a kind of detour on their road to success' (Devlin, 1982, 128) and 'a heavily incarnadined cul-de-sac' (Trewin, 1955, 50). Nevertheless, it seems that neither of them took much persuading.

For Sybil Thorndike it would appear that the attraction lay partly within the acting challenge that the Grand Guignol presented. Moving fast-paced between a number of roles and between comedy and horror was very different from the classical roles to which she had become accustomed, as was the ensemble way of working which Levy was keen to establish. In addition:

> Versatility was essential, because the same players would be called upon to jump from Comedy to Tragedy, Fantasy to Farce, and from all these to Horror, because, of course, the great horror play has to be the most important item in each Guignol performance. (Thorndike, 1950, 274)

The above is part of Russell Thorndike's recollection of the London Grand Guignol, and it clearly indicates the irresistible appeal inherent in this demanding form of theatre. Furthermore, the project afforded Sybil Thorndike the opportunity to work with her beloved brother Russell, with whom she had staged horror plays as a child, and whose involvement was determined at the very first meeting with Levy. London's Grand Guignol was to be 'a family reunion' (Trewin, 1955, 53). Linked to this, and certainly not to be underestimated, was Sybil Thorndike's sense of fun, and her enthusiasm for the project can be partly explained by this. As John Casson, a child at the time, recalls, after the deal was struck with Levy, his mother explained the idea to him:

There'll be lots of exciting murders and crimes and all sorts of other terribly quirky things and everyone will be terrified. Then we'll do one or two funny ones in the middle to let them get their breaths back and then more horrors. Uncle Russell's going to come too and he can frighten anyone! It'll be just like the plays he and I used to do in the attic when we were children. Lots of blood and agony! I'm not sure if we'll be able to let you see them all because you'll all have awful nightmares. But you like being frightened a bit, don't you? It's such fun! (Casson, 1972, 70)

Trewin too has no doubt that Thorndike acted her parts 'with intense relish' (1958, 21), and noted that, 'For two years and with the intensest pleasure, Sybil Thorndike would endure mortal agonies on the stage of the Little Theatre' (1955, 50).

Lewis Casson, it seems, was drawn to the project purely for artistic reasons. Again there was the challenge of taking on something that contrasted so strongly with his previous work. As Diana Devlin, Casson's granddaughter, says:

Much of Lewis's experience had been in theatres frequented by an intellectual elite. Grand Guignol gave him the chance to bring the same integrity and imagination to popular entertainment. Though his chief enemy in the theatre was commercialism, he was just as frustrated by a protective 'ivory tower' reaction to it. (Devlin, 1982, 131)

This is, though, in itself interesting because the opposite argument was made by Levy in his attempts to get the Lord Chamberlain to grant licences to certain plays. When *Collusion*, a play attacking the divorce laws by American playwright George Middleton, was banned because it featured a young man hiring a prostitute so that he could be caught *in flagrante* in order that his wife could seek a divorce and they could both be freed from an unhappy marriage, Levy made the following point in a letter to the censor:

As you are also aware, the audiences frequenting this theatre consist of the more thinking and cultured type of playgoers, and it is not as if the play would be seen by the masses, a point which I think is worthy of being taken into consideration. (letter from Levy to Crichton, 26 February 1921)

He made the same point during the difficulties of getting *The Hand of Death* licensed for the first season, claiming that he was 'only catering for special audience at Little Theatre no cheap seats' (telegram from Mr

Hertslet, Lord Chamberlain's secretary, to Viscount Sandhurst, 25 August 1920). Even H.F. Maltby suggested that the Grand Guignol was attracting a more sophisticated and open-minded audience when he declared in a letter to the Lord Chamberlain protesting about the refusal of a license for *I Want to Go Home*, 'What is there in either of my pieces that the Jazz loving inhabitants of the West End of London could take exception to?' (letter, 13 December 1920).

According to Devlin, though, the main attraction for Casson was 'the *structure* of the scheme as the closest thing to genuine repertory to be found in London: a vast range of plays and a permanent company in the most varied roles' (1982, 129). The project also allowed Casson to indulge his passion as a writer and translator, as well as a director and actor. Central to this was the model of the ensemble. Success was to be dependent on a group of actors, writers and technicians working equally together towards a common purpose. And so Casson set about recruiting a team that consisted of not only family, but long-established friends and colleagues with whom he and his wife could establish a fruitful and creative working relationship. This was evidently successful, at least according to Russell Thorndike who writes extremely positively about the team-feel of the Grand Guignol ensemble and how he and his fellow actors were all happy to play the lead role in one play and have a walk-on part in another. Russell Thorndike concludes: 'We got to know each other so well that we could tell what each of us was thinking about' (Thorndike, 1950, 274).

One of the key players in the ensemble was George Bealby. Bealby was forty-three at the time, two years younger than Lewis Casson. He was married to the sister of Aubrey Beardsley and was well known in theatrical circles. He had established a name for himself as an actor in farce, but he was well-built and barrel-chested and carried himself with a certain air of seniority and *gravitas* and so was well-suited to 'the heavy tragic roles of the horror plays' (Devlin, 1982, 129). The *Reynolds's Newspaper* (5 September 1920) remarked that Bealby's superb acting in the horror genre served to 'astonish those who have hitherto only seen him in ... lighter parts'. Others included the young Dorothy Minto, Nicholas Hannen and Athene Seyler, all of whom were personally known to Casson. Cyril Cattley was recruited as stage manager, a job which involved working with Casson to ingeniously design a series of sets that would enable five or more plays to be presented in a single evening. The ensemble ethos of the project also required Cattley to step into minor roles as and when required.

There is no doubt that between them Levy and Casson assembled an impressive ensemble, and the press reviews suggest that this was a key contributing factor to the overall success of the experiment. The theatre critic of the *People* paid tribute to the company's culture of collective endeavour:

> The company at the Little have never acted better than on this
> occasion. Their 'team' work is deserving of the highest praise, and
> alone is worth a visit to the little theatre in the Adelphi. (16 October
> 1921)

It was, ironically, also a key contributing factor to its ultimate downfall.
Unlike the actors at the Grand Guignol in Paris, Levy's team all had
successful careers outside of the Grand Guignol. Even during the busy
seasons at the Little Theatre, Sybil Thorndike 'kept herself occupied by
going to Paris to play Lady Macbeth' (Trewin, 1955, 53), and she would take
on 'remote classical parts on Sunday nights at such theatres as the Lyric,
Hammersmith' (Trewin, 1958, 21). For Thorndike, Casson and the rest of
the company, London's Grand Guignol was never going to be more than a
temporary, exciting and fun-filled experiment. For Thorndike, her famous
portrayal of Joan of Arc in Shaw's *Saint Joan* was only two years away, and
Casson was keen to develop his directorial career in the commercial theatre
to support their growing family. Russell Thorndike would continue as a stage
and occasional film actor before concentrating on his writing including, in
the 1930s and 1940s, a number of sequels to his novel *Dr Syn: A Tale of
the Romney Marsh* (1915). In other words, the Thorndike-Cassons all had
bigger fish to fry. Levy may have been ultimately disappointed that he was
unable to realize his dream of establishing a permanent Grand Guignol in
London, but when the project finally closed in 1922, there must have been
just the slightest sigh of relief from the key players that they were now free
to pursue other projects.

The Importance of Personality and the Actor/Audience Relationship

It is clear that the involvement of such luminaries of the British stage in
London's Grand Guignol gave the enterprise a certain respectability which
could be put to good purpose, given the suspicion of French plays generally
and the doubtful morality of the Grand Guignol specifically. There is
evidence to suggest that the involvement of the Thorndike-Cassons actually
led to the project being treated more leniently by the Lord Chamberlain than
it might otherwise have been. In his letter to Crichton regarding George
Middleton's *Collusion*, Levy made the following plea:

> It is hardly necessary for me to point out that Miss Thorndike, who
> has been cast for the part of the Woman, is an artist whose reputation
> is beyond reproach, and that Mr. Casson, who would play the Man
> and also produce the play, is a sufficient guarantee that the play
> will be handled in as sincere a way as possible. (letter, 24 February
> 1921)

On this occasion it was a plea that fell on deaf ears, but Lord Cromer, in his reply to the complaint made by The London Council for the Promotion of Public Morality concerning the possible revival of the Grand Guignol, was using the exact same argument to offer reassurance, claiming that 'given the standing of the artistes concerned, reliance may be placed upon their keeping within bounds the portrayal of their various parts' (letter, 14 June 1924). In fact, all the Lord Chamberlains who presided during the period between 1920 and 1922 were open to the influence of some people more than others. Casson was able to secure an interview with the Lord Chamberlain concerning *The Sisters' Tragedy*, and then entered into personal correspondence with him on the matter, whereas Levy was often unable to secure meetings with the censor, and his pleas were often summarily dismissed by the comptroller. Most successful in this was Eliot Crawshay-Williams who was able to call on his status as a former Member of Parliament[1] to gain favourable access to the Lord Chamberlain and even ensure the reconsideration of adverse decisions. Following his success in persuading Sandhurst to ease through the licence for *Rounding the Triangle* in early 1921, when *Cupboard Love* ran into difficulties later that same year, Levy wrote to the playwright suggesting that he might 'use any influence and get the decision [to refuse a licence] rescinded' (letter, 24 November 1921). Crawshay-Williams immediately wrote to Atholl, the new Lord Chamberlain, asking for an interview, beginning his letter with the words, 'You may remember me as being in the House of Commons with you about ten years ago' (letter, 27 November 1921). In the event no interview was necessary and Atholl replied to Crawshay-Williams in similarly obsequious tones:

> I am sorry that the office over which I preside decided to spin your play. I have read it carefully, and it is quite a clever, light little piece. (Letter, 30 November 1921)

In terms of the theatrical event the most significant consequence of having a company of established, respected and well-known actors was that it facilitated the sense of *familiarity* between actors and audience that was required in the intimate space of the Little Theatre and was necessary for the success and survival of the project. Levy would have been aware that both Max Maurey and Camille Choisy had been able to cultivate a group of regular audience members at the Grand Guignol in Paris. These *guignoleurs* would regularly heckle good-naturedly from the auditorium and counted out loud as other (presumably, non-regular) members of the audience fainted. It became like an unofficial club, an elite, the membership of which relied upon

---

[1]   Crawshay-Williams was Liberal MP for Leicester, 1910–13, and had served as Lloyd George's Parliamentary Private Secretary.

complete familiarity with the form and the actors. Quickly establishing a regular, committed and enthusiastic core audience was key to ensuring the financial success and sustainability of London's Grand Guignol. With an ensemble consisting of the likes of the Thorndikes, Casson and Bealby, the audience did not have to get to know their Grand Guignol actors. They were already familiar, which made the job of 'befriending' the audience that much easier.

We have already mentioned Reginald Arkell and Russell Thorndike's *Oh Hell!!!*, which includes a scene, set in Hell, where Dorothy Minto and George Bealby play themselves, acting in a parody of *The Hand of Death* which appeared on the same bill, whilst continually making fun of the controversy surrounding the Grand Guignol. This self-referencing and joking at one's own expense works as if the audience is being let in on a private joke. Only by being true supporters and aficionados of the form, only by being genuine *guignoleurs*, will they fully appreciate the piece. Consequently, laughing at the play confirms their expertise and membership of the elite. It breeds instant familiarity and brings the entire audience into the Grand Guignol fold. In so doing, it also allowed Levy to establish the notion of 'playfulness' between actors and audience, which is so crucial to the entire Grand Guignol event (see Hand and Wilson, 2002, 69–72). It is a playfulness that is also evident in the illustration on the theatre's publicity postcard, which depicts a terrorized audience running frantically from the theatre – a humorous exaggeration to those in the know. Crucially, though, it is also a playfulness that allows the actor to break through the fourth wall and acknowledge the audience at appropriate moments. A definite, but almost imperceptible glance at the audience, immediately prior to a premeditated horror, is a way of implicating the audience in the crime, drawing them further into the horror (see Hand and Wilson, 2002, 35–37), and is a not uncommon technique for the Grand Guignol actor. But turning the audience into collaborators and accessories in this way can only be done on the basis of familiarity. Nurturing that kind of familiar, trusting and playful relationship between actor and audience is a prerequisite not just for successful Grand Guignol acting but for the successful Grand Guignol *event*.

The Style of Grand Guignol Performance

When Richard Hughes wrote disparagingly about what he called 'the Grand Guignol manner' (1928, 3), it is clear that he was equating it with *bad* acting. Whilst we cannot be absolutely sure what Hughes means by this, it would not be unreasonable to assume that he is making reference to the *melodramatic* conventions of Grand Guignol performance. It is interesting to consider this in relation to Hughes's own play for the Little Theatre, *The Sisters' Tragedy*, the production of which was, it would seem, the motivation for his disparaging comments. The pace and suspense in the play raises a considerable challenge in performance inasmuch as the play could easily be performed in a heightened, over-the-top manner which could fatally detract from the serious social dimension to the play and its endeavours to present a family *'bitten with the prevalent Welsh piety of the neighbourhood'*. In other words, a social tragedy in a detailed regional setting could become a white-knuckle ride into melodrama. Another significant challenge presented by *The Sisters' Tragedy* is the characterization of Owen. Hughes's opening notes state:

> Owen *is about 24, tall and very thin, with the vacant peevish air of a blind and deaf mute. The only sound he makes is a sort of throaty chuckle (referred to as 'Owen's noise') by which he attracts attention to his wants, which he explains in dumb-show. His jaw droops rather.*

The challenge of convincingly portraying a blind and deaf mute character is enormous at the best of times and is merely compounded when one considers how focal the character is to the tragedy of Hughes's play. There are other blind characters in the British Grand Guignol, including Lucien Descaves's *Seven Blind Men* in the third series at the Little Theatre, while the brutally tragic combination of the blind and deaf in *Blind Man's Buff* was enough to get the play banned outright. Owen, however, is much more demanding and, interestingly, a very similar role appeared in the West End later the same year when Joseph Conrad's play version of *The Secret Agent*, in which the retarded Stevie is also murdered and similarly seals the tragic fate of the entire Verloc family, opened in November 1922. In Hughes's and Conrad's plays and, a generation later, in a play like Peter Nichols's *A Day in the Death of Joe Egg* (1967), the failure to convincingly portray the disabled can render the play ridiculous and even offensive.

To return to the dangers of melodrama, it is too easy these days for us to view melodramatic acting, with its exaggerated gestures and declamations, as bad acting, but even by the 1920s melodrama had largely gone out of fashion on the serious stage. The acting style of Henry Irving, which in its day was seen as a radical departure from melodrama towards realism, would have seemed histrionic to the 1920s audience who were already more used to the naturalism of the du Maurier generation. Whilst melodramatic acting lived on and continued to evolve in cinema until the late 1920s, the barnstorming productions of the old melodramas by Tod Slaughter and his company, which he toured around the provinces, would already have seemed wholly out-of-date and (along with the subsequent films) would have appealed primarily to a nostalgic audience. Nevertheless, melodrama still had a certain currency, or at least certain elements of it did, when used judiciously to express extreme emotions or passions, or to create moments of tension. As such, whilst not melodramas, both the thriller plays and the

Grand Guignol made use of melodramatic acting techniques, and it is these that observers most easily picked up on.

A.E. Wilson, writing in the *Star* after the opening night of the first series, commented upon George Bealby's 'remarkable display of strong and forceful acting' (2 September 1920), and Diana Devlin refers to the 'melodramatic grotesqueries' (Devlin, 1982, 132) of the horror plays. The existing production photographs are also suggestive of melodramatic acting styles. The photograph of Russell Thorndike in *Latitude 15° South* is reminiscent of the stills of Paulais acting in the French Grand Guignol. The tenseness of the body, the wild, large eyes, the contortion of the limbs are all out of the melodramatic stable. Likewise, the famous photograph of Sybil Thorndike performing in *Private Room Number 6* shows the contorted facial expression and exaggerated physicality required to express, not horror, but *extreme* horror. We should, however, be wary of attaching too much importance to the melodramatic aspects of Grand Guignol performance. The production photographs, especially if used for publicity purposes, are most likely to depict the climactic moments of the play where melodrama was brought to bear. Melodrama simply makes for a more exciting photograph than naturalism.

Figure 6. Lewis Casson and Russell Thorndike in *Latitude 15° South*, 1921

Figure 7. Lea (Sybil Thorndike) and Gregorff (George Bealby) in *Private Room Number 6*, 1920

Although Steve Nicholson is right to say that 'Grand Guignol productions were probably non-realistic in their style of presentation, and therefore unconvincing' (Nicholson, 2003, 181), it is worth remembering that aspects of melodramatic acting were used in Grand Guignol in order to intensify the emotional response, rather than to be realistic or convincing. We should perhaps be reminded of *The Times*'s attempts to define certain plays as being realistically or romantically 'creepy'. There is a level at which horror works best when it is unconvincing, when it revels in its own artifice. If the audience knows that this is not real horror, then it is better able to enjoy it and surrender to its emotional intensity. Certainly the critics were largely enthusiastic about the acting at the Little Theatre. The *Daily Telegraph* critic, commenting on *The Hand of Death*, declared that 'Mr Bealby's acting is a miniature masterpiece of the horrid' (2 September 1920), and 'Arkany' in the *Tatler* called it 'a really wonderful exhibition in the art of making the audience's blood curdle' (15 September 1920).

But the relentless intensity that Grand Guignol performance demanded of the actors and its effect, particularly, on Sybil Thorndike was a cause for concern amongst some critics. J.C. Trewin was relieved that she was able to 'refresh herself' (1958, 21) with her performances away from the Little, and one critic, writing in *Lloyds*, worried 'that Sybil Thorndike is suffering from the monstrous tension which Grand Guignol exercises on her nerves' (16 October 1921). Thorndike herself held the opposite opinion that 'when she played horrors at the theatre she achieved a release and cleansing that gave her much more patience and love outside' (Devlin, 1982, 133). Inevitably, Thorndike was compared, both explicitly and implicitly with Paula Maxa, the star of the impasse Chaptal. J.C. Trewin describes her Grand Guignol experiences thus:

> Mad women in a lunatic asylum gouged out Sybil Thorndike's eyes with knitting needles; she was a murdered *cocotte* stuffed into a trunk; as a war-widow she killed her scientist-brother, inventor of a bomb; she was neatly strangled; she did a little strangulation herself; with her lover she was crushed beneath a movable ceiling; her husband was tossed alive to the wolfhounds; and in *The Medium* she was encased in plaster. (Trewin, 1955, 53)

It is very redolent of the tribute paid to Maxa:

> All the humiliations that this charming artist has endured during her short, but already glorious, career cannot be ignored. Cut into ninety-three pieces by an invisible Spanish dagger, stitched back together in two seconds by a Samaritan; flattened by a steamroller; disembowelled by a slaughterman who steals her intestines; shot by firing squad, quartered, burned alive, devoured by a puma, crucified, shot with a pistol, stabbed, raped and still she stays happy and smiling. (quoted in Hand and Wilson, 2002, 19)

Famously, Maxa damaged her voice with the amount of blood-curdling screaming demanded of her. Sybil Thorndike's fans need not have worried for her health though. She emerged unscathed from her two-year ordeal at the Little Theatre and 'the Guignol helped to bring Sybil to her full height' (Devlin, 1982, 133). It is worth noting that she was not simply compared to Maxa. A review of *Private Room Number 6* declared:

> The piece is obvious enough, but Miss Thorndike's performance, in its tigress ferocity, has almost a Bernhardtian vigour. (un-sourced press cutting, Theatre Museum Archives)

To be compared to the iconic French stage performer Sarah Bernhardt (1844–1923) would be praise indeed at the time, but it is worth noting that such praise would be something of a mixed blessing in the context of the intentionally innovative Grand Guignol experiment, as it is a parallel that looks back to the achievements of a previous generation of melodrama.

The Complexity of Grand Guignol Acting: the Management of Tension

To dismiss Grand Guignol acting as melodramatic and one-dimensional is to do it a great disservice. What is particularly interesting about the evolution of the Grand Guignol in Paris at the end of the nineteenth century is that it straddled the new psychological realism with the older, impersonatory style associated with melodrama. In many ways the aesthetics of these two styles were not only contrasting, but often contradictory, and it is the primary tension between the two that the Grand Guignol actor is called upon to manage.

Of course the Grand Guignol is, in any case, essentially a form that embodies a mass of contradictions. It is comic and horrific, progressive and reactionary, realist and sensationalist, erotic and even pornographic. It is all these things and more besides. The job of the Grand Guignol actor, on the other hand, has been likened to the journey of a tightrope walker, trying to keep a balance between these opposing tensions, treading the fine line that maximizes the horrific effect of the moment, by taking it to the very edge (but not transgressing it) where horror meets comedy. The opposing forces at either end of the tightrope, which keep it tense, are those of melodrama and naturalism, and it is this tension that is the major preoccupation of the Grand Guignol actor. Indeed, in 1931 a journalist wrote of the Grand Guignol actor that 'he does not simply live his part. He is a chronometer' (Hand and Wilson, 2002, 47). Alongside the suggestion of tension in the image of the chronometer, is the perceptive insight that the job of the Grand Guignol actor goes beyond the demands of psychological realism that an actor should 'live his part'.

Any actor approaching the job of developing his/her character from a psychological realist standpoint needs to put the character's psychology at the forefront of that exploration. As psychological realism aspires to presenting real life upon the stage, then it necessarily follows that the characters on stage must have a life and a history off-stage. In other words, they exist outside of the play and must have psychologies which determine their behaviour. Stanislavski's exercises for the actor relating to emotional memory and the objective and super-objective all lay testament to a belief that the actor must approach the development of a character through the supposed psychology of that character and that it is the actor's ultimate aim to present a convincing performance by inhabiting the psyche of the character.

This emphasis on psychology places 'character' at the very centre of theatre. If the character has an existence outside of the play, then the play itself is determined by the psychology of the accumulated characters. That is to say, the play exists for the characters and not the other way round. Psychological realism, therefore, for the actor is characterized by the supremacy of the character over all else – over plot, narrative and, most certainly, the actor, since the actor is rendered invisible, completely subsumed in character. The actor must surrender him/herself completely to the character to the point that character and actor become indivisible and the actor becomes invisible, which in turn prevents the actor from commenting upon the action. If pre-realist forms are characterized by the character having no existence off-stage, then realist forms are characterized by the actor having no existence on-stage.

It is somewhat difficult nowadays to understand the radical approach to acting that psychological realism presented, but its very philosophical foundations contradict what went before in terms of acting. For the Grand Guignol, it is melodrama that provides the model for pre-realist acting, a form that is representational and impersonatory, in contrast to psychological realism. It makes quite contradictory demands upon the actor in relation to his/her approach to character. Indeed, character is not a particularly useful word when comparing melodramatic acting styles to psychological realism. The Victorians might just as likely have equated 'character' with moral fibre, such as is implied in the term 'character witness'. For a discussion of melodrama, the term 'role' is far more useful.[2] Its secondary meaning of 'function' or 'purpose' is far more suitable for describing the relationship between the actor and what s/he does on stage. As Thomson points out, where character exists purely to serve the plot, acting is necessarily *purposeful* (2000, 8). At the same time 'role' suggests an artificiality of character, that what is seen on stage is simply an actor fulfilling a function in relation to the play, rather than a character in actual reality. Role suggests a fundamental division between actor and character.

Melodrama is in part characterized by a primacy of plot and, as such, the key difference between the melodramatic role and the realist character is the absence of psychology of the former. The melodramatic role has no existence outside of the play and within the play only exists to serve the narrative. The melodramatic actor must give a purposeful performance, not a psychological one – the melodramatic actor impersonates, rather than inhabits, the consequence of which is a separation of actor and role, where each is equally visible.

With the Grand Guignol, however, life is not so simple. Violence, one of the form's defining features, is never motiveless. It is carefully prepared and signposted by the writer, and the motive usually resides within the characters' psychological selves. For example, in *The Person Unknown*,

---

[2]   See Thomson, 2000, 3–15, for a discussion of how this also applies to the model of the Elizabethan actor.

the eponymous character is driven to action by events and experiences that have occurred outside of the play, and Daisy is marked as a victim because of what she has done prior to the play. His motivation is determined by his past which forms his psychology. In other words, these characters have lives beyond the play and have psychologies that determine their behaviour and, as such, the actor playing the role has little choice but to approach the play through psychological realism, by building a character.

It is doubtful, though, that the audiences that packed the little theatre in Paris to see Paulais and Maxa or the Little Theatre in London to see the Thorndike-Cassons and George Bealby, did so to witness fully rounded, psychologically realistic and believable characters. They did not watch the plays wondering whether the internal traumas of the characters would be resolved in a happy ending or lead to emotional desolation. In most plays in the Grand Guignol we are dealing with largely recognizable *types* imported from melodrama or farce. The audience knew exactly how a horror play would turn out – in a climactic moment of violence – the only question that arose was the means by which the violence would be executed and the manner of that execution: are we in for a stabbing, a shooting, a poisoning, a decapitation or a death of fright? Will the journey to this inexorable denouement put us off our dinner or give us a damned good laugh?

The unfortunate former soldier in *The Person Unknown* may well be a psychologically complete character, but he is also a functionary, in that he would be immediately marked out as the perpetrator of violence by anybody familiar with the Grand Guignol form. He may well have a history beyond the play which predetermines his behaviour, but within the play he is there for no other reason than to take a terrible revenge on his victim. The same is true of Daisy. From her first appearance as a frivolous, insensitive and arrogant young woman, she is instantly recognizable as simultaneously the victim of forthcoming violence and also the villain who will 'deserve' what is coming to her. Daisy is a villain inasmuch as she is the emblem of the evils of a society which effectively brainwashed young men into conscription: her demise will be mortifying and ugly and she will not be able to redeem herself or be rescued by a melodramatic hero, but it is nonetheless a 'come-uppance'. This is character as role, existing purely to serve the narrative, and it demands not a psychological realist approach, but a representational approach to acting. This is one of the most significant contradictions of Grand Guignol drama: characters that emerge from naturalist assumptions, but demand stylized representation on stage. Similarly in *Private Room Number 6*, the General and Lea are the polarized melodramatic functionaries of evil and good respectively: but what Grand Guignol brilliantly delivers is its dramatic – indeed, post-melodramatic – twist whereby Lea is not a helpless victim but a ruthless and efficient assassin.

The shift towards melodramatic acting in performance, however, remains incomplete. It is certainly the most striking feature of Grand Guignol performance, and one can understand why Richard Hughes equated Grand Guignol acting with melodramatic acting. Psychological realism is never completely banished from Grand Guignol performance and rather acts to temper the extreme posturing associated with melodrama. Curiously, the two opposing styles are used against each other to maximize the effective use of both. It is almost as if the actor is like a dial, rather than a chronometer, swinging between psychological realism on the one hand, to high melodrama on the other. Whilst the dial may generally point towards melodrama, it is the juxtaposition of melodrama with realism that gives weight to the melodrama without resort to the most ludicrous histrionics.

Melodrama is largely reserved for the most significant and climactic moments in the Grand Guignol drama, with varying levels of melodrama used for moments of varying significance. Inevitably perhaps, the moment of highest melodrama is the enactment of violence – slow, measured and highly stylized. Realism is used for the scenes which link and lead up to those moments of significance (and melodrama), furthering the narrative and providing brief respite for the audience. Interestingly, the clues to identifying those moments of significance lie within the text, not within the character. Ultimately it is the narrative, not the psychology, that determines the drama. The Grand Guignol demands of its actors representation, not being.

The Grand Guignol actor works constantly across opposing styles of acting, seeking to manage and exploit the tensions that exist between psychological realism and melodrama in a creative way. It is a challenge that is encapsulated in the following comments by the theatre critic for the *Daily Chronicle*, commenting upon Sybil Thorndike's performance in the 1921 production of *The Unseen* at London's Grand Guignol:

> Miss Thorndike's playing was not only wonderful in the intensity of the rather needless agonies of the mad scene, but exquisitely sympathetic in the far better earlier moments. (13 October 1921)

Differences in Grand Guignol acting between London and Paris

We should, in discussing Grand Guignol acting as if it were a single unified style, be aware that there did exist differences between the way the plays were performed in France and in Britain. These would be due to two main reasons, the first being that the actors at the London Grand Guignol often drew, inevitably, on English popular theatre traditions, such as pantomime, especially in those plays written specifically for the stage of the Little Theatre. For example, the production photographs from *Oh, Hell!!!* show a set design, costuming and even the positioning of character groups as if they were from an English pantomime. In addition, Russell Thorndike's cross-dressing portrayal of 'La Borgnesse' in *The Old Women* has the unmistakable qualities of a pantomime villain.

The main reason for differences in acting, though, is attributable to the presence (if not the direct intervention) of the Lord Chamberlain and broad public opinion as to what was acceptable on the stage. The French were far more liberal in this respect, especially in matters of sex and violence. We have already discussed at length how the Parisian Grand Guignol has had a certain mythology built around it in terms of its levels of enacted violence (Hand and Wilson, 2002, 46–51). Very often it was a theatre of restraint, punctuated very carefully with well-placed theatrical trickery and sleight-of-hand, but held together by meticulously crafted dialogue which suggested acts of horror that were not always enacted. It was always a theatre of the Unseen, as much as a theatre of the Seen.

If that was the case in France, then it was doubly so in London. In France, the restraint was driven largely by theatrical and economic (the laundry bill for blood-stained costumes had to be kept under control) considerations, whereas Levy had to operate within the limits of good taste, as defined by the Lord Chamberlain. Stage blood was rarely if ever used and even the final moments of violence, if they were considered too visually disturbing, happened off-stage or obscured by the actors. As Russell Thorndike recalls:

> Now in regard to [Grand Guignol] horrors, Casson set himself a rule which I think made them. He produced them rather to create fear and panic than just sickening horror. He used suggestion rather than blood-dripping props. We frightened our audiences, rather than disgusted them (Thorndike, 1950, 274)

Climactic acts of violence were usually bloodless – strangulation was preferred to throat-slitting, for example. In Levy's French-language London production of *Le Baiser dans la nuit* in 1915, the curtain had to be brought down before the final vitriol attack had taken place.

Similarly, when Levy revived the Grand Guignol at the Little Theatre for a short-lived season in May 1928, he included Virginia and Frank Vernon's *After Death* (an adaptation of René Berton's recent offering at the Parisian Grand Guignol, *L'homme qui a tué la mort* (1928)). The play features a scientist reanimating the severed head of a guillotine victim called Morales, and in order to secure the licence for the play, Levy had to assure the Lord Chamberlain that the head of the executed man would not be visible to the audience, but would be obscured by the bodies of the actors, as they crowded around. It is fascinating to note that although Levy was forced to obscure the chilling tableau of the living head in the production, the role of Morales was played by James Whale who would soon emigrate to the US and would direct *Frankenstein* (1931) for Universal Pictures just three years later. It is not in the least fanciful to presume that Whale's own experience as a reanimated corpse at the Grand Guignol must have had a major impact on how he directed Boris Karloff in one of the most memorable, influential and meticulously *visible* sequences in horror cinema. Such revelations gives us valuable clues to the performance style and pace of British Grand Guignol as well as opening up generally neglected channels of legacy and influence.

The impact of censorship on what could or could not be displayed would always haunt the Grand Guignol in Britain. Even as late as 1945, when a licence was finally granted to Frederick Witney's *Coals of Fire* and the new Chief Examiner was criticizing the prudishness of his predecessor, the licence was only granted on condition that the climax of the piece – when the face of a character is pushed into a fire – should not be shown. Only once did the French Grand Guignol get into trouble, and that was when a guillotining was represented on stage in a production of *Au petit jour* by André de Lorde and Jean Bernac in 1921. This was considered to be 'an act of sacrilege towards a national icon' (Hand and Wilson, 2002, 123), and Choisy was hauled before the Chief of Police and was made to alter the play's ending.

These were not uncommon occurrences in London, and even when the censor did not directly intervene, as in these cases, the spectre of his restraining hand was ever-present. Levy, or any other manager for that matter, had no interest in deliberately antagonizing the Lord Chamberlain (having plays refused was a time-consuming and costly business) and so a consideration of what may or may not be permissible was ever-present during rehearsals. This culture of restraint was also evident in the way that Casson designed the sets. James Agate, the critic, described them as 'no more than a suggestion of the frame in which the thing portrayed might be supposed to happen' (quoted in Devlin, 1982, 131). Whilst much of this may have been driven by the practical and financial considerations associated with staging a programme of five or more plays, it appears to have added to the creation of a theatre of suggestion.

All this inevitably affected the approach to acting adopted by the company. Without the special effects and stage trickery at the disposal of the Parisian Grand Guignol, an even greater responsibility was placed upon the actors to evoke horror in the audience purely on the strength of their performances. The production photographs of Sybil Thorndike in the throes of murdering, or being murdered herself, suggest that perhaps even greater levels of melodrama were employed at the Little Theatre than at the rue Chaptal in Paris. But that is not to disparage their acting in any way. It would seem that, if they set out to thrill and chill their audience through acting alone, then they certainly achieved it and their efforts were appreciated by audiences and critics alike. Audiences came back, time after time, to enjoy the acting of Thorndike and the rest of the ensemble at London's Grand Guignol. As the critic of the *Daily Telegraph* wrote, 'Altogether, the acting at the Little Theatre is unsurpassed in London at the present moment' (13 October 1921).

4

Censorship and Reception

Theatre Censorship in Britain

In a consideration of the way that Levy's experiment was received by both the establishment and the wider public, there are two main sources of evidence available to us. The first of those is the files of correspondence of the Lord Chamberlain, the official censor, which are housed in the British Library. The second is the large collection of press reviews that appeared in the dailies and weeklies of the time. This chapter seeks to use that evidence to address specific issues around the reception of London's Grand Guignol. The Grand Guignol in Paris became, in many ways, a theatre of exploitation. It was a theatre that *lured* some members of its audience with promises of explicit violence and erotic titillation and, by the same token, it *defied* other potential spectators with the self-same menu, daring them to see if they were brave enough to witness the extreme acts that were to be enacted on its stage. In seeking to inaugurate an authentic Grand Guignol in London, José Levy was faced with a major challenge. In fact, any desire to create a theatre of exploitation in Britain in the first part of the twentieth century would immediately have been faced with a major problem: censorship. As has already been amply demonstrated in this book, the story of London's Grand Guignol is very closely tied up with the story of the censorship of the British theatre in the inter-war period and presents a particularly interesting case study in the 231-year history of theatrical censorship in Britain.

Although Britain may have boasted about its commitment to democracy and free speech, this stopped short of permitting a non-interventionist stance when it came to what could or could not be performed on the stages of the nation's public theatres. The key legislation in the history of stage censorship in Britain was the Theatrical Licensing Act of 1737 which was introduced in immediate reaction to Henry Fielding's scathing satire *The Historical Register for 1736*. The Act meant that all plays needed to be submitted to the Lord Chamberlain's Office for official approval at least fourteen days before any proposed public performance. Any defiance would cost £50 plus the loss of the offending theatre's licence for staging performances. The powers of the legislation were further clarified and consolidated most significantly by the 1843 Theatres Act which introduced regulations whereby playwrights not only had to submit all plays to the Lord Chamberlain's Office but now had to pay the Office for the privilege at the new rate of two guineas for a full play and one guinea for a one-act play. The shadow of censorship put enormous pressure on the artistic freedom of dramatists and put limitations on the kind of play they were able to produce. The legislation forced Henry Fielding to become a novelist, that medium of published fiction being unimpeded by the threat of suppression. It could be argued that the existence of stage censorship kept many writers away from the theatre for over 200 years, as partly corroborated a little over a decade before the establishment of the London Grand Guignol when Harley Granville Barker described the options open to writers in Britain to the official enquiry set up by Parliament in 1909, the Joint Select Committee on Censorship:

> [A writer] must either write purely conventional plays, which he practically knows the Lord Chamberlain will not object to, or he must take to some other form of literary work, such as book-writing – the writing of fiction – where he is not hampered by any such dictation. (quoted in Findlater, 1967, 107)

A number of prominent figures in the English literary scene volunteered their opinions on stage censorship for the 1909 investigation. Interestingly, although some of these writers were not known for their radical temperament or political views, when it comes to the existence and mechanism of stage censorship they pursue their quarry in no uncertain terms. Arnold Bennett regards it as 'monstrous and grotesque and profoundly insulting' (quoted in Findlater, 1967, 106); and Henry James, by 1909 a pre-eminent novelist and an experienced yet wholly unsuccessful playwright, is just as uncompromising when he describes 'the depth of dismay and disgust' of any aspiring English dramatist when they discover they have to deal with the Lord Chamberlain: 'an obscure and irresponsible Mr So-and-So' (James, 1984, 532). The implication of this is that there is greater freedom in other genres, and James goes on to stress that the repression of the stage has deterred writers who have 'any intellectual independence and self-respect' (ibid.). Similarly, in his high profile article 'The Censor of Plays: An Appreciation' (*Daily Mail*, 12 October 1907) – published some two years before the Joint Select Committee on Censorship – Joseph Conrad reveals that he was astonished when he learned of the existence of the Lord Chamberlain's Office and its exceptional powers of censorship. In describing it, Conrad says, 'I don't say inappropriate. I say improper – that is: something to be ashamed of' (Conrad, 1921, 76). Conrad regarded the Lord Chamberlain as 'the Caesar of the dramatic world' (1921, 79), with formidable powers to 'kill thought, and incidentally truth, and incidentally beauty' (1921, 78). Over all, however, opinion was divided. While the playwrights and other writers, by and large bitterly resentful of the restrictions imposed on their artistic freedom, were generally united in railing against censorship, the theatre managers, with their eyes fixed firmly on box office receipts, welcomed censorship as a way of curbing the risky excesses of playwrights. For these managers, theatre was a business, and very few had any interest in morally challenging or offending the audience (Findlater, 1967, 122; Shellard and Nicholson, 2004, 61).

Those opposed to censorship had started out with great optimism at the beginning of the 1909 enquiry, but what resulted was a classic fudge, which allowed for the continuation of censorship whilst drawing up guidelines suggesting how the Lord Chamberlain's Office should operate. It stated that plays should receive a licence unless the Lord Chamberlain considered them:

(a) To be indecent;
(b) To contain offensive personalities;
(c) To represent on the stage in an invidious manner a living person, or any person recently dead;
(d) To do violence to the sentiment of religious reverence;
(e) To be calculated to conduce to crime or vice;
(f) To be calculated to impair friendly relations with any foreign Power; or
(g) To be calculated to cause a breach of the peace

(from the Report of the 1909 Enquiry, quoted in Shellard and Nicholson, 2004, 63)

Whilst it placed the burden of proof, as it were, upon the Lord Chamberlain, it was what George Bernard Shaw called 'a capital illustration [of] the art of contriving methods of reform which will leave matters exactly as they are!' (quoted in Findlater, 1967, 112) and did nothing to quell the debate, but rather encouraged it (Findlater, 1967, 114). In November 1911 a question was asked in Parliament concerning the introduction of possible legislation to abolish theatre censorship, and Sir Douglas Dawson, the then comptroller, was forced into a robust response and defence of the censor:

My belief is that the abolition of the censor would mean ruin for all connected with the drama, the authors included, for the only alternative is action by the police, *after the harm has been done*, and where international questions are at issue this would involve great risk.

(private memo to the Home Office, quoted in Shellard and Nicholson, 2004, 65) [1]

This is not to say that the Lord Chamberlain's Office was an entrenched, conservative force, incapable of reform or moving with the times. Dawson was fully aware of the controversy surrounding censorship and had introduced a series of reforms upon his appointment in 1907, including the establishment of an additional Examiner of Plays and an advisory committee made up of 'experts', including Squire Bancroft who was an octogenarian former actor-manager (Shellard and Nicholson, 2004, 63). He also required each reader's report to contain a brief summary of the play to ensure evidence that each script had been properly read and considered.

When George Street – the censor who would be most involved with the London Grand Guignol – was appointed Joint Examiner of Plays in 1914, following the death of Charles Brookfield, it was seen as an enlightened appointment. Street was 'an enthusiastic supporter of Ibsen and Wilde, and a man of rather more progressive theatrical tastes' (Shellard and Nicholson, 2004, 65), who began with a rather ambivalent attitude towards the necessity for stage censorship and was only later fully converted to its cause (Findlater, 1967, 130).

It is important to note that some people viewed the censor (including those who worked in the Lord Chamberlain's Office) not as the enemy of the theatre, but as its champion and protector. When the censor refused a licence to examples of the British Grand Guignol repertoire and plays now acknowledged as masterpieces such as George Bernard Shaw's Mrs Warren's Profession (first performed privately in 1902), some defenders of censorship regarded this as not merely being inspired by a sense of moral outrage, but emanating from a genuine desire to protect the broader integrity of the theatre as a whole. When the Lord Chamberlain did grant licences to potentially controversial plays, then those plays were given an added protection precisely because of that implied endorsement. For example, in the uproar that followed the staging of G. H. Q. Love at the opening night of London's Grand Guignol in September 1920, much of the venom from what we would now call the religious right and other self-appointed moral crusaders, such as the Westminster Catholic Federation and The Public Morality Council, was directed at the Lord Chamberlain himself, and there were calls for his dismissal (Nicholson, 2003, 209). As Steve Nicholson comments, 'the Office realized it could not afford to endorse the reductive

---

[1]   An interesting example of an 'international' issue is the proposed revival of Gilbert and Sullivan's The Mikado in 1907, which was banned because the Crown Prince of Japan would be visiting London. Ironically, the overzealous attitude of the Lord Chamberlain backfired: the Japanese noble was greatly disappointed as he was looking forward to seeing the production.

moral line some were urging on them' (Nicholson, 2003, 209), and the necessity of being seen to be enforcing a strict moral code on behalf of the public was one way of affording greater protection to those plays that were licensed. Rather than being on the opposite side of the fence to the theatre, the Lord Chamberlain's Office often found itself, ironically, sandwiched between those who argued for a relaxation in censorship and those who called for the imposition of a stricter moral line, and as a result absorbed the blows from both camps.

Although, as previously mentioned, Sir Douglas Dawson introduced some procedural changes to the licensing of plays in 1907, the process for obtaining a licence remained largely unchanged. The producer of a play (not the author) would submit a script to the Lord Chamberlain's Office for consideration, along with a fee. The script would then be read by one of the Examiners of Plays (in spite of Dawson's reforms, George Street was, in fact, the only Examiner from 1920–30), who would then produce a reader's report along with a recommendation for either a granting of a licence (with or without conditions) or for a refusal. The Lord Chamberlain would then act on that recommendation, with the option of considering the script himself or referring it to the Advisory Committee for 'special consideration'. Despite the presence of a stringent and long-standing system of stage censorship in Britain, most scripts were uncontroversial and were nodded through on the recommendation of the Examiner. Very few plays were banned outright. During the second half of the nineteenth century an average of one play per year was prohibited from public performance, and although this increased in the first years of the twentieth century, we are still looking at less than one percent of all submitted plays facing outright proscription. This changed when the Grand Guignol was established at the Little Theatre, with a relatively large number of scripts being denied a licence. However, it is important to understand that the Lord Chamberlain's Office had other powers at its disposal, and what was probably more insidious was the censor's notorious 'blue pencil'. The censor of British theatre was granted full powers of intervention on a submitted script. The stage censor – literally equipped with a blue pencil – was permitted to tinker with the script, rewriting or completely excising words and phrases, or even characters and stage directions, which were perceived as being offensive on moral, religious or political grounds.

A direct and profound consequence of the presence of this legislation was *self-censorship*. There were other options for playwrights inasmuch as the Lord Chamberlain's Office had no jurisdiction over performances of plays that took place in private arts clubs and theatre societies; most famous in relation to this is the banning in 1891 of Ibsen's *Ghosts*, which went on to find life and an audience in private society performance. Similarly, some of Frederick Witney's horror plays submitted to the British Grand Guignol were banned and only performed in private club performances. Typically, however, playwrights who wanted to see their plays performed on the public stage were obliged to write scripts which would not cause offence. For some dramatists this must have established a state of mind not dissimilar to what Augusto Boal would call 'the cop in the head' (Boal, 1995, 40), a mechanism of oppression whereby individuals censor their own thoughts or desires. Many playwrights must have written plays which they consciously or otherwise expunged of anything which ran the risk of challenging their audience.

It could be argued that there were only a couple of instances in British theatre history when clear lines of conflict were established, and playwrights and theatres sought to defy the powers of the Lord Chamberlain's Office. One was in the twilight of stage censorship before its demise by Act of Parliament in 1968, when the Royal Court Theatre staged productions of Edward Bond's deliberately provocative *Saved* (1965) and *Early Morning* (1968). We would like to argue that another instance of British theatre that was equally defiant when it came to taking a stand against the principle and powers of stage censorship was the Grand Guignol seasons at the Little Theatre.

One feature that may seem remarkable to us now is just how close to the planned opening night of a play scripts were submitted for consideration. Not only was it quite normal practice for scripts to reach the Lord Chamberlain's Office once rehearsals were well underway: sometimes it was a deliberate tactic whereby, it was hoped, pressure would be placed on the Lord Chamberlain to approve the play. Bearing in mind that the process of obtaining a licence could be a lengthy one, especially if it were referred to the Advisory Committee, and that late changes to the rehearsed script may well have been necessary at the eleventh hour, it might be assumed that producers were taking something of a risk. At the same time, they were equally unwilling to make an imposition on the Lord Chamberlain's time and to waste their own money by submitting a play for consideration before they could be certain that a production would be staged. It also meant that, should a play prove controversial, representatives from the Lord Chamberlain's Office could be invited to a rehearsal to make an assessment of the production. With these procedures in mind, let us look in depth at the opening season of London's Grand Guignol.

The Lord Chamberlain's Office and the Grand Guignol's First Season

When Levy submitted five plays at the beginning of August 1920 with a view to getting them licensed in time for the opening night of London's Grand Guignol at the start of the following month,[2] he was theoretically

---

[2]   It would appear from the licence applications that the opening night was originally scheduled for 30 August. However, due to the ensuing delays in obtaining

allowing plenty of time to overcome any difficulties. The five plays were *How to be Happy* by Pierre Veber, *The Hand of Death* by André de Lorde and Alfred Binet, *Save the Mark* by Wilfred Harris, *Oh, Hell!!!*, a revuette by Reginald Arkell and Russell Thorndike and *G. H. Q. Love* by Sewell Collins. Levy was presumably particularly unsure about *The Hand of Death* as it had previously been refused a licence in 1915 in its French original as *L'Horrible Expérience* when it might have expected an easier ride from the censor. Not surprisingly this was a fact that Levy tried to keep quiet. The sequence of events that followed is not exactly clear from the Lord Chamberlain's correspondence, but the story that emerges very much sets the scene for the ongoing relationship between London's Grand Guignol and the Lord Chamberlain, a relationship that ultimately contributed to the closing down of the project.

Having already compiled the reader's reports on the plays, a memorandum from Street, dated 7 August, asks for four plays (*The Hand of Death, Save the Mark, Oh, Hell!!!* and *G. H. Q. Love*) to be sent to the Lord Chamberlain for special consideration, which was done two days later. In the meantime, *How to be Happy*, which Levy himself had translated and adapted, and which Street described as 'a pleasant little comedy quite free from offence' (reader's report, 5 August 1920), was granted a licence on 12 August. *Oh, Hell!!!* received its licence on 16 August, as did *G. H. Q. Love*,[3] presumably after Viscount Sandhurst, the Lord Chamberlain, accepted Street's recommendations. For the remaining two plays, *The Hand of Death* and *Save the Mark*, the matter was more complex and Sandhurst decided to refer both plays to the Advisory Committee for further consideration.

The context of all this was that August was 'the dead season', a period of time when those with country homes and estates left the heat and poor air of a London summer to escape into the provinces. As a result the Lord Chamberlain and the members of the Advisory Committee were spread far and wide throughout Britain. This would account for the fact that it took a whole week for Sandhurst to initially respond to Street and also for the ensuing delay in gathering the opinions of the Advisory Committee on the two outstanding pieces. We may also conjecture that Levy took advantage of the situation, hoping perhaps that the plays would not receive as much scrutiny as they would if the Advisory Committee had all been readily available in London. In this Levy was mistaken.

Henry Higgins was the first member of the committee to receive the two scripts and he responded to them both promptly on 17 August. As

---

the licence for, in particular, *The Hand of Death*, it would appear that Levy found it necessary to delay by two days.

[3]   It is unclear why Street asked for *Oh, Hell!!!* to be given special consideration, since his report is very favourable. Street is less enthusiastic about *G. H. Q. Love*, and it is 'only dubiously, however, Recommended for Licence'.

regards *The Hand of Death*, he recommended refusal, but not without some reservation:

> It is difficult to contend that the performance of this play would do any particular harm, but it is an understandably peculiarly unpleasant specimen of the blood curdling playlet & one that in my opinion should not be licenced – if only because those who were induced to attend its performance without knowing its character, would be shocked and horrified beyond measure (handwritten memo, 17 August 1920)

When it came to *Save the Mark*, he was unequivocal in his support for Street, who had written in his report:

> This Grand Guignol effort is poor stuff and as it stands objectionable. It is a great pity the management should go to tenth rate French plays for their enterprise. This one is a hackneyed kind of immoral farce. (…) I think it is an inferior piece of nastiness which might well be refused. (reader's report, 5 August 1920)

Whether the scripts were circulated amongst other committee members is not clear, but by the time they reached Sir Douglas Dawson it was already 24 August and the proposed opening night was only six days away, a fact that greatly troubled Dawson. Feeling that the Lord Chamberlain's Office had taken too long in dealing with the matter, he proposed issuing a licence to *The Hand of Death* without further ado in order 'to avoid the hardship inflicted by refusing a licence' (handwritten memo, 24 August 1920), although he insisted that the play could be given a licence only if certain changes were made to the ending of the piece. It is an interesting fact that Dawson, a staunch supporter of the role of the censor, clearly sees the job in terms of providing a service to the theatre industry, rather than standing in opposition to it. Perhaps that is what Levy had hoped for.

In respect of *Save the Mark*, even the time delay could not persuade Dawson to support it. The very act of one character giving another a lovebite during an adulterous encounter was enough for him to declare that the play was 'sufficiently *"indecent"* to preclude the granting of a licence' (handwritten memo, 24 August 1920). With that the play's fate was sealed and Levy was informed that it could not be publicly performed. Clearly Levy was distraught and sought an interview with Sandhurst (who was still on his estate in Scotland), pointing out that the actions in *The Hand of Death* to which the committee had objected had already been licensed previously in two other plays, including F. Brooke Warren's *The Face at the Window*. This was communicated to Sandhurst by a telegram from the Chief Clerk, Mr. Hertslet, to the Lord Chamberlain's Office, sent on the morning of 25

August. Here, though, Levy dangerously overplayed his hand. Hertslet was clearly a fastidious clerk and returned to the archives to check Levy's claims and in doing so came across something that Levy had hoped nobody would remember – *The Hand of Death* had been refused a licence in 1915 under its French title. A further telegram was sent to Sandhurst that same day informing him of the fact.

This changed everything – it would be difficult to justify licensing a play in English that had been refused a licence in French only five years previously under his own watch. The following day Sandhurst sent another telegram to Hertslet, not only refusing an interview with Levy, but also confirming that *Save the Mark* was refused and imposing further conditions on the licence for *The Hand of Death*. This time Colonel Crichton, the current comptroller, was to be sent to observe a rehearsal, and only if he were satisfied would the licence be granted. But time was now running desperately short for Levy. It was already too late to substitute another play for *Save the Mark*, but he felt that he could still open with four plays on the programme. Everything depended on the licence for the de Lorde play. The opening night was now only four days away and he knew he would be unlikely to receive a decision before the 28th at the very earliest. It must have been around this time that Levy decided to delay the inaugural performances of London's Grand Guignol until 1 September. Crichton attended a rehearsal on 27 August and was accompanied by Street. The next day he sent his verdict to the Lord Chamberlain:

> [We] were both strongly of [the] opinion that it read very much worse
> than it played. We both expected to be thrilled & were merely bored,
> & I think the public will be the same. (letter, 28 August 1920)

The licence was eventually issued on 30 August and was received by Levy the following morning. It was a close-run thing. London's Grand Guignol finally opened the next evening.

The Lord Chamberlain's Office and the Grand Guignol's Subsequent Seasons

The build-up to the opening of the Grand Guignol at the Little Theatre was thus a somewhat tense and hectic process. It was, in no small measure, a sign of things to come. It was immediately clear that relations with the Lord Chamberlain's Office were never going to be easy and the constant wrangling gradually began to wear Levy down. The tone of that relationship was already set, and even by November 1920 Viscount Sandhurst was calling for plays submitted by the Little Theatre to be sent for special consideration, as he was already aware of 'the general trend of matters at this theatre' (handwritten note, 29 November 1920). A particular example is the case of

Figure 8. Aubrey Hammond:
Poster for London's Grand
Guignol, 1920

H.F. Maltby's play *I Want to Go Home*, which was scheduled to open as part of the Second Series at the Little Theatre. The plot concerns a husband who, suspected of adultery, gives himself away when his wife gets him drunk on champagne. In his initial report Street recommended a licence, claiming that it 'is not exactly a moral little comedy, but I think there is nothing in it absolutely harmful' (reader's report, 23 November 1920), but Sandhurst still insisted on gathering the opinions of the Advisory Committee. Henry Higgins's feeling that the play was 'loathsomely vulgar' (handwritten note, 29 November 1920) was universally shared by the committee, but only Lord Buckmaster and Squire Bancroft (who thought it a 'nasty little play') considered that this vulgarity was worthy of a refusal. Buckmaster in particular was adamant, and his argument won the day. The play was refused and another Maltby comedy, *What Did Her Husband Say?* (a play which had previously been passed only after considerable amendments and had been brought into the first series to replace the less successful *How to be Happy*) was substituted in the programme. Maltby was incensed and wrote a long letter of protest to the Lord Chamberlain, but to no avail. This was in contrast to Eliot Crawshay-Williams who, as previously discussed, was able to use his influence as a former MP to his advantage. A good example of this was *Rounding the Triangle* which was scheduled into the fourth series, to open in April 1921. As early as 1 March Levy had written to Crawshay-Williams expressing his fears:

> I am also having more trouble with the censor over one of my plays for the next series, and if I cannot get it through, I am thinking of sending in 'Rounding the Triangle', but they seem so particular with my plays that I am afraid they may not pass this one too. (private correspondence, 1 March 1921)

Levy's fears were confirmed when the play was initially refused, but Crawshay-Williams sought and received a private interview with Sandhurst, promised certain revisions and the play received its licence, much to the relief and pleasure of Levy.

Overall, however, one gets the impression that José Levy was frequently exasperated, and it seems that he never fully understood why he had such a difficult relationship with the censor. The producer's attitude is perhaps at odds with other members of the British Grand Guignol 'family'. There is no doubt that the Little Theatre thrived on the controversy it created. In *The Grand Guignol Annual Review 1921*, published as a souvenir programme by the theatre, Mervyn McPherson declared that 'we prefer to be ambitious and, if necessary, to die of too much daring, than complacently to endure the mediocre. This might well be the slogan of the Grand Guignol' (McPherson, 1921, 3). In the same issue, Lewis Casson wrote that the 'fascination of working for the Grand Guignol lies in the risks one runs' (McPherson, 1921, 32). He may well have been referring primarily to the job of acting in the Grand Guignol, but Casson was certainly aware of the risks involved in managing this kind of enterprise too. Some of the Grand Guignol playwrights were aware of the 'risks' of the Grand Guignol, not least in the presence of stage censorship. A number were intentionally defiant of it as is evidenced by Crawshay-Williams's 'Preface' to his *Five Grand Guignol Plays* (1924), in which the former MP – who, as we have seen, had demonstrated that he had a 'special relationship' with authority – openly attacks the Lord Chamberlain: 'the Censor continues to think that plays which apparently do not demoralize the French will have that effect on the more delicate-minded inhabitants of these islands ...' (Crawshay-Williams, 1924, 3). With his Grand Guignol project, Levy sought not only to introduce the form, style and technique of a French theatrical genre to the British stage but also, whether he was fully aware of its implications or not, he had to import a degree of French morality too. Having said that, the British Grand Guignol repertoire – even in the banned plays – seldom explores the taboo to the extent that the Parisian repertoire does. With this in mind, it is little surprise that some of the most literal translations of the French Grand Guignol's more violent and unsettling pieces were mutilated with the blue pencil shortly before being banned outright. For example, Charles Hellem and Pol d'Estoc's *Aveugle!* (1907) – translated as *Blind Man's Buff* for the British Grand Guignol – was condemned by G.S. Street: this is 'a horrible and revolting Play and in my opinion there should be a limit to the extent to which managers should be allowed to sicken normal minds or to pander to the depraved' (reader's report, 22 February 1921). Similarly, just under a year later when Levy submitted *The Regiment* by Robert Francheville, a version of the Parisian Grand Guignol play *Le Beau Regiment* (1912), in January 1922, Street called it, in tones of exasperation, 'Another painful play for this troublesome Theatre' (reader's report, 3 January 1922).

A further example of a banned play is *Dr Goudron's System* (submitted to the Lord Chamberlain's Office in May 1922), which was yet again a translation of a French Grand Guignol masterpiece: this was an adaptation of André de Lorde's classic *Le Système du Docteur Goudron et du Professeur Plume* (1903). De Lorde's play was itself a dramatization of Edgar Allan Poe's short story 'The System of Dr Tarr and Professor Fether' (1845), the horror tale which established the paradigm of the 'lunatics taking over the asylum' scenario. The British version of the play does not re-anglicize the French characters into Tarr and Fether but retains the French names Goudron and Plume: it is as if the French play has become more of a classic paradigm than Poe's original. Even if the play finds its roots in a classic mid-nineteenth-century 'Tale of Mystery and Imagination', it was still banned outright. Interestingly, the play – like *Blind Man's Buff* – was not banned before the censor had taken particular exception to a few lines which were excised with the blue pencil before he decided that the play was completely unacceptable for performance. The lines that censor strikes out include the stage direction that '*All the lunatics howl*' offstage during the thunderstorm, and provides an example of how even auditory material was sometimes deemed to be as offensive as visual material. Other lines that were excised from *Dr Goudron's System* include this section:

> GOUDRON [...] Wait, give me a knife to jab in his eye. (*He takes a paper knife from the table*)
> PLUME: Yes. Tear out his eye.
> JEAN (*struggling on the table*): Help! Henri!
> PLUME: Blood! Ah! Ah! (*They laugh*)

The offensiveness of this scene of eye-gouging was no doubt compounded by the fact that two women – the lunatics Joyeuse and Eugenie – help to hold the victim down. It is probably no surprise that this episode of extreme violence was automatically struck out before the whole play was completely forbidden. It is a pivotal moment in the script and it is quite possible that the whole play went unlicensed partly because the removal of this scene fatally compromises the overall drama. Interestingly, a very similar sequence

– eye-gouging at the hands of inmates in a lunatic asylum – *was* successfully staged at the Little Theatre in June of the previous year, 1921. The play was Christopher Holland's *The Old Women*, a translation of André de Lorde and Alfred Binet's *Un crime dans une maison de fous ou Les Infernales*. The fact that a play containing an explicit eye-gouging was permitted seems surprising until one knows the fuller context to *The Old Women*, a play which endures as a masterpiece of the Grand Guignol form and is perhaps the single most significant play in the history of the British Grand Guignol: after *The Old Women* was staged at the Little Theatre, the British Grand Guignol's precarious relationship with the Lord Chamberlain's Office came to a head.

The Beginning of the End: *The Old Women*

In the Spring of 1921, Levy was offered the opportunity to produce de Lorde and Binet's *Un crime dans une maison de fous*, a play which had not, as yet, been performed in Paris. The chance to première a play written by de Lorde, the French 'Prince of Terror' and writer most synonymous with the rue Chaptal, was to be a first for London's Grand Guignol and a genuine endorsement of Levy's project from one of the most important figures in the Grand Guignol. The resulting translation, *The Old Women*, was the work of 'Christopher Holland'. It seems likely that the name of the playwright was a pseudonym for José Levy or Lewis Casson. Furthermore, the seeming innocuousness of the title ('Crime in the Madhouse' would be a literal, and perfectly adequate, translation) and the distinct absence of the names of de Lorde, Levy, Casson or the Little Theatre from the copy of the script submitted to the Lord Chamberlain's Office reflect the fact that a cunning ruse was afoot.

Up until that point the most extreme on-stage horrors displayed in the British Grand Guignol had been restricted to poisonings and strangulations. *The Old Women* culminates in an eye-gouging, an act of violence that the Lord Chamberlain's Office would have found intolerable despite the fact that the brutal action finds a precedent in the blinding of Gloucester in Shakespeare's *King Lear*: on the other hand, we must remember that classical plays were not new plays and therefore did not need to be submitted to the censor for scrutiny. The chance that *The Old Women* would be passed without intervention was negligible: most likely, the play would have been completely prohibited. H.F. Maltby takes up the story:

> Then George Bealby got an idea. A friend of his, a clergyman somewhere in Suffolk, had a hall licenced for stage plays in his parish at Little Snookington, we will call it where he sometimes produced local efforts. To him was sent a script of *The Old Women*, together with the reading fee and the draft of a letter he was asked to send

July 20, 1921 *The Sketch*

The Most Horrific Horror of the Grand Guignol.

THE SANE LOUISE (MISS SYBIL THORNDIKE) OVERHEARS THE MADWOMEN PLOTTING HER DEATH:
THE OPENING OF "THE OLD WOMEN."

TORTURED TO THE ACCOMPANIMENT OF A REQUIEM MASS: LOUISE (MISS SYBIL THORNDIKE) AND THE LUNATICS
(MR. RUSSELL THORNDIKE, MISS ATHENE SEYLER, AND MISS BARBARA GOTT).

The fourth series of London's Grand Guignol at the Little Theatre offers one item whose horror is more horrific than anything before presented on the London stage. The scene is laid in a French lunatic asylum. The nun in charge neglects the living in order to pray for the dead, and leaves Louise, the young girl who has recovered her sanity and is awaiting discharge, to sleep in the same room with deformed and horrible lunatic women. She hears them plotting her destruction and, reinforced by La Borgnesse, they do their grisly will upon her—gouging out her eyes — to the accompaniment of the strains of the Requiem Mass, heard off the stage.—[Photographs by Stage Photo. Co.]

Figure 9. Above Louise (Sybil Thorndike) in *The Old Women*, 1921; and *below* La Borgnesse (Russell Thorndike) and Louise (Sybil Thorndike) in *The Old Women* (*The Sketch*, 20 July 1921)

Figure 10. The 'Eye Gouging' Scene in *The Old Women*, 1921: Russell Thorndike and Athene Seyler look down upon Barbara Gott and, with bandaged eyes, Sybil Thorndike

to the Lord Chamberlain, stating he wished to produce the play at his Parish Hall in aid of his Girl Guide's Jamboree, or something of the sort. To everyone's amazement the licence was issued at once and the play was produced at the Little Theatre in the next bill. The play created an enormous sensation, the Press next morning was full of it. (Maltby, 1950, 185)

John Casson, the eldest son of Lewis Casson and Sybil Thorndike, gives a more accurate, if less humorous, version of events:

Russell at that time had a week-end cottage at Wrotham in Kent. Lewis announced that they would stage a theatrical performance in the Parish Hall for the benefit of the Wrotham villagers and duly submitted the script to the censor. Apparently the psychological balance of the villagers of Wrotham was of no great concern to the Lord Chamberlain's Office and the script was passed for their edification. (Casson, 1972, 71)

Given the nature of the request and the mischievous, if not ingenious, exploitation of context, the script was licensed for performance without any censorial intervention. Clearly, the play had been rubber-stamped without being read properly.[4] As it was *scripts*, rather than *productions*, that were licensed, the Little Theatre was then free to stage its own production. By the time the Lord Chamberlain realized that he had been tricked it was too late, as the play was already being performed on the stage of the Little Theatre. Although the victorious hoodwinking of the official censor may have been amusing and triumphant, it was not without grave consequences and was ultimately a Pyrrhic victory for the Little Theatre. The embarrassment caused to the Lord Chamberlain's Office was enough for London's Grand Guignol to come under even greater scrutiny. As H.F. Maltby recalls, the censor would never forget this very public humiliation:

> [The Lord Chamberlain] had carefully scrutinised our plays before, but he put them under the microscope after that and that finished Grand Guignol in this country for many years. (1950, 185)

Maltby's argument is certainly persuasive. *The Old Women* is the most extreme play within the staged repertoire of the London Grand Guignol, and although the play would become one of the classic – if not most beloved – offerings of the Parisian Grand Guignol, the British censor would not be fooled again, and it marked the beginning of the end for this example of British horror theatre. It is worth noting that in the event, it would seem that audiences were not overly shocked by the spectacle. J.C. Trewin argues that the spectators at the Little Theatre 'took serenely the blinding of Sybil Thorndike in *The Old Women* and other excesses of Grand Guignol' (Trewin, 1958, 29). This is an apposite point at which to turn our attention to the contemporary critical reception of the British Grand Guignol.

---

4   No reader's report for *The Old Women* can be found in the British Library, a fact which certainly reinforces the possibility that the script was not read thoroughly.

5

London's Grand Guignol
and the Reviewers

The Grand Guignol seasons at the Little Theatre happened at a time when the reviewing of West End theatre in the London press was a thorough and impressive mechanism and perhaps witnessed the pinnacle of theatrical reviewing in the British press. The number of licensed newspapers significantly exceeded those available in our own time and the space devoted to drama reviews was far more substantial. Reviews were a standard feature in tabloids, broadsheets and numerous periodicals. It was also a time that saw important literary and theatrical figures, and influential critics such as J.T. Grein, writing for the press as well as the numerous anonymous reviewers. The consequence is that when it comes to the British Grand Guignol we have a bountiful amount of material that gives a fascinating insight into all aspects of the Little Theatre's horror seasons.

J.T. Grein and the Grand Guignol

Reviewing the Grand Guignol's opening season in the *Illustrated London News* (18 September 1920), the highly influential man-of-the-theatre, impresario and journalist J.T. Grein (1862–1935), abounds with encouragement:

> London's Grand Guignol, as Mr José Levy calls the Little Theatre, has begun its career fairly well. It is likely to become a permanency when the pieces are as uniformly interesting as 'The Hand of Death' and when English playlets, of which there is an abundance in waiting, are the main fare.

Grein's comment is interesting in that it praises Levy's experiment for staging adaptations of French classics such as *The Hand of Death* (i.e. André de Lorde and Alfred Binet's 1909 play *L'Horrible Expérience*)[1] and at the

---

[1]   In this play, the surgeon Dr Charrier's daughter has been found dead, having died of a cardiac seizure. Her father and his assistant doctor (his daughter's fiancé) attempt to resuscitate her through the use of electricity. Eventually, the dead

same time supports Levy's intention to establish a repertoire of British short drama. It is also remarkable that Grein believes that the Little Theatre will become a permanent Grand Guignol venue. This bears testimony to how refreshing and necessary London's Grand Guignol must have felt to many people at the time.

Later in the same article, Grein analyses the genre of Grand Guignol drama – especially the plays of de Lorde – and makes the following assertion:

> It is easily said that these plays are sheer melodrama. It would be both an injustice and a misnomer. De Lorde's way is not merely to thrill for the sake of sensation. He is a scientist fond of research and experiment, and he likes to test his theories on stage. In 'The Hand of Death' he holds that electricity applied to the heart after sudden death may cause resuscitation.

After this, Grein starts watching the English audience:

> Knowing the play, I was wondering how our audience would take it. It was horrible and haunting yet it was so plausible, all so subtly prepared, that no one seemed shocked and everybody deeply interested although – and I have this on the authority of a well-known doctor who sat next to me, that strictly, in a medical sense, the end was wrong. *Rigor mortis* no longer functions after hours of death. Here de Lorde indulged in poetic licence, because there was no other issue to the play (had the daughter returned to life, all science would have been angry and up in arms), and because, possibly, he wanted to drive home a symbolic moral.

This section of the review is interesting because it reveals a certain degree of contradiction in Grein's interpretation and defence. Grein has already contended that de Lorde is a scientist and yet he acknowledges that the science here displayed is, in fact, ultimately implausible. Grein thus sees de Lorde as a scientist who uses poetic licence when a 'symbolic moral' needs to be driven home to a Grand Guignol audience. The emphasis on *morality* from an English critic is interesting here. In stark contrast, a critic of the

---

woman's hand begins to move – whether through 'electrification' or 'rigor mortis' is deliberately ambiguous – and seizes Dr Charrier by the throat and strangles him to death. Confronted with the spectacle of the two dead people, Charrier's assistant declares 'Death has had her revenge'. The play is a classic of the original Grand Guignol repertoire, and remains a masterpiece of suspense drama, including paradigmatic examples of the techniques and strategies of performance horror. *The Hand of Death* received the most extensive press coverage in the Little Theatre's first Grand Guignol season.

French Grand Guignol such as František Deák consistently argues that the Grand Guignol is an *amoral drama* (Deák, 1974, 34–44). Perhaps a more accurate reading is to see Grand Guignol as lying somewhere between the two poles of morality and amorality:

> ... the Grand Guignol as morally erratic, taking place in an indifferent universe where there is no justice but definitely retribution albeit far from the divine. (Hand and Wilson, 2000, 272)

The issue of morality, or the lack of it, is as much of a preoccupation for some English reviewers as it was for the censors. However, in the reception of the opening season, the concept of Grand Guignol as a 'scientific' theatre is not an issue of interest for J.T. Grein alone, a fact that reflects one aspect of the novelty of this new import: it is as if a theatre of science is being offered in London. This is taken furthest by the *Daily Graphic* (13 September 1920) which conducted its own experiment by sending its 'Medical Correspondent' to see *The Hand of Death*. After a detailed description of the play, the medical expert notes:

> Opening the abdomen and massaging the heart through the diaphragm is a recognised mode of treatment in chloroform syncope, and has been successful more than once. In *The Hand of Death* the experiment was certain to fail because the professor's daughter had been dead some time and her blood was already clotting, as is intimated to the audience. The main point to which I took exception was the professor's attempting a delicate operation with his back to the only light in the room.

It is with some relief that we read that the 'element of the supernatural introduced into the play has to be borne in mind' – an equivalent to J.T. Grein's 'symbolic moral' – which liberates the play from being regarded as an entirely realistic display. Whatever the shortcomings of the play's medical science, the Medical Correspondent is thankful that the portrayal of the stage doctor has improved enormously in the four decades he has been attending plays:

> Times are changed since there were but two types of stage doctor: the grey-haired old gentlemen of domestic drama, who pronounced [...] 'past human aid' without adequate examination; and the farcical comedy young practitioner who concealed compromising lady patients behind the many doors of his consulting-room.

The melodrama and farce of previous traditions of London theatre were evidently being superseded by the Grand Guignol which, despite its medical inaccuracies, poetic licence and supernatural elements, was offering a breath of fresh air in its realism. In other words, the Grand Guignol was offering a modern drama for a modern world.

London's Grand Guignol: Enemies and Defenders

If some reviews in September 1920 explored the scientific accuracy and the dramatic efficacy of the Grand Guignol with an overall mood of encouragement, others were less than sanguine. The *Daily Mirror* (4 September 1920) offered an article penned by John Burton with the eye-catching title:

WHY WE DON'T WANT HORRIFYING PLAYS
WOMEN NOT ATTRACTED BY THE MORBID

Burton offers a critique of *The Hand of Death*, although he chooses not to mention the title of the play in an attempt to deprive the Little Theatre of the oxygen of publicity. Having described the plot of the play he concludes:

> Such an episode as this on the stage is as horrible as it is foolish. Calmly considered in any spirit of critical judgment it might be dismissed with a smile or a shrug of the shoulders. But audiences that pack a playhouse are not in the mood to consider matters either calmly or coolly.

This argument takes us back to some of the concerns we have already seen, as it is a familiar one in the history of the justification of theatrical censorship which has typically regarded a collective audience as irresponsible and dangerous. Robert Goldstein, for instance, argues that the history of theatrical censorship in nineteenth- and early twentieth-century Europe is predominantly a class issue inspired by concern about the illiteracy of the spectator and the dangers of the 'crowd' (Goldstein, 1989, 113–22). Despite his evident abhorrence of the Grand Guignol, Burton nonetheless warmly acknowledges what he recognizes as the *raison d'être* of London's Grand Guignol: a theatrical enterprise designed to offer the theatre-going public something different from the type of plays – 'ragtime rubbish and the nastiness of the bedroom farce' – the London audience was forced to endure during the First World War. However, although this experiment may be well-intentioned it is not without severe danger. Burton argues that with 'the nation's nerves still acutely at post-war tension', there is a minority of men and women with a sinister desire to be 'thrilled and horrified': their resulting 'excursions into morbid pathology' offer a so-called 'pleasure that is bad for them and for us all' and should 'not be supplied by a British theatre that has any respect left for its name'. This is a fascinating criticism in that it reveals, by suggestion, the erotic dimension of the Grand Guignol. Despite the subtitle of the article – 'WOMEN NOT ATTRACTED BY THE MORBID' – Burton is clearly terrified of the minority of women (and men) that *are* attracted by the morbid. The desire for the morbid and macabre that Burton sees, or at least fears, in the Little Theatre's audience reveals that the 'sex and death' eroticism exploited in Paris is inherent in the form as a whole. The British Grand Guignol would never come anywhere near to being as explicit as the French original with its notorious use of stage blood, onstage nudity and salacious narratives (and neither should we forget its location near place Pigalle), but Burton's article reveals that, even in its anglicized version, the Grand Guignol can be perceived as dangerous and titillating and should be banned.

In contrast to John Burton writing in the *Daily Mirror* on 4 September 1920, Archibald Haddon's review in the *Sunday Express* on the very next day (5 September 1920) clearly relishes the whole Grand Guignol experience:

> Blood-red illuminations at the entrance to the Little Theatre symbolise the fare within. Not all of it, because the programme is diversified – first a domestic pleasantry (*How to be Happy*), then a piece of serio-comic realism (*G. H. Q. Love*), next a morbid shocker (*The Hand of Death*), and finally a topical song-show (*Oh, Hell!!!*). If you are overcome by the realism or morbidity, you may obtain relief during the entr'actes in spacious lounges, where your fair companion is encouraged to soothe her nerves with a cigarette while an orchestra discourses 'Swanee' and 'Alice Blue Gown'.

Haddon enjoys the ominous lighting outside the theatre, the *douche écossaise* of the plays on offer and the safety foyers that Levy always promised. He praises the conception of the Grand Guignol package at the Little as well as some of the 'brilliant' writing and 'magnificent' acting: 'There are brains at London's Grand Guignol, both before and behind the curtain', he concludes. Less than a month later (*Sunday Express*, 3 October 1920), Haddon revisits the theatre to review the slightly revised programme (*How to be Happy* is dropped and replaced by a 'morbid shocker', Pierre Mille and C. de Vylars's *The Medium*, and an additional comedy, H.F. Maltby's *What Did Her Husband Say?*). Once again full of praise, Haddon concludes that 'The Grand Guignol is one of the most fascinating entertainments in London'.

Within a few months, the opinion offered by the *Express* newspaper franchise has changed, at least it has if we read the *Daily Express* in June 1921. In a review of *The Old Women* entitled 'HORROR AND HEALTH', the *Daily Express* takes a morally superior stance similar to John Burton's condemnatory article in the *Daily Mirror* (4 September

1920). The anonymous reviewer in the *Daily Express* claims – and this is at odds with J.C. Trewin's account of the nonchalance of the same audience – that the 'terror aroused in the audience was such that women rushed out of the theatre to avoid hearing the blood-curdling screams of Miss Sybil Thorndike'.[2] The paper subsequently demands the opinion of an 'eminent London physician' who gravely advises the reader:

> It goes without saying that those with heart trouble or neurasthenia might suffer most seriously from the effects of acute fear and excitement such as are said to be aroused by this new piece.

Emphasis on the dangers of Grand Guignol horror previously expressed by the *Daily Mirror* has now been adopted by the *Daily Express*, and once again there is something of an erotic inference: the respected yet anonymous doctor warns us of the perils of the *excitement* that can be *aroused* by the play. As with the reviews of the first season, some quarters of the British press ensure that medicine is tied in with morality, and yet the tone is no longer as charitable and supportive as it was when someone like J.T. Grein offered his first review of the British Grand Guignol.

If the *Express* newspapers seemed to change attitude, the *Observer* newspaper is consistent in its opposition to the Grand Guignol. This is thanks, not least, to St John Ervine, the principal theatre reviewer for the *Observer*, to whom we have already devoted some attention. In his review of the opening night of the British Grand Guignol in the *Observer* (5 September 1920), the somewhat Francophobic Ervine unsurprisingly singles out *The Hand of Death* for condemnation, commencing with a note of irony:

> The genuine 'Grand Guignol' piece (of the evening) is entitled *The Hand of Death* and its authors, MM. André de Lorde and Alfred Binet, have contrived it with great skill. They have packed more of the horrific into it than was packed by the bloodiest of the Elizabethans into his most gruesome work, but they have omitted one element which the Elizabethans never omitted – the element of beauty.

After recounting the plot, Ervine pronounces with an inference which once again signals the disturbing erotic potential of the material:

---

2   An un-sourced and undated (circa June 1921) press cutting in the Theatre Museum Archives provides an even more colourful description: 'The score or more people who hastily left as Sybil Thorndike reached the culminating point of agony may have had last trains to catch, but more probably they left because they could not stand any more. Frankly, the episode, entitled *The Old Women* ... is much too horrible.'

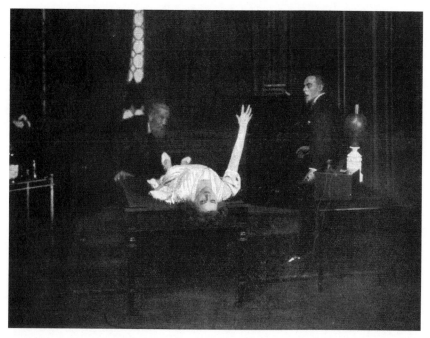

Figure 11. George Bealby, Sybil Thorndike and Lewis Casson in *The Hand of Death*, 1920

I think we in these islands are right in our refusal to accept this sort of horrific literature with anything but disrelish. The excitation of horror for the exclusive purpose of frightening the timid or stimulating jaded emotions is a fundamentally immoral act.

Despite the square condemnation of the play, the reader may be surprised when Ervine concludes his substantial review with a sentence that states that 'Mr George Bealby gave an exhibition of really great acting ... and fully deserved the ovation with which he was received at the end of the play'. The French play may be ugly and morally dubious, but was still a vehicle for brilliant (English) acting. The *Observer* would never lose its respect for the quality of the actors at the Grand Guignol, even if the plays were morally reprehensible. In a review of *The Old Women* (3 July 1921), a reviewer named 'H.G.' asserts:

If the Grand Guignol is not on its own merits useless, dangerous, and in need of abolition ... it should be at least forbidden to employ artists of more than a certain level of achievement.

To return to Ervine, his tone had not changed by the following year – if anything his opinions became more entrenched – as is evident in his vicious criticism of H.F. Maltby whose anti-war play *The Person Unknown* was staged as part of the Little Theatre's second Grand Guignol season in January 1921. In reviewing the play for the *Observer*, Ervine takes advantage of the situation to denounce the London Grand Guignol as a whole:

> Too much of the stuff given at the Little is concerned with neurotic prostitutes and lust and drink and general horror. This sort of thing may interest over-fed voluptuaries and creepy-crawly people with flabby insides, but I cannot imagine that this fashion will continue to be popular. (23 January 1921)

Given the stinging nature of Ervine's comments, it is nothing short of astonishing that in the following year he wrote his own anti-war play for Levy, *Progress*, which was performed as part of the Seventh Series of London's Grand Guignol in April 1922. On the same programme was the comedy *Amelia's Suitors* by H.F. Maltby.

One of the staunchest defences of the Grand Guignol to appear in the British press was one of the first: 'DRAMA AND DREAD: GUIGNOLLERIES at the LITTLE' was a review penned by 'Agravaine' in the *Era* (5 September 1920). Far from seeing the Grand Guignol as immoral, the author sees it as heartily welcome: 'in a stage-world where there is practically no alternative to sweet-stuff of one sort or another ... I frankly confess to welcoming the establishment of a specific "thrill-box" in John Street'. Agravaine regards the 'Guignolleries' as, in a neat turn of phrase, 'artificial, high-pitched shocks for the sophisticated' which are not in the least 'abnormal or degenerate' but 'perfectly natural'. The reference to the audience as 'sophisticated' would seem to contain certain implications of social and economic class, but the reviewer places his defence of the necessity of aesthetic horror in a broader context:

> So long as most people in their hearts enjoy a 'norrible tale' and feel the better for it afterwards, and so long as it is not imposed upon them, and so long as it does no harm to any living thing, I should say 'go ahead'. The amount of horror that can be enjoyed obviously varies. Even apart from the overdose most of the world has been having lately in real life, sedentary modern citizens show no particular liking on the stage for what the more robust, open-air taste of our Elizabethan forefathers, or of the average healthy schoolboy, or [...] of the well-sunned rustic could or can relish.

Agravaine's review implies that the Grand Guignol will always be a niche art form, as many have an aversion to horror in contrast to the Elizabethan (interesting to see the same cultural period used to very different ends from St John Ervine's), schoolboys and 'rustics'. What is most impressive is, censorship notwithstanding, Agravaine's assertion of a democracy of culture here: the Grand Guignol is only going to appeal to a minority audience and yet that audience has every right to attend: after all, there is 'nothing more exhilarating to a healthy temperament' than fear, which is a 'stimulant' as well as a 'moral and physical purgative'.

The press coverage of the London Grand Guignol by both its supporters and detractors may have been substantial and eager in its early days, but towards the end of its existence, it was much diminished. For example, its imminent last days received little more than a few lines in *The Times* (19 June 1922):

> The end of the 'Grand Guignol' productions at the Little Theatre is in sight. The present series is the eighth, and the venture has continued for nearly two years. It will be recalled that after a long association with the company Miss Sybil Thorndike recently left for a holiday, at the end of which she had decided not to return to the Little Theatre owing to her intention to start management on her own.

It is particularly interesting that this news item regards the end of the Grand Guignol as being wholly due to Sybil Thorndike's departure, as opposed to the pressures of censorship or the controversy of the repertoire: it would seem that from the point of view of *The Times*, the British Grand Guignol was less significant as a theatre of writing, a theatre of science or a theatre of controversy than, at the end of the day, a theatre of acting.

6

Aftermath and Legacy

Resurrections of the Grand Guignol

The final performance of London's Grand Guignol on 24 June 1922 may have been the end of a chapter in the history of Grand Guignol performance in Britain, but it was not entirely the end of the story. By the time the season closed, arrangements had already been made for a provincial tour, beginning with Brighton Theatre Royal on 24 July and ending in Bristol on 4 December, in between taking in venues as far north as York and Harrogate, and as far south as Plymouth, Torquay and (for three performances) Ilfracombe. The tour also included an Irish leg with performances in Belfast, Dublin and Cork.[1]

---

1   The company also played at the Cardiff Playhouse from 6–11 November 1922, playing two shows per evening, at 6.30pm and 8.45pm, each show consisting of three plays. From 6–8 November, the programme consisted of *Haricot Beans*, *The Hand of Death* and *Progress*, in that order. It is a slightly odd running order, as it ignores the principles of the *douche écossaise* and the gradual ratcheting up of horror – a more natural running order might have been *Progress*, followed by *Haricot Beans* and culminating with *Hand of Death*. The review of the show, which appeared in the *Western Mail* (7 November 1922), echoes many of the press reviews for the London seasons, namely high praise for the acting and writing (described as 'extraordinarily fine' and 'of exceptional quality'), tempered with moral reservations concerning the intensity of the horror (described as 'simply wanton'). Interestingly, it seems that, although the Thorndike-Cassons remained involved in the management of the tour (evidenced by correspondence between Sybil Thorndike and Eliot Crawshay-Williams), members of the London company were not involved, at least in the Cardiff performances. It is notable that all three plays on the bill have small casts, and the main parts in all the plays were taken by Farner Skein and Molly Veness. The programme changed for the second half of the week, but no review exists to tell us what that may have been. Incidentally, the Cardiff Playhouse (which had originally been the Theatre Royal and later became the Prince of Wales) played host in its time to the likes of Henry Irving and Sarah Bernhardt. In the 1960s and 1970s it became a porn cinema before falling into disuse. It was finally rescued from dereliction by the public house chain, A.J. Wetherspoon, and

The programme varied from venue to venue, but was a kind of 'greatest hits tour', a revival of some of the company's greatest successes from the previous two years. Bearing in mind that the tour had been scheduled at the beginning of the year, the Grand Guignol season at the Little Theatre would have had to close in June (or July) in any case to allow for rehearsals for the touring programme, and Levy could not have contemplated trying to run a further season in the autumn without the Thorndike-Cassons.[2] If a ninth season had been planned, it could not have happened until early 1923 anyway. In that sense, it could be argued that London's Grand Guignol closed its doors on 4 December 1922 in Bristol and that, with such a long break in the London performances, it had merely run out of steam.

Perhaps inevitably, the success of Levy's experiment at the Little Theatre encouraged other Grand Guignol productions, both in the professional and amateur spheres. In September 1921 Levy received a request from the British Rhine Army Dramatic Company, which wished to mount a production of the entire bill of the fourth series, which was running at the time and included *The Old Women*. Sewell Collins, who had been intimately involved in London's Grand Guignol, translating and adapting a number of plays from the original French, told Levy in November 1923 that he planned to take a number of one-act Grand Guignol plays to tour America. Whether Collins was ever successful in realizing this project is unclear, but it was a serious and realistic enough proposition for Levy to telephone Crawshay-Williams to tell him of the plans.

The continuing fashion for Grand Guignol and the use of the title by theatre managers as a marketing device, long after Levy had closed London's Grand Guignol, is evident in the exchange of correspondence which took place in June 1924 between Howard Tyrer, secretary to The London Council for the Promotion of Public Morality (an organization largely run by senior members of the London clergy), and Lord Cromer, who had begun his sixteen-year reign as Lord Chamberlain in 1922. In reference to a proposed staging of *Private Room Number 6* (licensed in December 1920 as part of Levy's second series), Tyrer expressed the Council's 'deep regret at the revival of the Guignol plays' (letter, 5 June 1924) and their hope that it would not be 'too late to prevent the presentation of at least plays

---

was converted into a pub, whilst restoring many of the features of the original Victorian theatre. Much of the planning and discussions which were an important part of the writing of this book, took place, we are proud to say, beneath the roof of that very same establishment.

[2]   None of the various Thorndike-Casson biographies mentions the tours and during the summer and autumn of 1922 Sybil Thorndike was also involved in productions of Ervine's *Jane Clegg*, Sardou's *La Tosca*, Lady Bell's *Scandal*, *Medea*, and Shelley's *The Cenci*. Nevertheless, correspondence between Sybil Thorndike and Eliot Crawshay-Williams suggests that they remained part of the touring company.

like "Private Room Nº 6" if it is identical with those previously produced.'
In response, Cromer sought both to explain his own inability to prevent
the production of a play that had already been granted a licence and to
reassure them by arguing that they should 'not attach too great significance
to the title "Grand Guignol" which is used by the producers and in the
Press mainly with the object of drawing audiences' (letter, 14 June 1924).
In addition Cromer explained that it was 'impossible to restrain theatrical
managers from naming their plays "Grand Guignol" as the title is in itself
one that attracts a certain section of the British public.'

Levy himself attempted to re-launch London's Grand Guignol at The
Little Theatre in 1928. He had, in fact, attempted to stage occasional plays
in the Grand Guignol vein after 1922, and then in the autumn of 1927 he
staged a season of 'Four Grand Guignol Plays' at the Arts Theatre Club.
As this was a private theatre, the plays performed did not require licences
and the programme consisted entirely of plays that had been refused licences
for the 1920–22 seasons: *Collusion*, *Blind Man's Buff*, *Save the Mark*
and Frederick Witney's *Coals of Fire*, which Street had described as 'an
exhibition of disgusting savagery and quite unfit for public presentation'
(reader's report, 30 March 1922). The express purpose of this 1927 season
was to test the water in advance of a possible revival at the Little Theatre
the following year, not only with the audience, but also with the Lord
Chamberlain's Office. Levy invited members of Cromer's office to attend
the plays and there followed a series of discussions with Levy.

Whatever the outcome of those discussions, Levy must have been
sufficiently encouraged to plan a revival of London's Grand Guignol for
May 1928. Nevertheless, the preparations were not without their problems.
Anticipating some difficulties, Levy submitted at least eight plays for
consideration. In the first instance, two of these were refused licences:
Her Mother's Daughter by Frederick Witney and an adaptation of René
Berton's *L'homme qui a tué le mort*, entitled *After Death*. Berton's play
concerns a doctor who takes the head of a recently guillotined murderer,
wires it up to an electrical apparatus and is so able to 'revive' the head
for a few brief seconds – long enough to ask the man to confirm his guilt
or innocence. This was to be the centrepiece of Levy's programme, and
he was, understandably, keen to secure a licence for it. C.L. Gordon, the
comptroller, was invited to see a rehearsal, after which he wrote to Cromer
on Levy's behalf, arguing for a licence on the grounds of both precedence
and, curiously, morality:

> ... no blood or anything was visible. It was conducted entirely as a
> medical demonstration and I think we had something very similar
> in a previous play entitled 'The Hand of Death' some years ago. In
> one way the play has a moral. That the English method of execution
> by hanging causes instantaneous death, while, by the guillotine

method, if the medical theory advanced in the play is correct, it is not so, but vitality remains in certain parts of the body for a time. (Memorandum, 8 May 1928)

Levy also gave an assurance that if the play proved too controversial, he would withdraw it from the programme and that the severed head would not be visible to the audience. After some further correspondence a licence was finally granted, and on 14 May 1928 London's Grand Guignol returned to the Little Theatre with a programme of five plays.[3] They were *The Old Firm's Reawakening* by A.J. Talbot (a deliberately ironic choice, perhaps), *Something More Important* by H.F. Maltby, *A Private Room* by Arthur Wing Pinero, *Wedding Day* by Frederick Witney and the aforementioned *After Death*, translated by Virginia and Frank Vernon. Two further plays, *An Honest Penny* by Witney and *Little Johnny* by John Drinkwater, were licensed but not included.

Many of 'the old firm' returned to the Little Theatre for the enterprise. Maltby was more centrally involved and produced his own play. *Wedding Day* was produced by Sewell Collins, another veteran of 1920–22, and George Bealby returned to perform in both *Wedding Day* and (inevitably) *After Death*. Securing the involvement of a now aged Arthur Wing Pinero was a great achievement for Levy, who no doubt hoped that the playwright's participation would bring with it the same respectability that had previously been provided by the Thorndike-Cassons. Pinero not only wrote a new play for the season, but also produced the play himself. Other talented 'new blood', but of a younger generation, included James Whale who acted in *After Death*: later the same year Whale would direct the massively successful *Journey's End* (1928) by R.C. Sherriff before emigrating to Hollywood and becoming a seminal film director, not least in the area of horror with films such as *Frankenstein* (1931), *The Old Dark House* (1932) and *The Invisible Man* (1933). Although Whale's future was as auspicious as Pinero's past was impressive, the 1928 Grand Guignol revival was to be a disappointment. Crucially Levy was unable to lure the Thorndike-Cassons back to the Grand Guignol, and without its lead actors the enterprise was always likely to face difficulties. It was not a great success and the project was short-lived, closing down within three weeks.

---

[3]   It is interesting to note that the Little Theatre continued to be perceived as the ideal location for London's Grand Guignol. Indeed, although the Grand Guignol may have last played at the Little Theatre in 1922, the theatre's association with horror and sensationalism continued undaunted: 'A run of the play *Dracula* at the Little Theatre in London in 1927 saw 29 people faint and a uniformed nurse was stationed on permanent duty in the foyer' (*Guardian*, 1 November 2006). Incidentally, the Little Theatre – London's great venue for horror – came to a horrifically real and tragic end, being completely destroyed in a bombing raid during the Second World War. It was never rebuilt.

Some of the plays first performed in the 1920–22 seasons continued to have a life outside of the Grand Guignol, especially some of the comedies. Of particular popularity was Eliot Crawshay-Williams's *E. & O.E.* which played in Levy's Fifth Series between October 1921 and January 1922. The play enjoyed a production at the Warrington Arts Theatre in 1929, where it was described as 'an original and brilliantly-written play with a real Grand Guignol ending' (*Warrington Examiner*, 27 April 1929), and even an Irish-language production at the Abbey Theatre in Dublin in 1926.[4] The play was also performed in the 1930s in New York as part of an attempt by George K. Arthur to establish a Grand Guignol in the Chanin Auditorium on the 50th floor of the Chanin Building. Crawshay-Williams also had some later success with *Cupboard Love*, part of the Sixth Series staged between January and March 1922, which was made into a film in 1931, directed by Bernard Mainwaring.

The next serious attempt to establish a Grand Guignol in London, though, was not until 1945, when two programmes of plays were performed at the Granville Theatre between May and October of that year. The programmes, which benefited from some typically barnstorming acting from the legendary melodramatic actor Tod Slaughter, included plays by Frederick Witney, such as *Coals of Fire*, which had originally been accepted by Levy in the early 1920s, but had been refused a licence at that time and again in 1929.[5] George Street's successor as Chief Examiner of Plays, Henry Game, took a far more liberal position and happily recommended licences with only minor amendments. Indeed, Game's reports criticize Street's attitude as 'grandmotherly', and claim that Grand Guignol was a form to which his 'predecessor was particularly allergic' (reader's report for *Coals of Fire*, 7 April 1945). Six years later Kenneth Tynan attempted a Grand Guignol season at the Irving Theatre,[6] but again this was not to be an enduring venture. Whilst it is interesting that Levy's venture thrived in the horrific aftermath of the First World War, and the experiments at the Granville and

---

4   The continually hard-pressed Crawshay-Williams almost missed out on his royalties for the Abbey production, as the request for rights had been (perhaps slightly mischievously) sent to Samuel French Ltd (who had published the script), but written in Irish. As nobody at the offices of Samuel French could read Irish, the letter was ignored.

5   In May 1929 Nancy Price applied for a licence for *Coals of Fire* for the Embassy Theatre. Street maintained his earlier objection, claiming that 'Anything more horrible and disgusting can hardly be imagined' (reader's report, 10 May 1929). Gordon was less damning, but the licence was refused on the grounds that it would be inconsistent to issue a licence for an unaltered play that had been refused only seven years earlier and under the same Lord Chamberlain.

6   Tynan's programme, which opened on 6 November 1951, included five plays: *Andronicus* by Peter Myers and Kenneth Tynan; *Before Breakfast* by Eugene O'Neill; *Coals of Fire* by Frederick Witney; *Dalgarni* by Griffith Jones; *The Mask* by H.M. Harwood and F. Tennyson Jesse.

Irving enjoyed some success in the aftermath of the Second World War, it is perhaps inevitable that they were only ever going to be one-off events. The competition from cinema and the post-war culture, which was not enamoured of melodrama, had already sealed the fate of the Grand Guignol in Paris. The Grand Guignol was hopelessly out-of-date in post-war Europe and, as the Parisian Grand Guignol descended into a camp parody of its former self, there was little chance for a sustained revival anywhere else.[7]

The Grand Guignol and the Thriller

While the one-act horror plays of the Grand Guignol failed to enjoy sustained revival after 1922, the broadly linked genre of the thriller (conforming to the longer format of three acts or more) burgeoned into a distinctive, established genre. If it was the Bulldog Drummond plays that began the fashion for thrillers from 1921 onwards, then the success of Levy's 'thrilling' Grand Guignol most probably also contributed to its further development by a number of other writers, in particular Edgar Wallace, but also exemplified by Arnold Ridley's *Ghost Train* (1925), James Bridie's *The Anatomist* (1930) and, most significantly, Patrick Hamilton's *Rope* (1929), *Gaslight* (1938) and *The Duke in Darkness* (1942). Wallace even gains the grudging respect of Pellizzi as 'a clever purveyor of thrills' (Pellizzi, 1935, 278). More interestingly, perhaps, Pellizzi also describes Wallace's plays as being 'derived on one hand from Grand Guignol, on the other from the American "drama of action" [...], including detective plays, secret service plays, and so on' (Pellizzi, 1935, 278). Whilst there are certain parallels to be drawn between these thrillers and the Grand Guignol, not least in the way that they reflect 'the social unease precipitated by the political climate, even though plays rarely confronted such unease directly' (Barker, 2000, 29), there are also key differences that are worth identifying. In spite of Barker's claims, Ridley's *Ghost Train* is not 'exemplary Grand Guignol' (Barker, 2000, 30). It is not even Grand Guignol at all.

---

[7]   Since Tynan's season in 1951, there have been occasional stagings of Grand Guignol plays, especially in recent years which have seen a revival of interest in the form. These have been largely by small-scale professional and semi-professional theatre companies. The most sustained attempt at establishing regular Grand Guignol programmes has arguably been that of Adam Meggido and The Sticking Place, which have, at the time of writing, just commenced their fourth annual horror theatre festival in The Union Theatre, Southwark, a perfect Grand Guignol theatre, housed beneath the railway arches. The theatre holds an audience of about seventy, and performances are regularly punctuated by the eerie rumbling of trains as they pass overhead. Their programmes include both Grand Guignol and supernatural horror plays. In 2006 and 2007 special Halloween programmes included some horror improvisation from British actor Ken Campbell who, incidentally, attended the Grand Guignol in Paris shortly before it closed in November 1962.

It is tempting to draw close parallels between the thriller and the Grand Guignol play, even perhaps to the extent of considering the latter as a sub-genre of the former, as both forms clearly built their popularity upon an exploitation of a post-war cultural phenomenon, which manifested itself in 'a surprising relish for horrors of other kinds' (i.e. not of the war) (Nicholson, 2003, 179). Certainly we can reasonably assume that the audiences who sought out the latest Bulldog Drummond play at Wyndham's were motivated by the same thrill-seeking urge as those who visited London's Grand Guignol, or even those who, as tourists, made their way to Paris to see the real thing.

At the same time, elements within the Lord Chamberlain's Office, whilst perhaps reserving particular contempt for the Grand Guignol, were alarmed by what Lord Buckmaster (a member of the advisory committee) called 'the growing tendency to depict sheer naked horror' (quoted in Nicholson, 2003, 182), and clearly made no specific distinction between different kinds of horror/thriller play. Instead the Chief Examiner, George Street more generally declared that 'the growing taste for horrors needs discouragement' (quoted in Nicholson, 2003, 180).

The Grand Guignol was heavily influenced by three distinct, and often contradictory theatrical traditions: the melodrama, radical naturalism and the Scribean well-made play (Homrighous, 1963, 25), and it required of its actors a unique blend of melodramatic and naturalistic techniques as they made the perilous journey, during the course of a performance, 'from bourgeois security to mortal danger, from the rational to the insane, from – in effect – Naturalism to Melodrama' (Hand and Wilson, 2000, 269). By the same token, Gerald du Maurier, 'whose carefully careless manner, calculated to each tap of the cigarette upon its case, was bred of an intricate technique' (Trewin, 1958, 10), absolutely embodied a naturalistic approach to acting in the British theatre at the time. His portrayal of Bulldog Drummond betrays a style of acting that owes more to nineteenth-century melodrama:

> There was no room for elaborate philosophising or speculation on the destiny of man. You acted and reacted without the possibility of deep thought. Good was good and bad was bad. (Harding, 1989, 113)

The photographic documentation of du Maurier's productions suggest a clear link with melodramatic acting styles; as one arm extends forward in a murderous lunge, the other arm stretches backwards in an opposite movement, or as a murderer grips the throat of his victim with outstretched arms, a leg stretches backwards to balance the action (see Barker and Gale, 2000, 43–44). In both examples, the action serves to enlarge the movement and maximize the physicality of the actor. The idea that an actor balances any action, by himself or by another actor, by an opposite and equal reaction is a common technique in melodramatic performance.

Yet the Grand Guignol, as a form, departed from its melodramatic traditions in a number of ways, whilst the thriller remained loyal to them. Most striking perhaps is the concept of morality. As previously indicated by Harding, the melodramatic concept of an uncomplicated, black and white morality was successfully imported wholesale into the thriller, and along with it came the stock characters of the (male) Hero, (male) Villain and helpless (female) victim. In the Grand Guignol the situation is more complex, with characters inhabiting an amoral – or at best morally erratic – universe, where there are no easily defined heroes and villains (see Hand and Wilson, 2000, 272). Certainly there are plenty of victims (of both sexes) in the Grand Guignol, but here everyone is capable of both heroic (rarely) and villainous (more commonly) behaviour. In thrillers, as in melodrama, the hero always arrives to save the heroine in the nick of time, so leaving open the possibility of a sequel (Stokes, 2000, 50), whereas in the Grand Guignol help consistently arrives a few moments too late. Whilst both forms have a well-paced, forward-moving narrative[8] (Stokes, 2000, 52), Grand Guignol plays have a grim inevitability which is missing from the thriller. Steve Nicholson's observation on 1920s horror drama, that it 'always has the potential to be viewed as exploitative and pornographic, and the number of plays which showed women suffering as victims of torture is striking' (Nicholson, 2003, 187), is more true of the thrillers than it is of the Grand Guignol.

As J.C. Trewin says, it was through the 1920s that the thriller as a genre 'had its panel-creaking hour' (1958, 10). What may have begun with Bulldog Drummond, and was encouraged by the Grand Guignol, then benefited from the talents of the likes of Edgar Wallace and Patrick Hamilton and soon became something of a craze. Many of these plays were from American dramatists and were more properly described as detective plays or secret service plays, such as John Willard's *The Cat and the Canary* (1922). *The Cat and the Canary* premièred in New York in February 1922 and enjoyed similar success when it opened in London later the same year. The play has become a classic of popular theatre and would go on to be a favourite for film adaptation.[9] There was also work

---

8   The Detective Drama or 'Whodunit', specifically, is an exception here, as it is normally backward-looking, attempting to unravel events after they have taken place (see Stokes, 2000, 52).

9   Paul Leni's film version of *The Cat and the Canary* (1927) is a paradigmatic work, above all in its construction of 'the old dark house' and its benighted residents. *The Cat and the Canary* was frequently remade in the era of sound, including the Bob Hope vehicle directed by Elliott Nugent in 1939. Although *The Cat and the Canary* was mischievously deconstructed in James Whale's pastiche *The Old Dark House* (1932), Willard's play and Leni's first adaptation of it had an enormous and earnest influence over Universal Pictures' classic horror films of the 1930s, and continues to inform the horror film genre up to the present day: indeed,

by British writers, such as the 'whodunits' of Agatha Christie, including *Alibi* (1928) and *Black Coffee* (1930), which also began to appear on the London stage.

Pellizzi complains that dramatists 'are forced very often to comply with the needs of the times and insert a horrible or macabre element in a play which could otherwise be treated on quite different lines' (1935, 280), and Trewin sees the trend as employing increasingly preposterous devices and scenarios:

> Never were faces more hideous. Walls opened, doors flew back, masked figures appeared, bookcases moved. There were shots in the dark, screams in the twilight, cats among the pigeons, and bats in the belfry [...] Each had [...] the masked figure in a gloom bitumen-black, the sudden powdery phosphorescence, the scrawny hand groping round the wall [...], the comic maidservant for relief who quavered into hysterics, the fixing of suspicion on each member of the cast in turn. (1958, 37)

Trewin hints at the growing abundance of such plays on the London stage by declaring that 1922 was 'the first harvest-year of the mechanical shockers' (1958, 37), but he very clearly distinguishes the form from the more serious work of the Grand Guignol, which always sought to thrill and chill its audience, not simply to make them jump and shriek. Furthermore, the Grand Guignol in Britain remained true to its French counterpart in that it steered well clear of the supernatural. All violence in the Grand Guignol was perpetrated by human agency.

Where a degree of commonality might be expected to be found between the thriller (and its sub-genres) and the Grand Guignol is in its use of real-life crime as material for its dramas. The publication in 1926 of William Bolitho's *Murder for Profit*, a series of case studies of serial killers, tapped into the public's thirst for sensationalism, as well as providing dramatists with source material (Stokes, 2000, 47), not unlike the use made by the French Grand Guignol writers of the *faits divers* published in newspapers such as *Le Petit Journal* or *Le Petit Parisien* (Hand and Wilson, 2002, 7–8), nor indeed by the writers of melodrama exploiting the Victorian 'penny dreadfuls'. London's Grand Guignol, on the other hand, offered 'possible' rather than 'factual' crime for its dramas, though Eliot Crawshay-Williams, its most prolific playwright, kept a file of newspaper clippings for just such a purpose.

---

even '*Alien* (Ridley Scott, 1979) is a variation on *The Cat and the Canary*' (Hand, 2004, 119).

Cinema, Radio and Later Stage Drama

As with the French Grand Guignol, the legacy of Levy's experiment can also be detected in the cinema and radio. Levy's company produced a number of short films based on the 1920–22 repertoire and, whilst Crawshay-Williams had only limited success with cinema (Fox British Pictures rejected his Grand Guignol plays as film material in 1935), H.F. Maltby enjoyed a distinguished film career as occasional actor and the author of dozens of screenplays from the early 1930s to the 1950s, including several screen adaptations of classic stage melodramas starring Tod Slaughter.

The success of the Grand Guignol at the Little Theatre can partly be gauged by the attempts at imitation. In June 1921, the Maggri Company (owners of the Little Theatre) took Hubert Woodward to court for touring his 'Grand Guignol Players' in the provinces. The trial, as reported in *The Times* (18 June 1921), centred on the implications of the phrase 'Grand Guignol': the defence argued that the phrase was 'only descriptive of the type of play produced at the Paris theatre', while the plaintiffs insisted that Grand Guignol was now 'in this country distinctive of the Little Theatre'. The defence countered with the claim that the Little Theatre called itself London's Grand Guignol and so the path was open for a 'Bristol Grand Guignol', a 'Manchester Grand Guignol' or 'Woodward's Grand Guignol'. The judge, Mr Justice Russell, revealed that he understood the term to mean plays which provided 'either short periods of amusement or short periods of thrills and shocks'. He passed an injunction which prevented Woodward from publicising the work as Grand Guignol but did not prevent him from performing examples of the genre. The following month the Maggri Company was back in court complaining that Woodward was breaching the injunction by using the same posters for the 'Grand Guignol Players', with an attached slip clarifying 'No connection with London's Grand Guignol or the Little Theatre'. Mr Justice Russell decided that this was no infringement and 'dismissed the motion without costs' (*The Times*, 23 July 1921). Around the same time, the Maggri Company also took the British Exhibitors Films Limited to court for the same perceived infringement and once again there was a debate about whether 'Grand Guignol' is a 'descriptive' or 'distinctive' term, this time because a film-making company and an exhibiting company were advertising their films as 'Grand Guignol'.

The most interesting and certainly most prolific of the Grand Guignol imitators in film was Fred Paul, who directed some twenty-eight short 'Grand Guignol' films in London in 1921.[10] None of them is related to the Little Theatre or even the Parisian repertoire. Having said that, the few examples of the surviving films successfully animate themes, narratives and

[10]   The authors wish to express their warm gratitude to Michael Eaton who introduced them to the existing Fred Paul films.

characters that are distinctly Grand Guignolian. For example, in *The Last Appeal* a judge sentences a young man to be executed, only to discover, all too late, that the condemned man is his own son. In *The Jest*, a mild-mannered man is humiliated when his wife leaves him. Years later, some acquaintances play a prank by dressing up one of their number to look like his departed spouse. In a gruesome, yet off-screen, denouement, the 'gentle' old man bludgeons his 'wife' to death. Interestingly, in an article about the Grand Guignol films, Fred Paul implies that there was a specifically social dimension to his output:

> I attempt to show life as it really is, its sordidness and cruelty; the diabolical humour of the destiny we call fate, which plays with us as it will, raises us to high places or drags us to the gutter; allows one man to rob the widows and orphans of their all and makes a criminal of the starving wretch who in his misery has stolen a mouthful of bread. (*Kinematograph Weekly*, 24 March 1921)

In this regard, Paul's films are closer to plays like *Eight O'Clock*, *The Sisters' Tragedy* or *The Person Unknown* in their post-war social consciousness. By the same token, none of them lacks a Grand Guignolian exploitation of suspense and/or violence and dramatic twists and irony.

In 1923, Richard Hughes was invited by the BBC to write what 'is usually taken to be the world's first specific radio play, Richard Hughes's *A Comedy of Danger*[11] (January 15, 1924)': the play is a thriller set in a Welsh coal mine during a power cut and 'demonstrates how suspense is not merely a generic choice in radio drama, but it was there from the form's inauguration' (Hand, 2006, 9). American broadcasting took the genre of short horror performance into a new era from the early 1930s so that by the late 1940s, as Martin Grams Jr states, 'U.S. Radio [...] fired at least 80 programs of horror and bloodcurdling adventure at its listeners every week' (Grams, 2002, 34). Much of this wholly live output could be regarded as Grand Guignolesque, and one series in particular – *Mystery House* (1944) – is remarkable for offering overt adaptations of plays from the French Grand Guignol Theatre. Although British radio does not compare with the vastness and diversity of the American output, the BBC's most famous horror radio programme, the ten series of *Appointment with Fear* from 1943 until the mid-1950s, is a classic of its kind. There is at least one example here where the Grand Guignol at the Little Theatre lives on. Along with classic fare such as adaptations of *The Tell-Tale Heart* (13 January 1944) and *The Monkey's Paw* (28 May 1946), *Appointment with Fear* broadcast a radio version of *The Nutcracker Suite* (26 March 1946), a play by Eliot

---

[11]   Sometimes referred to as simply *Danger*, the title under which it was published in Hughes, 1928.

Crawshay-Williams which had been staged at the Little Theatre in 1921 as part of the Seventh Series.

The Grand Guignol as a spirit and a genre continued to live on in British theatre even if the Little Theatre's horror seasons came to an end. Just a few months after the final performance of London's Grand Guignol, Joseph Conrad's play version of his novel *The Secret Agent* was staged at the Ambassador's Theatre in London. Conrad insisted that the play was not a 'Guignol horror but something which has a larger meaning' (Conrad, 2002, 596). A key role in the play, however, went to Russell Thorndike, and it would seem that this is one way that the producer J. Harry Benrimo hoped to realize, despite his protests, Conrad's intention of making his audience 'sup on horrors'. Thorndike's presence in the play is no doubt a major reason why a number of critics referred to the Grand Guignol quality of the play.[12] *The Secret Agent* was not a success and closed after a few performances. Whether it was Grand Guignolian or not, it was nonetheless influential on a future generation of Grand Guignolesque artists: the young Alfred Hitchcock was among the spectators at the Ambassadors in 1922, and much of the film director's work has qualities that could be associated with the possible horrors and white-knuckle ride of the Grand Guignol.

A play such as Emlyn Williams's *Night Must Fall* (1935) might well be a ground-breaking example of the psychological thriller and a classic of its kind, but it nonetheless owes a great debt to what London's Grand Guignol had established in the previous decade. The play is a narrative of bleakness and cruelty with the psychopathic yet charismatic Dan inexorably exploiting and eventually murdering the formidable yet utterly vulnerable Mrs Bramson. In addition, the play is laced with an unsettling eroticism, with Dan's role-play with the invalided old lady and, ultimately even more disturbing, his relationship with the young, alienated Olivia. The three acts of *Night Must Fall* permit an impressive psychological complexity (the character of Dan is almost certainly the most psychologically complex serial killer in stage drama), but there are moments of Grand Guignol flair, such as the murder of Mrs Bramson, and probably the most notorious prop in the history of stage thrillers: the weighty hatbox that Dan keeps in his room and the audience knows must have something to do with the headless corpse found in the woods. Critically, the audience never sees inside the hatbox and its impact is all the stronger for that: as in Grand Guignol, suggestion and inference often has a greater impact than the explicit. *Night Must Fall* paved the way for other taut psychological thrillers with dramatic set pieces

---

[12] Although it may have been to Conrad's chagrin, the Grand Guignolian aspect of the play was received positively in some influential quarters. J.T. Grein, writing for the *Illustrated London News*, praised Russell Thorndike's 'Grand Guignol spasms in the part of the cowardly agent' (Hand, 2001, 58), and the *Stage* celebrated Thorndike's 'vividly Grand Guignolesque final exit' (Hand, 2001, 56–57).

such as Frederick Knott's *Dial M for Murder* (1952) and *Wait Until Dark* (1966), both of which became highly successful films for Alfred Hitchcock (1954) and Terence Young (1967) respectively.

Conclusion

The Grand Guignol has had a sporadic history in Britain, beginning with the French company's tour in 1908 and ending forty-three years later with Kenneth Tynan. The most significant and sustained period of production, however, is the establishment of José Levy's London Grand Guignol in the Little Theatre between 1920–22. In that time it drew on the talents of over twenty-five writers to produce forty-three plays. Supported by a team of exceptional actors, it drew large audiences of devoted, thrill-seeking theatregoers, but its fate was ultimately sealed by its ongoing problematic relationship with the Office of the Lord Chamberlain. Nevertheless, Levy's brief experiment has left an indelible mark upon British Theatre history of the 1920s. The final word should go to the critic James Agate who, writing in the *Saturday Review*, paid the following unequivocal tribute to the London Grand Guignol:

> The essence of Grand Guignolism is, I take it, not horrible action but horrible motive. These little plays are really spiritual affairs like Shakespeare's or Ibsen's or Maeterlinck's. The door is a different one, but it is what goes on behind it that matters. (22 October 1921)

SECTION 2

TEN PLAYS OF
LONDON'S GRAND GUIGNOL

Figure 12. Programme cover featuring the logo of London's Grand Guignol by
Aubrey Hammond, 1921

Figure 13. Stockwell Hawkins,
Ralph Neale, Russell Thorndike
and Lewis Casson in *Eight O'Clock*,
1920

Eight O'Clock

by
Reginald Berkeley

Preface

In his report for the Lord Chamberlain, the censor G.S. Street wrote of
Eight O'Clock:

> This is called 'a sordid Play' and so it is; it is also extremely painful.
> [...] The audience's feelings are not spared in the treatment of this
> theme and the whole thing is meant to be realistic. It is painful and
> unpleasant, but no more so than many scenes of ordinary melodrama
> and better done.

The play is a work of social criticism focusing as it does on a condemned
man on death row. The play is in the tradition of Victor Hugo's prose
study *The Last Day of a Condemned Man* (1875) and is a precursor to
Richard Wright's epic novel *Native Son* (1940) and Krzysztof Kieslowski's
A Short Film About Killing (1988). All of these works present their doomed
protagonists with empathy: *Eight O'Clock* is more precisely *sympathetic*
towards it hero and as such is more obviously a work of melodrama
than a work of measured distanciation that the other artists managed
to create. In this respect, Berkeley's play is reminiscent of another short
work of drama, W.S. Gilbert's final play *The Hooligan* (1911), inspired
by the 1910 Dr Crippen murder trial, a surprisingly powerful and, given
the dramatist's track record, surprisingly serious work of tragic drama.
Like *Eight O'Clock*, Gilbert's one-act play depicts the last moments of
a condemned murderer in his prison cell. Unlike the central character in
Eight O'Clock, Gilbert's protagonist is successfully reprieved but, after the
psychological torment he has been forced to endure, dies of a heart attack.
Rogers, the condemned man, is a murderer who admits his guilt – this is
no tragedy of the miscarriage of justice – and Reginald Berkeley presents
a society in which it is impossible to 'go straight'. Rogers reveals how it is
impossible to secure employment when one has a background of felony. It
is a world determined by money: unable to afford the membership fees of

the trade union, Rogers loses his job and cannot afford a lawyer to support his claim of unfair dismissal, and so he is forced back into crime. Rogers is a criminal from the lumpenproletariat, but he is shown as having a clearer insight into the mechanics of society than Mr Dalton, the simplistic and bourgeois Chaplain:

> PRISONER: (…) I 'eard all I wanted to abaht Society from the Judge. (*warmly*) Wot 'e couldn't see, and you can't see, is that Society made me kill that bloke.

Interestingly, Rogers's miserable revelation about the nature of his society is in parallel with a journey away from religious faith. Rogers used to believe that lightning was 'God opening 'Eaven and lookin' out to see what the world was doin'', until he met an astronomer who explained the scientific facts and also demonstrated that it was impossible for heaven to exist as an actual place. Rogers refuses to believe that there could be a God to allow the injustices of the world to happen or, at least, if there is a God who cannot make 'allowances for me, after the trouble I've 'ad … I don't want nothin' to do with 'im'. Ironically, when it seems that Rogers has been reprieved he turns to prayer only to discover it was a false hope and his fate is sealed. Perhaps the final damning social criticism of the play is embodied in the figure of the Hangman, '*a man in seedy black clothes, who looks rather like a disreputable lay preacher*'.

Before Rogers is trooped out to his grim fate, the Warder utters the last spoken word in the play: 'Silence!' This is perhaps an allusion to Hamlet's final words 'The rest is silence'. Like the Prince of Denmark, Rogers is, provocatively, the victim of another evidently rotten state, and his demise is similarly tragic and immutable. There are also classical principles to the play in addition to allusion: *Eight O'Clock* is a play that adheres to the classical unities of time, place and action. The inexorability of time structures the piece: the dialogue reveals to us that it is 'Twenty-six minutes left'; 'twenty-three minutes left'; 'I've got to be 'anged in twenty minutes'; 'Eighteen minutes'; 'Quarter to'; 'Nearly five to', and ultimately the final stage direction informs us that, as the curtain descends, '*the deep chime of the prison clock … strikes eight o'clock, the hour of execution*'. The strict unity of time gives some interesting options regarding pace when it comes to practical interpretation, not least at moments of suspense such as when, the stage directions state, '*The stage remains empty for the space of about half a minute*' or when we are informed with precision that '*the Chaplain remains on his knees a second longer than the other*'.

The play has a stark visual quality from the very beginning, with the prisoner's face 'ghastly white in the half light' and appropriately under-lit so that 'your eyes are just beginning to take in the detail of the cell when there is the click of a key in a lock …'. In its dialogue, the play strikes a balance between melodrama (such as when Rogers asks *with a queer break in his voice at the mid of the question*': 'Do it 'urt much ... do you think?') and Grand Guignol (Rogers describing his dead victim: 'It makes me feel sick like afterwards ... 'E 'ad white 'air, all bloody ...'). Like Victor MacClure's *Latitude 15° South*, Berkeley's play makes an intricate, at times phonetic, use of dialect in an attempt to capture the voice of this doomed Londoner from 'dahn Moile End'. This quality to the play evidently caused some reaction from its audience, the *Stage* reporting that the 'Cockneyisms' moved 'to mirth the unthinking persons in the audience' (23 December 1920). But over all, the play was very well received: the same review in the *Stage* celebrated Berkeley's 'full command of detail' and the staging of the play, including its 'appalling realism' especially in the 'dull thud of "the drop"' at the end which served 'to complete our horror'. For the *Sunday Times* (19 December 1920) the play was peopled with 'real folk' and the *Observer* (19 December 1920), not usually an aficionado of the Grand Guignol, was impressed by this play's serious and realistic exploration of its subject through 'thoughtful emotion' and 'fine psychological' observation. Many reviewers were keen to celebrate Russell Thorndike's performance in the role of Rogers. Indeed, in *The Times* obituary of Russell Thorndike (9 November 1972), the newspaper recounts the Grand Guignol phase of his career, stating that he made 'his chief success as an actor in Richard Berkeley's *Eight O'clock*, a drama set in the condemned cell during a prisoner's last half hour'.

Eight O'Clock

A Sordid Play in One Act
by
Reginald Berkeley

First Performed: 15 December 1920

The Prisoner
The Chaplain
The Warder
The Attendant
The Governor of the Prison
The Prison Doctor
The Prison Chaplain
The Hangman

Scene: *A condemned cell in Aldgate Prison. The cell, about twelve feet by ten by say, nine feet high, is entered by a heavy wooden door strengthened with steel in the middle of the back wall of the stage, and, above the door, there is a barred grating for ventilation. The furniture is very sparse. In the far left hand corner of the cell there is a bed, unmistakably the property of His Majesty's Government, a hard angular looking thing. In the middle of the room there is a small deal table without a cloth, upon which may be seen a penny ink bottle, with a pen sticking in it, and some sheets of paper – also a strip of blotting paper. Beside the table, so placed as to face in a direction at right angles to the audience and with its back towards the bed, is a chair of the kind usually termed 'kitchen chairs' a stiff uncomfortable affair with a wooden seat and no arms. In the right hand corner of the cell there is a metal frame supporting an enamelled basin. On the floor, beside the frame, are an enamelled jug, with a brown towel thrown carelessly over it, and an enamelled soap-dish. There is no other furniture. It is half past seven on a raw winter's morning. When the curtain goes up, very faint grey daylight is filtering in through the grating above the door. In the gloomy corner, where the bed is, you can just distinguish, lying upon the bed, the figure of a man. He has the bedclothes pulled tightly up near his ears, but his chin is outside the coverlet, and, the coverlet being a heavy brown blanket, the prisoner's face shews ghastly white in the half light. He is lying on his back looking straight up at the ceiling with open eyes. For a perceptible period of time nothing moves, and your eyes are just beginning to take in the detail of the cell when there is the click of a key in a lock and the heavy clang of a bolt being drawn. As the key fumbles in the lock, you hear distinctly a hissing intake of breath from the man on the bed. The door of the cell then swings open, admitting the* Warder *and the* Chaplain. *The light faintly increases.*

WARDER   (*speaking in a tone of assumed cheerfulness*): Now then young feller, it's time for you to get up. (*in an undertone to the* Chaplain) Try and 'earten 'im up a bit, sir.

PRISONER   (*in a voice that strives to be natural and very nearly succeeds in the endeavour*): Wot time is it, any'ow? (*He stretches his arms above his head and yawns prodigiously.*)

WARDER   (*briskly*): 'Arpast seven. (*very slight pause*) I'll be bringin' yer breakfast along in a few minits. (*no answer from the bed – in an undertone to the* Chaplain) I'm afraid 'es goin' to take it pretty bad.

CHAPLAIN   (*speaking in a clear pleasant voice without any trace of affection whatever – rather in the manner of a young doctor speaking to a patient*): Now then old man (*he goes to the head of the bed*), come along and tumble up. (*The* Prisoner *suddenly jumps out of bed and stands up in his night clothes only.*)

PRISONER: Ugh, my Gawd it's cold! (*He shivers and hugs himself – the* Chaplain *picks up some clothes from near the head of the bed and hands them to the* Prisoner *silently – the* Prisoner *takes the coat and begins to put it on.*) Thank you, sir! (*He stops and takes it off again.*) I think I'll 'ave a bit of a swill first. (*The* Chaplain *takes the coat from his hands.*)

WARDER   (*gruffly*): 'Ere, I'll pour it out for yer. (*He goes to the washhand stand and pours water into the basin.*) It's nearly froze! (*He puts jug down again.*)

PRISONER: 'Alf a minit! (*He goes to the basin, picking up the soap on the way, and puts his hands in the water, withdrawing them with a muffled exclamation.*) Oh Gawd it ain't 'arf cold! (*He washes quickly, smearing some water on his face, and then rubs himself vigorously with the towel.*) (*Meanwhile the* Warder *has walked across and is standing by the*

Chaplain *and, while the* Prisoner *is performing his ablutions conversation is going on.*)

WARDER   (*in his former undertone*): Pore devil, 'e don't look up to much.

CHAPLAIN: I don't know what to say to him. He's so completely unrepentant.

WARDER   (*rather fiercely*): Oh! I 'ate these damned 'angings.

PRISONER   (*his voice coming suddenly from the corner of the room causes his hearers to give a slight start*): Wy don't yer try an' stop them then? (*with an attempt at jocularity that falls horribly flat*) I'm not too particular about bein' 'anged let me tell yer.

WARDER   (*gruffly*): That wasn't meant for you to 'ear. (*puritanically*) An' it isn't a thing to joke about. (*slight pause*) I'm goin' to leave you with Mr. Dalton now, and I'll bring in yer breakfast in about ten minits.

PRISONER   (*sobered by the other's precision*): Wot time are they goin' to do it, did yer say?

WARDER   (*curtly*): Eight!

PRISONER   (*with a note of eagerness in his voice*): Wot's the time now?

WARDER   (*curtly – he looks at his watch before he speaks*): Twenty-six minutes to. (*He snaps the watch case and pockets it.*)

PRISONER: Twenty-six minutes left. Gawd, it feels rum I tell yer!

WARDER: Don't get talking silly now. You talk to Mr. Dalton, and say a bit of a prayer. (*He goes to the door.*)

PRISONER   (*unintentionally striking an attitude mentally*): Naow, not me! I ain't a sniveller!

WARDER   (*just about to close the door*): Oh go on! (*He slams the door and fastens it from the outside.*) (*Meanwhile the Chaplain, you notice, has sat down on the bed.*)

PRISONER   (*respectfully*): I'm afraid it ain't much good us getting on to religion again, sir. (*He sits on the chair and begins to put on his socks and boots.*)

CHAPLAIN   (*pleasantly*): I'm sure I don't want you to talk about religion if you'd rather not. (*He gets up and puts his hand on the other's shoulder.*) Talk about anything you like, old man!

PRISONER   (*looking up, with his left boot half laced, and speaking very seriously*): It's a terrible funny thing to think as this is the last time I'll ever put them boots on.

CHAPLAIN   (*solemnly*): It is a terrible funny thing indeed, Rogers. And it's a terrible funny thing to think that in a few minutes you will be with your Maker.

PRISONER   (*with a little catch in his voice*): Did you ever ... see a man 'anged ... before sir?

CHAPLAIN: Yes.

PRISONER   (*eagerly, but with a queer break in his voice at the middle of the question*): Do it 'urt much ... do you think?

CHAPLAIN   (*sitting on the table facing the audience and looking kindly at his questioner*): Not much I think, old chap. It's all over very soon. (*He snaps his fingers.*) Like that!

PRISONER   (*with a little shudder*): I 'eard them tryin' the drop last night ... (*He pauses and gulps a little.*) It weren't a nice sound. (*He licks his lips.*)

CHAPLAIN   (*sympathetically*): No, I expect not. (*The* Prisoner *works his mouth convulsively.*) There old chap, the doctors say it's nothing – simply nothing.

PRISONER   (*hoarsely*): It's my life!

CHAPLAIN: Only your carnal life! Your spiritual life doesn't begin properly until you're dead.

PRISONER   (*hoarsely*): Yes ... an' from wot you say, I've got a nice time coming to me ... in the next world.

CHAPLAIN: 'Only believe and thou shalt see That Christ is all in all to thee'. That's a hymn it's true, but it's founded on Our Lord's own words. Only believe Rogers. Christ will do the rest for you.

PRISONER   (*desperately*): 'Ow in the name of Gawd *am* I to believe, when I don't know the way 'ow?

CHAPLAIN   (*pleasantly*): I don't know ... It just comes! Suddenly you believe; and then you simply can't understand why you haven't believed all your life.

PRISONER: Was you ever a 'eathen, sir?

CHAPLAIN: Surely! I didn't take orders till I was thirty-five.

PRISONER: An' did you start believin' ... an' ... an' all that after you was thirty-five?

CHAPLAIN: I didn't believe in anything much, until I was about thirty.

PRISONER: 'Ow did you come to do it?

CHAPLAIN: I don't know ... It just came – the same as it'll come to you to day.

PRISONER   (*decidedly*): Not it! Wot 'ud the time be now, sir?

CHAPLAIN   (*looking at his wrist watch*): Twenty-three minutes to.

PRISONER   (*gripping his hands together and twisting them nervously*): That's twenty-three minutes left ... It's not long sir.

CHAPLAIN   (*earnestly*): No old man, it's not long! Now we'll leave it that you don't believe. All the same there's no harm in facing the situation seriously and bravely.

PRISONER   (*nervously*): I 'ope I shall do the last any 'ow, sir.

CHAPLAIN: Are you going to meet your end unrepentant? Do remember that in the eye's of God and the world, you committed a foul murder.

PRISONER: Well, supposin' I did, I'm being 'anged for it, ain't I?

CHAPLAIN (*rather taken aback*): Er – that's not quite the same thing.

PRISONER (*looking furtively round the cell – he speaks half to himself*): It's a 'orrible thing!

CHAPLAIN (*kindly*): Aren't you at all sorry?

PRISONER: I'm sorry it's come to this.

CHAPLAIN: Yes, but don't you repent the sin at all?

PRISONER (*after a short pause*): Naow! It's no good my saying I'm sorry, 'cos I'm not.

CHAPLAIN: My dear fellow, that is a very unchristian spirit in which to go to God.

PRISONER (*in a puzzled tone*): 'Ow do you mean, go to Gawd, sir?

CHAPLAIN: I mean, to go to your Father which is in Heaven, God, the blessed Trinity, the Creator of this World, the Creator of everything living or inanimate, the God who made the man you killed.

PRISONER (*still puzzled*): Go before 'im where, sir?

CHAPLAIN (*impressively*): Up there! (*He points with his finger above his head.*)

PRISONER (*very puzzled*): That's only one of the things that troubles me. There was a parson that used to teach us kids dahn Moile End. 'E 'ad a way of pointing up in the air and saying 'Eaven was up there. Then once I met a gent as taught some science in the London University – Astomery I think 'e called it – (*He breaks off and looks interrogatively at the* Chaplain.)

CHAPLAIN: Astronomy?

PRISONER: Ah! That were it! I 'appened at the time to 'ave a job as 'and on one of the L.C.C. steamers. I was just takin the wheel for a minute or two, to 'elp the mate, when this gen'l'man come and stood close by. (*He pauses for a moment.*)

CHAPLAIN (*interested*): Yes?

PRISONER: As I was walkin' away, when the mate come back, the gentleman ses 'It's a fine night' ... It was too, a wunnerful fine night ... An' we got talkin' –

CHAPLAIN: Yes?

PRISONER: 'E told me no end of things. One thing, we got on to lightning. 'E aked me what did I think it was. I told 'im I'd always thought it was God opening 'Eaven and lookin' out to see what the world was doin' – which I 'ad always thought ... It ended in 'is drawin' me a lot of diagrams and shewin' me 'ow impossible it was for such a place as 'Eaven to exist anywhere.

CHAPLAIN (*in a chilling voice*): I'm afraid he must have been an Atheist.

PRISONER: Wot's that, sir?

CHAPLAIN: A man that doesn't believe in God.

PRISONER: The funny part was 'e *did* believe in God. At least, 'e *said* so.

CHAPLAIN: Ah well, it doesn't matter what he thought. We were talking about your position.

PRISONER: Oh Gawd, sir, *can't* you let me ferget that I've got to be 'anged in twenty minutes?

CHAPLAIN (*earnestly*): I'm sorry old man. But you want to die in a proper spirit, don't you?

PRISONER (*passionately*): 'Ow does it 'elp me to die in a proper spirit, if you keep on talkin' abaht it?

CHAPLAIN: You're overwrought – upset. That's because you can't meet your end in the consciousness of your belief in God and Christ.

PRISONER (*wistfully*): D'yer think ... Would it be more easy like, if I believed in Gawd?

CHAPLAIN (*unctuously*): Surely! If you believed in the Holy Trinity, you would know that death was just a swift passage from Earth to the kingdom of God. You would mount the scaffold with the knowledge that but a few seconds of carnal life separated you from the arms of your Father in Heaven.

PRISONER (*reflectively*): You want me to believe –?

CHAPLAIN (*very impressively*): I don't – *God* does. (*He gives time for the remark to soak in.*) Come now, man, is it very hard to believe in an Eternal Father full of love for you, hungering with you, sorrowing with you – as he does with me too, and every other poor sinner in the world. What is it that guides and comforts us all, strengthens us in tribulation, softens our hearts in wrath?

PRISONER (*respectfully but prosaically*): I'm sure I dunno', sir.

CHAPLAIN (*in a ringing voice*): God's love, man! His wonderful incomprehensible love for every single human being that was ever born.

PRISONER (*perplexed*): 'E takes a bloomin' funny way o' shewin' it sometimes.

CHAPLAIN (*severely*): What d'ye mean?

PRISONER: Well, take my ole 'ooman, 'Oos going to look after the kids for 'er when I'm turned off? There's four o' them.

CHAPLAIN: What's that got to do with God?

PRISONER: I can't rightly say, sir, not being edicated. And I can't argue. But it seem's a bit funny, don't it?

CHAPLAIN: Who are we to question God's purposes? (*He makes a rhetorical pause.*) Who *are* we? *What* are we? (*pause*)

PRISONER (*getting a little interested*): Did Gawd arrange like for me to kill that bloke?

CHAPLAIN (*piously*): No doubt he had some inscrutable purpose to fulfil.

PRISONER (*getting a little out of hand*): Then why am I being 'anged for fulfillin' Gawd's purpose?

CHAPLAIN (*a little nonplussed*): That's God's will too!

PRISONER: Is it? Gawd didn't make the law.

CHAPLAIN (*seeing his way out*): It was God's will that the law should be made. (*The* Prisoner, *his reasoning powers overcome leans his head on his hands upon the table. Short pause – the* Chaplain *lays his hand on the* Prisoner's *shoulder.*) Everything is God's will! Won't you believe in Christ and cast the burden of your sins on his shoulder? He's waiting to bear them for you, man, just waiting to bear them. Think of the comfort of being relieved of your sins.

PRISONER (*rather desperately*): 'Ow can I do it?

CHAPLAIN (*tenderly*): Just try. Say after me, 'I believe in God the Father Almighty' –

PRISONER (*with a gulp*) I believe in Gawd ... the Father Ormity –

CHAPLAIN (*with exquisite solemnity*) 'Maker of Heaven and Earth' –

PRISONER: Maker ove 'eaven ... 'n earth –

CHAPLAIN (*almost intoning the words*): 'And in Jesus Christ his only Son Our Lord' –

PRISONER: And in Jesus Christ ... No sir, I can't do it. I been to church 's often as the next man, but I never could unnerstand –

CHAPLAIN: You aren't required to understand. You've only got to believe.

PRISONER: Well I can't do that sir, unless I unnerstand. That wot you was sayin' is all rigmarole to me.

CHAPLAIN: I'll try to put it more simply. It simply means that you believe Jesus Christ was the Son of God.

PRISONER (*helplessly*): Yes, but 'ow do I know 'e was?

CHAPLAIN: How do you know there was such a person as William the Conqueror?

PRISONER (*with a puzzled expression*): It's in the 'Istry Books.

CHAPLAIN: Quite so! And Christ is in the Bible.

PRISONER (*nervously*): Wot's the ... time, sir?

CHAPLAIN (*looking at his watch*): Eighteen minutes to.

PRISONER (*scraping his feet*): I wish they'd 'urry up an' ... an' get done with it.

CHAPLAIN: Don't think about that, Rogers. (*softly*) Think of your soul. Don't kill that too!

PRISONER (*with a violent start*): I wish you wouldn't 'arp on killin' ... I keep seein' 'im lyin' on the floor with 'is face all bloody.

CHAPLAIN: Him? Who?

PRISONER   (*huskily*): The bloke what I put away. (*He shudders.*) It
makes me feel sick like afterwards ... 'E 'ad white 'air, all
bloody ... Pore devil, I didn't go in to kill 'im ... (*little
pause*) 'e was such a silly fool, wot 'ud he want to come at
me for.

CHAPLAIN   (*prosaically*): You had no business to steal his property.

PRISONER   (*derisively*): Oh yes, it's all bloomin' fine for you to talk. Wot
chance 'as a man got o' goin' square once 'e's been in the jug?
Nix! (*He snaps his fingers.*)

CHAPLAIN: Whose fault was it you got jugged?

PRISONER: Mine o' course! I ain't blamin' anyone for that. I pinched a
cove's watch, an' they run me in.

CHAPLAIN: Well?

PRISONER: W'y wouldn't they let me alone when I got out? Fine chanst
I 'ad o' goin' straight, I can tell you. There's a nasty sneakin'
cove called 'Arding in the force, 'oo'll ferret and ferret until 'e
can get you in again.

CHAPLAIN: Oh, nonsense!

PRISONER: Nonsense? It's not nonsense. It's a fact. I 'adn't been out
six weeks afore I found myself bein' watched by this cove
'Arding. 'E thought I'd pinched a 'and bag from the Tube,
just because I 'appened to be rahnd abaht at the time. 'E got
me arrested on suspicion. After that I give it best.

CHAPLAIN: That was cowardly of you.

PRISONER   (*with a snort*): Cowardly? 'Scuse me sir, but you don't know
wot you're talkin' abaht. 'Ow was it cowardly?

CHAPLAIN   (*unctuously*): God tries no man above his strength. You
should have resisted temptation.

PRISONER   (*rousing at the recollection of his wrongs*): My Gawd, to 'ear
you talk! 'Ave you ever 'ad a missus workin' 'er pore 'ands
to the bone to feed 'er kids, and you doin' nothing? (The
Chaplain *is silent.*) No – I should think not! Wot was I to do?

CHAPLAIN   (*tersely*) Work!

PRISONER   (*derisively*): Work! (*He laughs harshly.*) You seem to think
gettin' work's as easy as kiss yer foot. Wot work, I'd like to
know?

CHAPLAIN: Manual work. Navvying!

PRISONER   (*with bitter sarcasm*): 'Ave you ever 'eard of Trades Unions?

CHAPLAIN: Well?

PRISONER: Well! Yes it is well! You don't 'appen to know I suppose, that
a man's got to be admitted to the Union – and pay for it too.

CHAPLAIN: What of that?

PRISONER: You arst my friend Mr. 'Arding wot of that? (*bitterly*) Yer
see, I was known to the perlice.

CHAPLAIN: I'm sure a decent man like Harding wouldn't –

PRISONER: Ah, cheeze it, sir! It's 'Arding's job, an' I'm not blamin' 'im for doin' it. 'E ain't got no particular dahn on me ... I did get a job once, when I was about sick of the pore missus doin' all the work. It warn't a Union job, and I thought it was all clear for a straight run. (*wistfully and with a bit of a break in his voice*) yer see sir, the missus 'ad got me to promise I'd go straight for the kid's sake and 'ers. (*harshly*) Well, wot 'appened? I seen 'Arding, one day, talking to the boss, an' nex' day, the boss ses 'we shan't want you no more, Rogers', 'e ses, and gives me a day's pay to get rid of me.

CHAPLAIN   (*warmly*): If that's true, you could have sued Harding for –

PRISONER   (*quaintly*): 'Aven't you discovered yet, sir, that the law's only for them as can buy it? 'Ow was I goin' to prove that 'Arding said anything abaht me? Would the boss 'ave split on 'im? Not likely! An' where 'ud I get the brass to pay a lawyer? (The Chaplain *is silent*.) (*decisively*) Naow! ... I turned crook. An' beggin' your pardon, so would you, sir!

CHAPLAIN: You've had a hard row to hoe.

PRISONER   (*warmly*): I 'ave! (*a little hysterically*) An' it's something to know I'm at the end of it. (*The thought of the gallows suddenly chills him – He gulps and begins twisting his hands again.*) Wot's the ... time, sir?

CHAPLAIN   (*looking at his watch*): Quarter to. (*slight pause*) I say, why didn't you bring all this out at your trial?

PRISONER: I wanted ter. I told my lawyer to say I'd done it, and let me tell 'ow it all came abaht.

CHAPLAIN: What did he say?

PRISONER: 'E said there wasn't enough evidence to 'ang a dog on – Per'aps there wasn't, but there was enough to 'ang me though.

CHAPLAIN   (*shaking his head*): He was very sanguine.

PRISONER   (*muttering*): 'E was a damned fool! (*pause*) I'm not 'owling abaht it sir, but I 'aven't 'ad a fair go. Strite I 'aven't.

CHAPLAIN   (*sympathetically*): You've had hard luck certainly. But that doesn't excuse murder. Murder's a dreadful crime. Society –

PRISONER   (*respectfully but firmly*): Thank ye sir, but I 'eard all I wanted to abaht Society from the Judge. (*warmly*) Wot 'e couldn't see, and you can't see, is that Society made me kill that bloke.

CHAPLAIN: Oh nonsense, Rogers, you're talking rubbish!

PRISONER: Naow sir! I'm sayin' wot's true. If Society 'ad a little more time for a man when 'e's dahn, there'd be less men in the gutter –

CHAPLAIN: Well, never mind about that. (*seriously*) You don't defend murder, do you?

PRISONER: Naow! It's wrong! I've broke the law. I know that.

CHAPLAIN: Well then, aren't you goin to make your peace with God on this solemn and awful occasion? Don't go to your death with this weight of sin on your soul. Pray, Rogers! Go on your knees, man, and pray humbly.

PRISONER (*a little sullenly*): Pray? Wot for?

CHAPLAIN: For the forgiveness of God. You've broken His Laws.

PRISONER (*defiantly*): Yes, and I'm *paying* for it!

CHAPLAIN: Only an earthly penalty. Don't you repent at all?

PRISONER: I'm sorry I 'ad to do it.

CHAPLAIN: That's the wrong spirit. You're trying to justify yourself.

PRISONER (*doggedly*): I say I'm sorry I 'ad to do it.

CHAPLAIN: This isn't the time to be obstinate. Are you too proud, to ask God's forgiveness?

PRISONER: Look 'ere. It's this way. I've told you wot I 'ad to fight against.

CHAPLAIN: Yes?

PRISONER: Didn't you feel sorry for me?

CHAPLAIN: God knows I did.

PRISONER: Well, accordin' to you, God knows everything, and if 'e can't make allowances for me, after the trouble I've 'ad, without me snivellin', I don't want nothin' to do with 'im.

CHAPLAIN (*profoundly shocked*): Rogers, this is terrible! – (*The click of the* Warder's *key is heard in the lock and the bolt is pulled back with a clang – The door is partly opened and the* Warder *comes in, followed by an attendant carrying a tray on which are some rough breakfast utensils – the* Warder *stands near the table, and the attendant takes the things from the tray and puts them on the table. While the things are being set out, conversation proceeds.*)

WARDER (*looking from one to the other*): I'm sorry to intrude.

PRISONER (*affecting a gaiety which sets everybody's nerves on edge – he speaks in a mincing accent*): Not at all; delighted to see you!

CHAPLAIN (*pained*): Rogers!

WARDER: Stow that talk! I'm a bit late with your breakfast. I was kept sorting some letters.

PRISONER (*with painful eagerness*): Nothin' for me I suppose, sir?

WARDER: Yes, one! (*The* Attendant *leaves the cell, taking the tray.*) Come and eat your breakfast.

PRISONER: Can't I 'ave the letter first, sir?

WARDER: Yes, if you like. Now don't go and get upset about it. (*He hands an opened letter to the* Prisoner, *who retires with stumbling steps to the other end of the cell – the* Warder, *keeping an eye on him, talks in an undertone to the* Chaplain.) 'Ow's 'e takin' it?

CHAPLAIN: He's been telling me how he came to be a criminal. It's very sad.

WARDER: Chah! They're all like that! A man's got the power to go straight if he wants to.

CHAPLAIN: That's what I told him. He seems to have found the straight path too stony.

WARDER: Yes. I shouldn't think he tried very 'ard.

CHAPLAIN: Well, apparently he tried to get work and – (*There is a gasping sob from the corner of the cell – both face abruptly round to where the* Prisoner *is reading his letter – He is standing near the bed with his face to the audience, staring stupidly at the letter.*)

WARDER (*in a hoarse whisper to the* Chaplain): That letter says he'll very likely be reprieved. We did't know whether to give it to 'im or not. But it's from his wife, so we thought 'e'd better 'ave it.

CHAPLAIN: I hope to God he may be.

WARDER (*prosaically*): Erch! It means twenty years anyway. A man's just as well dead. Supposin' you –

PRISONER (*in a shaky voice*): Mr Dalton!

CHAPLAIN: Yes.

PRISONER (*walking forward unsteadily and holding out the letter*): Would you read that bit (*he points*) and tell me ... wot you make of it? (*He sits at the table.*) (*The* Chaplain *looks at the paper with puckered brows.*)

WARDER (*cheerily*): Come now. 'Ave a bit o' something to eat.

PRISONER: No, wait! (*He looks eagerly at the* Chaplain.)

WARDER (*firmly*): Come now. You'll want it anyway to 'earten you up. (*He puts the bowl of food in front of the* Prisoner.) 'Ere, you take a drink of cocoa. (*The* Prisoner *drinks the cocoa greedily and eats a small piece of bread.*)

PRISONER (*addressing the* Chaplain): Well, sir?

CHAPLAIN: As I read it, it means your wife and your lawyer expect you to be reprieved.

PRISONER (*getting up excitedly*): It's a bit of all right, ain't it? I –

WARDER (*taking him by the shoulder*): Now just you sit down. There's nothing official yet. Don't you be countin' your chickens before they're 'atched!

PRISONER (*sitting down obediently*): Do you know if it's come, sir?

WARDER: 'Ow can I possibly know what papers the Governor's got?

PRISONER   (*to the* Chaplain): You think it'll come all right, don't you
            sir?

CHAPLAIN   (*looks first at the* Warder, *lifting his eyebrows, whereat the
            other shrugs his shoulders, then, puzzled what to answer, he
            says*): Well, Rogers, your wife seems to think so.

PRISONER   (*eagerly to the* Warder): It means twenty years, sir, don't it?

WARDER: Hm! (*He nods his head.*)

PRISONER: That's nothing. Do that on me 'ead. (*He looks from one to
            the other.*) I'm only thirty-five now. I'll still be a young man
            when I get out.

WARDER: Finish your breakfast!

PRISONER: All right sir! (*Obediently he eats a few mouthfuls and drinks
            some more cocoa – suddenly he stops chewing and looks
            from one to the other again.*) O' course it mightn't come
            after all. (*to the* Chaplain) Just let me look at the letter
            again, sir. (*The* Chaplain *hands it to him in silence.*)

WARDER   (*in a whisper to the* Chaplain): I wish 'e wouldn't take on so
            over it. There's no certainty about it. There's nothing come
            so far as I know.

CHAPLAIN   (*also whispering – compassionately*): Poor fellow, let him
            think it's true if it eases his mind. (*The* Prisoner *looks up
            from the letter and sees their faces.*)

PRISONER   (*suspiciously*): This ain't a gag to–?

WARDER   (*harshly*): Stop that, now! You take it quiet.

PRISONER   (*wretchedly*): Yessir! (*slight pause*) Beg pardon, sir, but did
            you post that letter I gave you last night yet?

WARDER: No!

PRISONER: I'd like you not to post it until ... (*He pauses and gulps*) we
            know ... what's to 'appen.

WARDER: It won't be posted till after eight.

PRISONER   (*with a start*): Wot's the time now?

CHAPLAIN   (*looking at his watch*): Nearly five to.

PRISONER   (*nervously*): It's getting close! (*to the* Chaplain, *after a little
            pause*) I think it'll be all right sir. I feel it some 'ow.

CHAPLAIN: That's right, Rogers! Hope for the best! (*There is a pause.*)

PRISONER   (*breaking the silence suddenly and making his hearers jump*):
            Gawd ain't so bad after all!

WARDER   (*sharply*): No profanity here. Talk sense or not at all.

CHAPLAIN: Wait a bit, warder! (*to the* Prisoner) Why do you say that?

PRISONER: Well, it *do* look as though He must have worked this
            reprieve.

CHAPLAIN   (*eagerly seizing the opportunity*): You do believe then?

PRISONER   (*slowly*): Well, sir, what's a man to say, when he gets saved at
            the last minit?

CHAPLAIN: I'm sorry that only the thought of your own bodily benefit can move you to belief, but it's better than nothing. Do you repent your sin now? (*The* Prisoner *is silent.*) Won't you ask for God's forgiveness?

PRISONER: Yes, I'm sorry I done it, now.

CHAPLAIN   (*very earnestly*): Let us pray together.

PRISONER   (*respectfully*): Very well sir! (*They go over near the bed and kneel with their backs to the audience – the* Warder *removes his cap and bows his head respectfully, when they kneel, and then begins to clear the table noiselessly, walking on tip toe – When the table is cleared, he stands beside it with his head bent and his eyes on the floor – His cap is in his hand – After a longish pause, footsteps are heard echoing along the corridor.*)

WARDER   (*in a firm even tone*): It's time now, please! (*The* Prisoner *starts violently and rises to his feet, looking furtively about him – the* Chaplain *remains on his knees a second longer than the other, and then rises reverently and with a very grave face – The steps are heard just outside the door.*)

PRISONER   (*gripping his hands tightly together and pressing his arms close in to his sides – He speaks in a kind of broken mutter*): Oh Gawd ...! 'elp me! (*The door to the cell is opened and flung back, so that the audience sees through it a flight of stone stairs just outside. The* Governor *of the Prison enters, followed by the* Sheriff, *the* Doctor, *the* Prison Chaplain *and a man in seedy black clothes, who looks rather like a disreputable lay preacher – the* Governor *carries in his hand a white stiff paper sealed with a black seal, the* Governor *stands in the centre of the cell and reads the warrant – At its conclusion, the seedy-looking man comes forward.*)

PRISONER   (*brokenly*): Sir! Sir! (*While he is speaking, the man in black has caught his arms at the back.*)

GOVERNOR   (*in solemn tones*): Yes, my man? Have you anything to say?

PRISONER   (*eagerly*): Isn't there a reprieve for me, sir?

GOVERNOR: No, there's no reprieve.

WARDER   (*addressing the man in black*): Now then! Get a move on yourself!

PRISONER   (*looking helplessly round at the faces*): In the letter ... it said ... (*He gulps and glares round like a trapped animal*) it said there 'ud ... b ... be a reprieve, sir.

WARDER   (*sternly*): Silence!

(*The man in black has by this time finished binding the* Prisoner's *arms behind his back – the* Prisoner *realizing that there is no hope of a reprieve, gives a little whimper of terror*)

DOCTOR   (*apprehensively to the* Governor): I told you he'd better not
            have that letter. There'll be a scene now, I'm afraid.
WARDER   (*to the* Governor): All ready, sir!
GOVERNOR   (*nodding his head*): Right (*He looks at his watch.*) Bring him
            along! (*The* Warder *and the* Attendant *each take an arm of
            the Prisoner.*)
PRISONER   (*in a tone of frightened expostulation*): 'Ere ... ! 'Ere I say!
WARDER: Silence! (*They all troop out through the door and up the
            stairs outside it — The last person to leave the stage is the
            Chaplain — His face is very white and set. The stage remains
            empty for the space of about half a minute — Then the
            silence is broken by the deep chime of the prison clock — It
            strikes eight o'clock, the hour of execution — The prison bell
            begins to toll and the Curtain falls slowly.*)

CURTAIN

A Man in Mary's Room

by

Gladys Unger

Preface

The American writer Gladys Unger (1885–1940) was a moderately significant figure in theatre writing by the time she submitted this one-act comedy to the Little Theatre. She would later enjoy success as a screenwriter, producing the scripts for Cecil B. DeMille's first talkies, *Dynamite* (1929) and *Madam Satan* (1930), and going on to produce the screenplays for films such as *The Countess of Monte Cristo* (1934), directed by Karl Freund (director of one of the great Grand Guignolesque movies *Mad Love* (1935)), and Charles Dickens adaptations *Great Expectations* (1934) and *Edwin Drood* (1935).

A Man in Mary's Room is the first produced example of a Grand Guignol play by a woman writer. Indeed, it is the *only* example throughout the British and French repertoires. *A Man in Mary's Room* is a fine example of British Grand Guignol comedy. It is a well-written and well-crafted play with a sense of comic language, not least in its sharp repartee and use of accent and dialect. The play is never more than gently risqué – as such it forms a fascinating comparison with H.F. Maltby's outrightly banned *I Want to Go Home* – and functions as a satire with a number of targets and provides an engaging insight into early 1920s preoccupations. For example, the play satirises fashions such as 'keep fit' and exercise. The play also satirises fashionable ideology targeting the high-minded morality of Ronald who instinctively thinks the worst of Mary, despite the fact that he and Victoria are unmarried, because of his Fabian principles. In this respect, the play is a comic journey into personal morality.

The play is also a delicate satire of Grand Guignol form, which is perhaps most interesting in this context. In particular, there is the story of the baby murdered in the house and Ronald contemplating using a revolver, before choosing a poker, to confront the unwanted 'man in Mary's room'. These elements function as a successful parody of Grand Guignol suspense narrative and its strategies. Ultimately, *A Man in Mary's Room* is a playful farce, not least with the comic device of gender confusion so beloved in

British comedy when the 'man' turns out to be Mary's aunt, a middle aged woman.

The censor G.S. Street welcomed the play most warmly, reporting:

> This is an amusing and in my opinion quite harmless little Play and if the Little Theatre would only stick to such things by reputable English authors it would save us much trouble. [...] The language is never in the least degree indelicate and the moral is sound. The scene is necessarily a bedroom (in a small cottage) but the bed has nothing to do with the play.

Critical reception was similarly warm, with the *Sunday Express* regarding the play as 'audaciously amusing' (19 December 1920) and the *Reynolds's Newspaper* praising this 'brightly written [...] spoof farce'.

A Man in Mary's Room

A Comedy in One Act
by
Gladys Unger

First Performed: 15 December 1920

Ronald
Victoria
Mary, a General Servant

SCENE: Victoria's bedroom in Thornberry Cottage, Little Eppington
TIME: The Present Day.
SCENE: A bedroom in an old country cottage.

An irregularly shaped room with a sloping ceiling and oak beams. Up centre a recess in which is a window centre. A dressing-table stands in front of window. The bed is right in the recess, but only the lower of its four posts can be seen. Below recess to right, at an angle, is the fire place. Lower down right another window. In front of it a table on which stands a lighted lamp. Down right centre front a cushioned wicker armchair. Up left, to left of recess, a door leading to hall. Against left wall, a chest of drawers; above it hangs a mirror. Down left front a small table and an occasional chair. The furniture is all odd as if it had been picked up at sales; the curtains and cushions are bright, old fashioned chintz. A few middle class feminine touches: an antimacassar on the armchair, a china cat with a rainbow bow about its neck, a florid picture calendar adorned with angels, etc.

It is night. The curtains of both windows have been drawn, there is a log fire burning and the room looks cosy and inviting.

Discovered: Victoria. She is a comely young women of the lower middle class; twenty five years old; very neat about her person. She speaks with a slight cockney accent; her intelligence is somewhat slow; her sense of humor unreliable. But she is earnest and warm-hearted and has a pretty, ingratiating manner very flattering to Man. She is wearing pale blue pyjamas; her hair is braided back for the night. Her dressing gown is thrown across occasional chair left; her slippers lie neatly on the ground beside it. At rise Victoria *is standing centre facing mirror on left wall; her right foot is forward; she is twirling her arms and breathing hard. She repeats movement with left foot forward, then anxiously consults chart, which is open on table down left front. Having traced the next movement with her finger; brows bent and tongue out, she proceeds to carry it into execution. She lies down on floor and waves her legs in circles.*

Suddenly, a knock on door. She continues exercise, unheeding. Knock repeated.

VICTORIA   (*pausing in her exercise*): Is that you, Mary? (*raising her head from the ground*) Aren't you in bed? Whatever do you want?

A MAN'S VOICE (*outside*): It's I.

VICTORIA: Oh! I thought you were going to work another hour. (*lowering her head again*) You can't come in yet, lovely. I haven't finished my improvers.

RONALD   (*outside; impatiently*): Victoria! Let me in!

VICTORIA   (*sitting up*): But I've only got to the twelve kicks each way.

RONALD   (*outside*) It's urgent! (*rattling door handle*) I must speak to you at once! Let me in!

VICTORIA   (*rising*): All right, lovely. Don't fidget yourself. I'm coming.

(*She slips on her dressing-gown and shuffles across floor in her bare feet, while* Ronald *continues to rattle handle impatiently. She unlocks the door and admits him.* Ronald *is an attractive looking young man of 27; slightly conscious of his own intellectual superiority. He wears an old house jacket, carries an unlit lamp in his hand and seems highly perturbed*)

VICTORIA   (*shocked at his appearance*): Ronald! Whatever is the matter? You've never gone and gotten another chill? Not since I came upstairs?

RONALD   (*impatiently*): It's worse than that.

VICTORIA   (*applying her hand to his forehead*): Your temperature! It's gone up! I'll get the thermometer. (*moves towards dressing table*)

RONALD   (*pulling her back*): You'll do nothing of the sort. Put on your slippers and listen to me. (*closing door left behind him*) Why didn't you let me in before? I've been knocking for five minutes.

VICTORIA   (*putting on her slippers*): I couldn't hear you, lovey, I was holding my breath.

RONALD: Holding one's breath doesn't affect one's hearing! (*comes down left*)

VICTORIA: But it tells you in the Perfect Physic Chart –

RONALD: Perfect Physi*que* – not physic. (*trying to put his lamp on table left front and obstructed by the chart*) Damn the chart!

VICTORIA   (*rescuing the chart*): Oh! Ronald! How can you! (*folds chart lovingly and puts it neatly under table*) I thought you wanted me to deepen my chest.

RONALD: Yes, but not to-night. (*seizing her by the arm*) Victoria, I've just made a horrible discovery.

VICTORIA   (*quaking*): Not – not the body?

RONALD   (*puzzled*): What body?

VICTORIA: I never meant for you to know. To *my* way of thinking authors get enough ideas of their own without being made nervous extra.

RONALD: But what is it? What body?

VICTORIA: The body of a baby what was burnt to death by its cruel stepmother here in this very house. She – she baked it in the oven and from that day whenever anyone's 'ad the darin' to bake bread in this house – the loaves have come out with a dark red stain!

RONALD: Who told you this?

VICTORIA: Our baker.

RONALD: What utter nonsense! Unfortunately there's no dead body in our house. It's far worse. There's a live man.

VICTORIA: A *man*?

RONALD   (*snorting*): A Man in Mary's room!

VICTORIA   (*shocked*): A *Man* in *Mary's* room? (Ronald *nods*.) It isn't possible!

RONALD: Why not?

VICTORIA: She's a chapel girl.

RONALD: My dear child, that may be only a blind.

VICTORIA: But she'd three years' character with an old lady who never allowed followers – not even cousins!

RONALD: Ah! Then *this* is the reaction.

VICTORIA   (*excited*): Well, if I say it who shouldn't, *I* ought to know a good reference if any one should. Not that general service can be mentioned in the same breath with waiting on gentlemen in a restaurant, still –

RONALD: Yes, yes, dear, and I'm not attempting to blame you, but the fact remains – there's a Man in Mary's room!

VICTORIA: Well, you could knock me over with a feather, reely you could. (*pushing him into armchair right centre*) Sit down lovey, and tell me (*sitting on his knee*) – however did you find it out?

RONALD: Well, I'd just written the heading to Chapter III, 'Petty Tyrannies of the Marriage Tie' when suddenly my lamp began to flicker.

VICTORIA: There! This very identical morning did I tell that girl to fill your lamp. Reely as mother used to say 'One servant is more bother than two twins.'

RONALD: The clock struck ten. Thinking Mary might still be in the kitchen –

VICTORIA   (*shaking her head*): She's mostly up by nine; she's what I call an early sleeper.

RONALD: I took the lamp and went out into the hall.

VICTORIA   (*with breathless interest*): And then?

RONALD: The flame died out completely and as I groped my way along the passage I distinctly heard, going up the twisted staircase that leads to Mary's room – *two sets of footsteps*!

VICTORIA: Two sets of footsteps?

RONALD: Yes. Mary's usual little shuffle and a heavy masculine tread following her up the creaking flight to her room.

VICTORIA: I can't believe it! A girl I've taken such pains with! Taught her her Bible lessons and how to fold napkins into boats and do her hair like the young ladies in the Refreshment Room and what not. Ronald, are you sure Mary knew the man was after her?

RONALD: Unless she's lost her sense of smell. The passage reeked of beer. And when I paused and listened Mary and her – accomplice – were *giggling* outside her door! And then they opened it and went into her room. Pah!

VICTORIA   (*philosophically*): To think that if she'd filled your lamp properly we might never have known! It shows that if we only do our duty in this world –

RONALD: Yes, and ours is before us. (*lifting Victoria from his knee*) Get up, dear.

VICTORIA   (*following her train of thought*): I can't get over girls nowadays with their brazen faces and their higher wages. What would mother have said to such goings-on – well, there, pretty much what she said to me when I first walked out with you.

RONALD   (*rising and putting armchair abruptly to right*): We needn't go into all that again, Victoria. Your mother never understood me.

VICTORIA: You can't blame her, lovey. Old fashioned, she is. 'No good ever come to a girl through walking out with a real gentleman,' she said. And true enough it turned out, to 'er way of thinking. (*sighs*)

RONALD   (*wincing*): Victoria, how many times have I asked you not to say 'walking-out?'

VICTORIA   (*patiently*): Very well then, keeping company. Though we *did* a lot of walking while you were reading at the Museum didn't we?

RONALD: I've no time to quibble. There is work ahead of me. (*goes resolutely up centre to dressing-table*)

VICTORIA   (*watching his back apprehensively*): Whatever are you going to do? (*He stoops and opens lower drawer of dressing-table.*) Your handkerchiefs aren't there, lovely.

RONALD: I am not looking for a handkerchief. (*He takes out a revolver.*)

VICTORIA   (*going up; alarmed*): Ronald! No! No! Don't take that thing! (*clutching his arm*) It might go off!

RONALD: It will if you do that. (*removes her hand and comes down*)

VICTORIA   (*following him down*): You're never going to kill him?

RONALD   (*making sure that revolver is loaded*): Not if he goes quietly. But if he proves an ugly customer – Why, for all we know Mary may have been victimized by some cunning thief! (*slips revolver in pocket of his jacket*)

VICTORIA: A thief! The silver spoons!

RONALD: Georgian, with our crest. And a country burglar's capable of melting them! (*makes a movement*)

VICTORIA   (*keeping between him and the door*): But, Ronald, how could Mary have picked up with a thief? She never goes nowheres except to her old Aunt's on the 'ill – hill.

RONALD: Have you noticed anyone – suspicious hanging about the place?

VICTORIA: Only the policeman.

RONALD: There's nothing in that. I asked him once to keep an eye on the house.

VICTORIA   (*shaking her head*): When a policeman starts keeping an eye on a house it generally ends on the Cook.

RONALD: Perhaps you're right.

VICTORIA: But, Ronald – (*smiles*)

RONALD: Well?

VICTORIA: If it is the policeman we needn't worry about the spoons.

RONALD: No, it's far worse. Do you realise that there's *only one policeman in the village*?

VICTORIA: Well?

RONALD: Well, suppose anything happens in Eppington while the policeman's here?

VICTORIA: Nothing ever *does* happen in Eppington.

RONALD: If it's ever going to, it will to-night.

VICTORIA: That's true. My word! A nice lot of talk there'll be!

RONALD   (*making a movement*): Come, we must settle this question.

VICTORIA   (*throwing her arms about him*): Ronald!

RONALD: What?

VICTORIA: If it *is* the policeman promise me you won't shoot!

RONALD: Why not?

VICTORIA: If you shot him, 'e'd arrest you!

RONALD: Never mind about that. Now come along. I want you to knock on Mary's door for me.

VICTORIA   (*surprised*): Me?

RONALD: Make some excuse – say you're ill – say you want her – insist on being admitted.

VICTORIA   (*very shocked*): Oh! Ronald!

RONALD: As soon as she unlocks the door I'll go in and drag the fellow out. While I'm seeing him off the premises I depend on you to say a few firm words to Mary. (*He crosses to fireplace and picks up the poker.*)

VICTORIA   (*standing left; watching him*): What's that for?

RONALD: In case it is the policeman. (*taking lighted lamp from table right in his left hand*) Are you ready?

VICTORIA: No!

RONALD: Eh?

VICTORIA: Ronald, I don't want to go.

RONALD   (*amazed*): Why not?

VICTORIA   (*stubbornly*): I don't want to go.

RONALD: I'll go first.

VICTORIA   (*tossing her head*): Oh, I'm not afraid.

RONALD: Then what is it?

VICTORIA   (*taking occasional chair from left, planting it left centre and sitting resolutely*): I'm not going!

RONALD: Victoria! In the three years we've lived together this is the first time you've ever opposed me.

VICTORIA   (*folding her arms*): There's a beginning to everything.

RONALD   (*centre behind her*): I don't understand this at all.

VICTORIA   (*tossing her head*): Per'aps I have my reasons.

RONALD   (*right side of her*): Reasons? Then tell me what they are?

VICTORIA   (*turning to left away from him*): Per'aps I don't choose to.

(Ronald *looks at her back, goes to table right, puts down lamp, sticks poker under his arm and then returns to the attack*)

RONALD   (*tenderly*): Victoria, don't let us disagree, I've grown so proud of my little woman – her wise head and her clever fingers and her loving, cheerful disposition.

(Victoria, *touched, looks up at him gratefully*)

You've tried so hard to please me; you've improved so splendidly – and now to meet this sudden obstinacy in you – this – this capriciousness –

VICTORIA   (*hard again*): I can't 'elp it, Ronald, I'm not going to Mary's room to-night, not for you nor nobody.

RONALD   (*using poker to emphasise his remarks*): You realise that this blackguard mustn't remain under our roof till morning, don't you?

VICTORIA: Yes.

RONALD: You understand why I need you, why Mary must hear *your* voice at her door and not mine?

VICTORIA   (*shifting in her chair*): Oh, yes.

RONALD   (*losing patience*): And yet you refuse! When I think how my dear mother behaved once in similar circumstances at home – *she* didn't even consult father. She marched straight into cook's room and with her own hands dragged the new gardener out from underneath the bed where he was hiding. I can hear the fellow begging for mercy now.

VICTORIA   (*touched to the quick*): It was all very well for your mother. *She* was married.

RONALD   (*completely surprised*): But as far as Mary knows you and I are as legally married as my mother and father were.

VICTORIA: Ah! I'm not so sure. I've caught Mary watching me sometimes in a very peculiar manner. Only yesterday she threw such a look at my wedding-ring – much as if she knew it wasn't real.

RONALD: Pardon me, your wedding-ring is not only real but 18 carat gold.

VICTORIA: No amount of carats make the ring real without the marriage lines.

RONALD: But not a soul knows the truth in Eppington or anywhere else – except your people and one or two of my Fabian friends. Who on earth could have told Mary?

VICTORIA: Ah! As mother used to say to us girls, 'It's an ill wind that blows nobody any news.'

RONALD   (*patting her on the shoulder*): My dear child, this is pure self consciousness. And even if Mary is aware that no legal tie binds us – which is highly improbable – what has that to do with your reproving her for her own immoral conduct?

VICTORIA: Don't you see?

RONALD: I most certainly do not.

VICTORIA: Well, if I was to say to Mary 'Who's the Man in your room?'
Mary might say to me 'Who's the man in yours?'

RONALD: Victoria! (*He puts the poker down on table right.*) It – it
shocks me to hear you put yourself on a level with this
– this village Messalina. To begin with Mary is guilty of the
meanest fraud. She's deceiving us.

VICTORIA   (*placidly*): Well, we're deceiving Little Eppington.

RONALD   (*blazing out*): Not by my wish! There's only one rule for
me, 'Do nothing you are ashamed of and be ashamed of
nothing you do!' I'm proud of the fact that we are still free,
unfettered human beings. If I haven't proclaimed from the
house-tops of Little Eppington that we are not married, you
know why!

VICTORIA: Yes; we couldn't have kept a cook!

RONALD: Nothing of the kind! Don't be sordid, Victoria. I consented to
appear conventional so that other women should call on you
– so that you shouldn't be always alone in the long hours I'm
at work.

VICTORIA: It is very kind of you, Ronald, and I'm sure I have nothing to
complain of.

RONALD   (*mollified*): Then be a good girl and come with me to Mary's
room.

VICTORIA   (*with deeper obstinacy*): Ronald, I'll do anything in reason
for you; I'll haspirate my h's and take cold baths and breathe
through my nose – but one thing you cannot make me do is
lecture other girls who are no better than they should be.

RONALD   (*walking up and down; profoundly disturbed*): This is too
horrible! Do you mean to say that you feel yourself in the
wrong – that you're secretly ashamed of your own courage?
After all the trouble I've taken to explain the pitiful thraldom
of being married?

VICTORIA: It's no pitifuler then being in love.

RONALD: What! But love is natural! Free as air! God-given! Marriage is
artificial – manufactured – it's love packed in tins for 'home
consumption!'

VICTORIA: Yes, lovey, I'm sure it must be.

RONALD: Heaven knows I'm thinking more of you than of myself.
How would you like to be tied to me for life if I committed a
crime or went mad?

VICTORIA: You're not mad. Whatever my sister says.

RONALD: As for the moral aspect, remember this, Victoria: As long
as you're true to me you're just as worthy of respect as if a

bishop had blessed us. You're my wife in the eyes of God.

VICTORIA (*simply*): Yes, dear, but not in the eyes of mother.

RONALD (*straightens up; moves back a few steps; in a strange voice*): Come here to me. (*Holds out his arms. She rises obediently and goes into them. Bending his head down to her; anxiously.*) Tell me something; three years ago did I talk you down? Was I unfair? Did I take advantage of your inexperience?

VICTORIA: What an idea! No young lady could serve refreshments in the British Museum and not have her eyes opened, believe me! What with the language of the Egyptologers, *and* the statues, *and* the Art Students, male and female – But there, I mustn't run the place down; I might never have met you without our two and sixpenny luncheon.

RONALD (*his conscience twinging badly*): I never promised you marriage, I never misled you as to my views, did I?

VICTORIA (*touching his face*): Lovey, Don't take it so! You never deceived your Vicky, never! You made quite free with your ideas. All you ever promised me was a servant of my own and that I have had and often wished I hadn't with the worry and bother they are.

RONALD (*catching her hand; insistent*): Victoria, you still love me, don't you?

VICTORIA: Of course I do.

RONALD: As much as when you used to let me have three helpings of the sweet?

VICTORIA: More.

RONALD: Then what is your regret?

VICTORIA: Why nothing, lovey, nothing. (*leaving him; gently*) I'm sure you've been as good a husband as a girl could wish for, in everything but license.

RONALD: I see it all. You're suffering from a conviction of sin! And I've given it to you. How grotesque! Oh, Victoria, why did you pretend to agree with me? Why did you let me think I'd converted you?

VICTORIA (*humbly*): I was afraid if you knew how old-fashioned and respectable I was you wouldn't love me.

RONALD (*bitterly*): Here I've dedicated my life to breaking down barriers and all I succeed in breaking is the heart of the woman I love.

VICTORIA (*going swiftly to him; very repentant*): Oh, no, no, darling, no! I'm sure there's not a girl happier than me anywhere's. It's only sometimes I get a little fretted when I think what mother and my married sister are calling me to each other.

RONALD   (*very serious*): If it hadn't been for the Man in Mary's room I might never have found out. I've not given you my standards, I've simply made you false to your own. Victoria, we must get married.

VICTORIA   (*gasping*): But your ideas?

RONALD: They're not as important as your feelings.

VICTORIA: But your friends? Won't they be shocked if you get married? The ones that are so intellectual? Those Fabians?

RONALD: Oh, they're all married too.

VICTORIA: Then you mean it?

RONALD: Mean it? We'll go up to London to-morrow and be quietly married at a registrar's.

VICTORIA   (*still incredulous*): It's not a joke?

RONALD: A joke? Damn it all we'll ask your mother to the wedding!

VICTORIA: And my married sister?

RONALD: *And* your married sister!

VICTORIA   (*breaking down and crying*): Oh, Ronald, you do spoil me! I never was so happy.

RONALD: Then stop crying, there's a good girl.

VICTORIA   (*putting her arms around his neck*): My darling! Just think! You and I together for ever and ever! (*They embrace tenderly. Suddenly; disengaging herself; in a business-like manner.*) And now I must go to Mary's room.

RONALD   (*amazed*): What? But you said you wouldn't.

VICTORIA   (*lightly*): Did I?

RONALD: Why, you positively refused to knock on her door!

VICTORIA   (*with complete finality*): Yes, but that was before I knew we were going to be married. (*As he still looks at her; surprised at his density.*) Now I have my position to consider. (*picking up lighted lamp from table right*) I'll carry the lamp, lovey, you take the poker. I shall give that girl a month's notice and a piece of my mind.

RONALD   (*arming himself with the poker again*): Oh, very well, if you insist.

VICTORIA: Better let me go first with the light. Are you ready?

(*As the solemn procession of Victoria with the lamp and Ronald with the poker reaches left centre there is a knock on the door. They step back and look at each other in surprise. Knock repeated*)

VICTORIA   (*loudly*): What is it?

MARY   (*outside*): Only me, 'm. Can I speak with you, please, 'm?

(Victoria *hastily replaces lamp on table right* Ronald *conceals poker behind his back*)

VICTORIA   (*with an effort to make her voice sound natural*): Come in!

(*Enter left centre* Mary, *an apple-cheeked, hobbledehoy country girl*)[1]

MARY   (*coming in*): Beggin' your pardon, 'm, but (*seeing* Ronald, *slightly awed*)– oh! excuse me, sir. (*to* Victoria, *very respectfully*) Beggin' your pardon, 'm but I was wishful to ask, if it's not asking too much, for Hellaman.

---

[1]   The script from this point to the end of the play was submitted, late, to the Lord Chamberlain as a replacement to the original ending of the play. The original script ends thus:

MARY   (*coming in*): Beggin' your pardon, 'm, but (*slightly awed by* Ronald) – oh! Excuse me, sir. (*to* Victoria; *very respectfully*) I was wishful to tell you, 'm, as my aunt, Mrs. Porter's 'ere and she's been took bad if you don't mind, please.

VICTORIA   (*with a side glance at* Ronald): Your Aunt, the fat one, who goes out by the day?

MARY: Yes 'm.

VICTORIA: What's she been took with?

MARY: 'Er ankle, please. It's swollen something sudden. Livin' alone on the 'ill she gets lonely like so thought she'd look in for a chat this evening but passin' the Cow and Feather turned 'er foot on a stone in the dark and –

RONALD   (*sympathetically*): Where is the poor woman at present, Mary?

MARY   (*surprised at his interest*): In my room, sir, thank you, sir. (Ronald *surreptitiously gets rid of the poker.*)

VICTORIA: I hope you've got her foot up?

MARY   (*encouraged by their attention*): Yes 'm, please, she's lying on my bed. Though, 'owever I get 'er up I couldn't go for to say. What with 'er bein' wide and the wind blowin' out my candle and me tellin' 'er to keep quiet so's not to disturb the Master in 'is study, I couldn't 'elp but laurf (*pulling herself up*) – I 'ope we didnt make too much noise, sir?

RONALD   (*genially*): Not at all, Mary, not at all.

VICTORIA: But will your aunt be able to get home to-night?

MARY: No, thank you, 'm, and I was to ask as 'ow if you'd no objection to 'er stayin' on all night –

RONALD   (*cordially*): Tell your Aunt we shall be delighted.

MARY   (*confused*): Oh, thank you, sir. (*going to door*) Is there nothing more I can do for you, 'm?

VICTORIA   (*with a note of suppressed triumph in her voice*): Nothing more you can do for me, Mary. Good-night.

MARY: Good-night, 'm. Good night, sir.

RONALD: Good-night, Mary, good-night. (*Exit* Mary *door left centre* Ronald *and* Victoria *look at each other.*)

RONALD: I think I ought to apologise to Mary.

VICTORIA: I think I ought to raise her wages.

RONALD: What man? We haven't got a man in *this* room.

MARY   (*surprised*): No, sir?

VICTORIA: She means the Hembrocation.

RONALD: Oh! What do you want Elliman's for, Mary?

MARY: Please, sir, for a sprain.

VICTORIA: You've never been and hurt yourself, Mary?

MARY: Oh no, 'm, it's not for me; *I'm* quite steady on my feet.
             (*tearfully*) But it does upset me to see others suffer and a
             twisted ankle ...

RONALD: Where is this sufferer – at present – Mary?

MARY: In my bed, sir. I hope you don't mind?

RONALD: Mind? Not at all. We shall be delighted to start a hospital for
             your friends.

MARY   (*apologetically*): I'd never ask to put a friend in my bed, sir,
             but I did think I might put a cousin.

VICTORIA   (*murmuring*): Well! Whatever girls are coming to nowadays ...

RONALD: A cousin, you say? You're sure it's a cousin?

MARY: A very close cousin, sir –

RONALD: So I should judge.

MARY: Only once removed

RONALD   (*weighing the poker in his hand*): At present once – presently
             twice.

MARY: Properly speakin', sir, she's my mother's cousin, but being
             elderly I always call her my Aunt.

RONALD AND VICTORIA (*together*):   Your Aunt! It's your Aunt? (Ronald
             surreptitiously gets rid of poker.)

VICTORIA: The fat one who goes out by the day?

MARY: Yes, 'm. Living alone on the hill she gets lonely-like so
             thought she'd look in for a chat this evening but turned her
             foot accidental-like passin' the Cow and Feathers and now
             it's swollen something sudden.

VICTORIA   (*who has gone to the dressing table*): Here's the
             hembrocation, Mary.

MARY: Oh, thank you, 'm.

RONALD: And here's an old handkerchief to bandage her foot. You
             must take great care of your Aunt, Mary.

MARY   (*overwhelmed by their attentions*): Oh, thank you, sir. I
             hope we didn't disturb you in your study, sir. But what with
             'er bein' wide and the wind blowin' out my candles and my
             havin' to push her upstairs, I couldn't 'elp but larf –

RONALD: Yes, I think I heard you laugh. But don't apologise, Mary, I
             like a laugh – even when it's against me.

THE END

Private Room Number 6

by

André de Lorde and Pierre Chaine

Preface

The Glove by José Levy, adapted from André de Lorde and Pierre Chaine's *Au Rat mort, cabinet 6* (1907), was approved for licence on 8 October 1920 and premièred on 15 December 1920 as part of the second series of London's Grand Guignol. However, by the time the play was staged it was re-titled *Private Room Number 6* and Pierre Chaine's credit was cut. The play is a melodramatic treatment of a political theme and is set in a Czarist political context — a context which was contemporary in 1907 but had become historical by the time of the London production. The play portrays a brutal and drunken Russian general with a supposed courtesan, Lea. In fact,

Figure 14. Aubrey Hammond: Poster for *Private Room Number 6*, 1920

Lea is the sister of a political prisoner whom the general tortured to death, and has come to exact her revenge. The play is a taut and claustrophobic melodrama, and yet, despite clearly emerging from a melodramatic, even operatic, tradition (one thinks of Tosca's murder of Scarpia in Verdi's 1900 *Tosca*), the scenario of the play can be seen as a precursor to the similarly lethal and gendered stand-offs in plays such as Howard Barker's *Judith* (1990) and Ariel Dorfman's *Death and the Maiden* (1991) or films such as *Hard Candy* (David Slade, 2005).

It is a violent play with an onstage murder, but this is a strangulation deemed acceptable by the censor. Writing the Lord Chamberlain's Office report, G.S. Street declared that *Private Room Number 6* 'is nothing worse than a bit of violent, old-fashioned melodrama', adding that although it is 'a brutal sort of Play, (it is) not of a kind to be banned. The brutality might be overdone, but I think these players, who are very good, will keep within bounds.' Nevertheless, the blue pencil was used in a number of places. The censor took exception to two particularly violent moments in the play. One incident is when the General sexually assaults Lea:

> LEA   (*struggles and her dress is torn*) Stop it, stop it, you're hurting me.
> GENERAL: Ah! Your skin drives me mad … it's so soft and velvety as a peach … I should love to bite it.
> LEA: Ah! You brute! You filthy brute!

The other violent moment deemed too strong by the censor was Lea's murder of the General:

> LEA   (… Lea *puts her foot on back of armchair to give her more strength – A long struggle – during the last convulsions of* General*'s body, she shouts and laughs to deafen his groans*): Don't struggle, my darling! Don't struggle so much! You'll soon be all right!

Although the murder by strangulation was still permitted it was obliged to be 'toned down'. The excision of these violent moments is perhaps not surprising: more interesting is how the blue pencil extended to *descriptions* of violence:

> When they brought him to me I happened to be smoking a very excellent Havannah and as I pressed my questions on him I pressed the burning end of my cigar on his hand and face. (*He makes a gesture as if doing it, laughing brutally.*) He was securely bound of course … I didn't have long to wait.

Even in its slightly bowdlerised version, the play enjoyed particular success with its audience and close critical attention from the press. In particular, great delight was taken in Sybil Thorndike's performance as Lea. The *Observer* claimed that 'Miss Thorndike holds our attention absolutely. It is impossible to draw a deep breath until the tyrant has been successfully strangled by her long white gloves' (19 December 1920), and the *Stage* concurred with a review which gives a fascinating insight into Thorndike's evidently melodramatic performance practice:

> Brilliant emotional work was done in the character of the revenge-taking sister by Miss Sybil Thorndike, with realistic assumption of hysterical laughter before the deed and of enforced whimpering after its performance ... (23 December 1920)

A number of un-sourced cuttings in the Theatre Museum's Archives provide further examples of the play's success, including ones which may dismiss the play as 'very crude melodrama on familiar lines' but praise Thorndike's 'fine display of passionate hate and hysteria', while another playfully claims that all the actors 'play their parts in a purple style that causes casualties among the audience'. Another unsourced review comments:

> The story is of a modern Judith – a Nihilist girl of the time before the war. [...] The play itself is, of course, simply 'thrill', but the perfect coldness and nervous intensity of Miss Thorndike, as the girl – with her curious little squeals and prayers to her brother as she twists the handkerchief round the Grand Duke's neck – gives the whole thing an almost heroic distinction and poignancy.

A most interesting footnote to this play is that a revised *Private Room No. 6* was licensed for production on 26 June 1945 at the Granville Theatre, Walham Green in an updated version suitable for the recent context of the Second World War (which makes the play even more clearly a precursor to Ariel Dorfman's *Death and the Maiden*). The play remains the same, except that a number of very interesting changes are added as marginalia and pencil additions. For example, General Gregorff becomes a stereotypical German Nazi, General 'von Keller', who drinks 'kummel' rather than brandy and expresses his devotion to the 'Fuehrer'. Indeed, Lea describes how she has seen a picture of Von Keller 'stuck up between the Fuehrer and Goebbels'. Later von Keller threatens Lea by saying, 'I'll have you sent to Dachau!' The irony of the 1920s dialogue (such as when the General sarcastically calls Lea 'my fine lady') is replaced by 1940s robustness ('you bitch!'). Similarly, the previously banned 'foot on back of armchair to give her more strength' stage description is permitted in 1945. The single biggest addition to the revised version of the play is the following exchange:

> LEA [...]: Come and look at the Parade. (General *rises and goes to her.*)
>
> GENERAL: Isn't it wonderful to think that we will soon be marching like this through London. (Lea *opens window and noise of Parade is heard outside.*)
>
> LEA: Yes, but in the meantime you're enjoying the French wines!
>
> GENERAL: You see those two men there on the pavement?
>
> LEA: Yes.
>
> GENERAL: They are my bodyguard. Nothing else to do but to follow me wherever I go. You see there were so many attempts on my life when I was gauleiter of Moravia, that I've had to be guarded ever since. And damn efficient our Gestapo!

The play can be seen as drawing on and reflecting the anxieties and atrocities of recent history, whether it is de Lorde portraying the violent abuses of Czarist Russia or, in the revised version, of the Third Reich. Arguably, although the more recent analysis of state torture in *Death and the Maiden* or paedophilia in *Hard Candy* may be more postmodern in its moral complexities, both works share the archetypal revenge situation and gendered confrontations of de Lorde's Grand Guignol play.

Private Room Number 6

A Drama in One Act
Adapted from the French of André de Lorde and Pierre Chaine
by
José G. Levy

First Performed: 15 December 1920

General Gregorff
Count Lutzi
Victor, Head Waiter
Under Waiter
Lea
Alice
Two Detectives

Scene: *A private room at the 'Rat Mort', the celebrated night restaurant in Paris. Window right, door left, table centre.*

(*At the rise of curtain, the Under* Waiter *is discovered arranging the table. Through the open window sounds of a fete progressing are heard. Enter* Victor)

VICTOR: Is everything ready?
WAITER: Very nearly, sir.
VICTOR: Hurry up ... Hurry up ...
WAITER   (*arranging flowers*): I've nearly finished. I had to look after Number 4. They've gone.
VICTOR   (*seeing flowers on table*): Didn't I tell you there were to be no flowers? His Excellency doesn't like them ... They give him a headache.
WAITER: This is the first that I've heard of it.
VICTOR: How many times do I have to give my orders ... ? Take them away ... yes ... all of them.

(*The* Waiter *removes flowers; exits with them; and returns immediately*)

VICTOR   (*who meanwhile looks round the room and sees that everything is in order*): You'd better shut that window with that noise going on outside.

WAITER   (*shutting window*): Not much good to our business this fete.

VICTOR: You're right. It's the wrong class of people. It keeps the decent ones away.

WAITER   (*still looking after the table arrangements*): I say, what's he like, this chap you all call your excellency?

VICTOR   (*helping him at the table*): He's General Gregorff the famous Russian General.

WAITER: What, the one there's been such a lot about in the newspapers lately?

VICTOR: Yes, about the Moscow affair ... That's the man.

WAITER: He's the brute who had the women and children shot in the streets.

VICTOR   (*very dignified*): Sssh ... You mustn't talk like that here. Don't forget he's a customer.

WAITER: Does he come here often?

VICTOR: Nearly every night.

WAITER   (*laughing*): Likes the ladies, eh?

VICTOR: I should say so.

WAITER: Plenty of money?

VICTOR   (*going along to sideboard and taking one of the small ice buckets and placing it on the table*): Rather ... He's spent a bit here in his time ... And tips (*smacking his lips*) My word ... Only everything must be just so-so. If it isn't, he just grumbles and growls like a bear with a sore head.

WAITER: No ...

VICTOR   (*tapping him on the shoulder*): I know a thing or two.

WAITER: Bit of a dog, eh?

VICTOR: A perfect devil sometimes.

WAITER: I pity his poor servants.

VICTOR: Oh it's bad enough with some of the women he brings up here. You ought to see him when he's had a drop too much. We've had some scenes here I can tell you.

(*Electric bell is heard off*) (Victor *exits quickly and returns immediately*)

VICTOR   (*continuing*): Sssh ... Here he is. Be careful. (*He stands near the door, his back to the public in a respectful and obsequious attitude. The waiter stands immobile at the back of armchair. Enter General.*)

GENERAL: Good evening Victor. (*He pauses in front of* Victor *and comes to the middle of the stage.*)

VICTOR   (*bowing low*): Your Excellency.

GENERAL: Anyone arrived yet?

VICTOR: No one your Excellency. Your Excellency is the first.

GENERAL   (*laughing*): I'm never late when there's any fun to be had.

VICTOR   (*to* Waiter): Emile ... Take his Excellency's coat and hat.
(Waiter *assists the* General *to take his hat and coat off.*)

GENERAL: I'm expecting someone.

VICTOR   (*with respectful smile*): Mademoiselle Suzanne?

GENERAL: Suzanne? Oh no ... She's a back number ... No, I've found something fresh ... young ... Sweet and appetising. (*brutally to* Waiter *who is still helping him with his coat*) Look out you fool. Do you want to break my arm? (*a pause*) What time is it? (*The waiter after having taken the* General's *coat, folds it on his arm, returns to behind the armchair and awaits orders.*)

VICTOR   (*looking at his watch*): A quarter past twelve, your Excellency.

GENERAL: She won't be long now. Get me a drink Victor.

VICTOR: Kummel, your Excellency?

GENERAL: Yes. (Victor *makes signs to the waiter, who exits carrying the* General's *overcoat*)

GENERAL: You shall keep me company.

VICTOR   (*smiling very obsequiously*): Thank you your Excellency.

GENERAL   (*sitting in armchair*): Yes Victor. I've found a pearl ... A delightful little creature. (Waiter *enters and gives* Victor *a tray on which are a bottle of Kummel and a large glass and exits.*) What a figure ... Lissom as a gazelle ... And hair ... A rope of gold which seems to entwine itself around one's heart.

VICTOR: And your pockets too, your Excellency.

GENERAL   (*laughing*): Ah ha ... What do I care? ... As long as I can kiss that pretty little mouth of hers and see the sparkle of those wonderful eyes ... I tell you she's a find, Victor ... a veritable find ... (*with a bestial expression*) And I'm a bit of a judge you know.

VICTOR: Your Excellency has always the very best of taste.

GENERAL: Why not?

VICTOR   (*bottle in hand*): Shall I serve your Excellency?

GENERAL   (*looking at what* Victor *is pouring out*): That's right ... In the big one ... You know how I like it. What I like about her is, there's something original – different from all the others ... I think she'll suit me down to the ground.

(Victor *at a sign from the* General *pours out another glass*)

VICTOR: She'll take jolly good care ... That she does.

GENERAL: I'm sick of the usual type of women one finds about here.
          The affectation they put on ... (*He drinks*) In my own
          country I have only to express a desire for any lady I might
          meet, and it is at once satisfied. My slightest wish in that
          direction becomes an absolute command.

VICTOR: And how did your Excellency come across this lucky person?

GENERAL: In the Rue de la Paix ...

VICTOR   (*jokingly*): That's where all the pearls and jewels come from.

GENERAL: I'd seen her two or three times before ... I followed her
          up one night and spoke to her. (*He rises, gives* Victor *his
          hat which he had kept on his head.* Victor *puts it on the
          sideboard.*)

VICTOR: Was she accommodating?

GENERAL: She will be. (*A pause. He looks at his watch.*) Ha ha I don't
          think I'm going to be bored tonight, my little Lea.

VICTOR: Lea?

GENERAL: That's the child's name. (*He takes glass.*) Go on; I'll drink to
          her health.

VICTOR   (*pouring out*): If you drink too much to her health your
          Excellency, I'm afraid you'll upset your own.

GENERAL   (*laughing*): You think so? (*He drinks.*)

VICTOR: Your Excellency doesn't remember the state you were in last
          Tuesday.

GENERAL: No ... (*laughing*) Was I drunk?

VICTOR   (*respectfully*): I don't think his Excellency quite knew what
          he was doing. The wine must have upset him ... Luckily
          his Excellency loses the use of his legs when he has drunk a
          little too much, otherwise I should not have the honour of
          speaking to him now.

GENERAL: Why? ... What did I do?

VICTOR: Your Excellency wanted to strangle me ... You didn't seem
          to recognise me ... You called me Yvan, and treated me like
          a dog. (General *gives him empty glass, which he places on
          sideboard.*)

GENERAL: Where the devil do my brains go when I'm drunk? (*puts his
          hand in his pocket*) Ah ... I wanted to strangle you did I?
          (*Gives him a louis.*) Here you are my friend.

VICTOR   (*after having pocketed coin, very obsequious*): Oh your
          Excellency, I didn't mean it for that ...

GENERAL: I know ... I know ... (*Walking towards left*) Why the deuce
          doesn't Lea turn up?

VICTOR: Did your Excellency make an appointment with her here?

GENERAL: Yes ... (*At this moment bell is heard off, and at same time a*

	knock is heard on door)
VICTOR:	Excuse me. (*He opens door; waiter enters on the threshold, and speaks to him in an undertone.*)
GENERAL	(*walking up and down, smoking*): If she doesn't turn up there'll be the devil to pay ... She'll have to learn she can't make a fool of me. (*Voices are heard off saying 'Is he here? I bet he was giving us up. This way ladies; room No. 6'.*)
VICTOR	(*back to public, holds door open, turning his head to speak to General*): Here are the friends you have been expecting, your Excellency.
GENERAL	(*butting cigar on ashtray*): Ah ... At last ... It's about time. (*Lea enters first and goes over to the General. She is dressed in furs, and carries a fur muff. She wears a very décolleté costume under same.*)
LEA:	Good evening.
GENERAL	(*kissing her hand lovingly*): Good evening. (*Alice enters followed by the Count.*)
GENERAL:	Ah here we are ... Where in the world have you been to?
COUNT	(*gayly*): You are always the first, General
ALICE	(*going up to General, whilst Lea places her muff on the sideboard*): Have you been here long? Have we kept you waiting?
GENERAL	(*kissing her hand also*): A little ... But Victor and some Kummel have kept me entertained.
ALICE:	That's right.
COUNT	(*shaking hands with General*): We've just been to see the latest dancer.
ALICE:	At Olympia.
LEA:	She's just splendid.
VICTOR:	Your coat, Madam? (*Waiter comes behind Lea and takes coat and puts it over chair.*)
GENERAL	(*looking at Lea*): You look perfectly charming ... What a lovely frock.
ALICE:	It'll cost you fifty louis, old boy.
COUNT	(*laughing*): Alice has introduced her to her dress-maker.
GENERAL	(*designating the two women*): They've only known each other for the last week, and now they are inseparable.
COUNT	(*laughing*): They make a pretty pair; but damned expensive.
ALICE	(*putting her arm round Lea's waist*): Don't listen to them, my dear. They're talking a lot of rot. You are young yet ... You don't know men as I do. You haven't had as much experience. I'll teach you.
COUNT:	Rather ... She'll teach you right enough. There's not much she doesn't know. (*He kisses Alice on the neck. Lea crosses*

to the General *who is sitting in armchair. He takes her hands and looks at her lovingly.*)

ALICE   (*to the* Count *in an undertone*): She's no fool, I can tell you.

VICTOR   (*coming to* Alice *and* Count): Your coats, M'sieur, and Madame?

COUNT: No, no, we are not staying.

(General *rises.* Lea *is standing at the corner of table*)

GENERAL: You are not staying?

ALICE: No ... We've promised to have supper with some friends. We're in the next private room to this, I think.

LEA   (*with an almost imperceptible movement*): What? Here?

COUNT: Yes this is No. 6. I believe we shall be in No. 4.

ALICE   (*gayly*): Don't worry ... The walls are thick. We shan't hear you.

GENERAL   (*with bestial laugh*): Oh, I don't care if you do.

COUNT: We'll leave you then. Have a good time both of you.

ALICE   (*disengaging herself from the* Count *and turning towards the* General): If you can't be good be careful ... And don't drink too much. I shall expect to see you quite sober in a couple of hours from now.

COUNT: Ah, yes ... We don't want a repetition of last Tuesday's business.

ALICE: It upset me.

GENERAL: Did I frighten you?

ALICE: Good heavens ... I was scared to death.

COUNT: He wanted to strangle poor Victor. (*At these words* Victor *bows slightly, smiling.*)

ALICE: You swore he wanted to kill you.

GENERAL   (*smiling*): Yes ... So it seems

COUNT: Your legs were all to pieces. You couldn't stand up straight. We had to carry you downstairs into your car.

GENERAL: Ah, this evening I'll be good. Lea is going to look after me. Aren't you, Lea?

LEA: Certainly, if you'll obey me.

GENERAL   (*laughing*): As if you were the Czar.

COUNT   (*going towards door*): Au revoir then. Will see you later. (Alice *before leaving goes to* Lea *and gives her a little tap on cheek – she then exits followed by* Count *and* Waiter.)

GENERAL: Bye bye for the present. We'll all go home together if you like. There's plenty of room in my car.

COUNT   (*off*): Right Ho! (Waiter *closes door.* Lea *goes to sideboard and slowly pulls off gloves which are very long ones and puts them inside muff.* General *goes to table and looks at menu.* Waiter *is standing near door.*)

GENERAL   (*to* Lea): What do you feel like eh?

LEA: Order what you like. I'm not hungry.

GENERAL   (*crossing to* Lea): Nor am I – except for you. (*a pause*) (*He suddenly bends down and gives her a long kiss on the neck. Turning to* Victor.) All right, Victor, we'll leave it to you. Give us just what you like only don't forget the liqueurs.

VICTOR: No, your Excellency. (General *sits on settee near table and looks at champagne on same.*)

GENERAL: I hope this is not the filthy muck you gave us to drink the last time we were here.

VICTOR: No, your Excellency, I specially ordered –

GENERAL   (*brutally interrupting*): Alright! Hurry up, get on with it.

VICTOR: At once, your Excellency. (*Exits.* General *takes cigarette out of case.*)

GENERAL: Lea! (*She is before glass arranging herself.*)

LEA: Yes, darling?

GENERAL: What are you doing?

LEA: Tidying myself. Putting a little colour in my cheeks. (*seeing cigarette case* General *still has in his hand*) Give me a cigarette. (*He opens case –* Lea *takes cigarette and goes to find a match stand on sideboard.*) It's nice and comfy here.

GENERAL: Not bad! Come over and give me a kiss.

LEA: That's all you think of. (*She pauses in front of table.*)

GENERAL: You look ravishing tonight –

LEA: I can never be beautiful enough for you, darling. (*She comes nearer to the table.*)

GENERAL   (*gazing into her eyes*): Are you going to be good to me tonight little one?

LEA   (*smiling*): I'm always good to you.

GENERAL   (*taking her hands*): You understand what I mean. (*He makes her sit down on his knees.*) You'll be a good little girl? You'll do everything I want?

LEA: Like a lamb.

(*Knock at the door – enter* Victor *and* Waiter – *The latter brings in supper all prepared on tray and places it on table.* Victor *uncorks champagne and pours it into glasses during following confab. Hearing knock* Lea *has risen, goes to window and looks out*)

LEA: Come and look at the Carnival. (General *rises and goes to her.*)

GENERAL: They're still at it! It's wonderful what energy some people have. (Lea *opens window and noise of fete outside is heard.*)

LEA: Good Heavens! What a crowd there is!

GENERAL (*leaning arms on window and looking out of window*): Ah, that's funny!

LEA: What?

GENERAL (*pointing with his hand*): You see those two men there on the pavement?

LEA (*looking*): Yes!

GENERAL (*gaily*): They're two detectives which the Foreign Office have placed at my disposal.

LEA (*laughing*): That's ripping! It's quite safe to go out with you, then, you're well looked after. (*She closes window.*) Do they follow you about everywhere?

GENERAL: Everywhere. I manage to give them the slip sometimes but they soon track me down again. They're perfect bloodhounds.

LEA: They could tell a few tales about you if they wanted, I bet.

GENERAL (*without leaving window – raising curtain of same*): Ah they little think that I can see them now. (*looking more attentively*) They're not the same men. They must have changed.

LEA (*drawing him to the table*): They relieve each other, I expect. You must lead them a fine dance too, poor devils. Come on, come on and have supper.

VICTOR (*who has prepared the supper and poured out the champagne*): Everything is quite prepared, your Excellency. (Waiter *exits.*)

LEA (*taking her glass*): I'm going to have a drink – I'm simply dying of thirst.

GENERAL (*raising his glass to* Lea): Here's to the prettiest lady in France.

LEA: That's awfully sweet of you. (*They drink.*) I say you know, when I saw your photo first stuck up between the Pope and the President I never dreamt that one day I should be sitting here with you drinking champagne. Oh no!

GENERAL: Are you glad?

LEA (*bending towards him*): Of course I am, you old darling – I say I sported five francs on one of those photographs.

GENERAL (*laughing*): Ha! Ha!

LEA: You'll write something on it for me, won't you?

GENERAL: Anything you like, my dear.

LEA (*looking around*): I wonder if there is a pen and ink here?

GENERAL (*motioning towards sideboard*): Yes, there's some there. (Lea *is about to rise but he holds her back.*) There's plenty of time – there's no hurry. (Lea *sits down again. Caressing her.*)

Look here, Lea, if you'll be a good little girl I'll make it my business to look after you.

LEA: Will you? Will you get me on the stage? I feel sure I could act drama especially ... I am simply dying to go on the stage.

GENERAL *(laughing)*: Yes, yes, of course I will, and you shall be a great actress one of these days.

LEA: And you will take me with you to Russia?

GENERAL: Whatever for? I'm in Paris

LEA *(whilst eating)*: Don't you ever go and see the old folks at home?

GENERAL: As little as possible

LEA: Do they bore you, then?

GENERAL: Yes ... and when I'm over there, there's always the danger of my never getting back.

LEA: Why? Are they so fond of you ... won't they let you go?

GENERAL: Ha, ha! On the contrary ... There are certain persons over there who are only waiting for the opportunity to blow my brains out.

LEA: They don't like you over there, then?

GENERAL *(eating)*: Oh! They're a lot of anarchists, dogs and revolutionists ... What swine!

LEA: What did you do to them then? You don't look a hard hearted monster, you know.

GENERAL: I'm not! Only I will have my own way and won't be interfered with. While I was Governor of Moscow, they got up a plot against me, under the pretext that I had violated their rights – the dogs.

LEA *(laughing)*: I don't suppose that's all you violated, eh?

GENERAL *(grunts)*: Ha, ha! They think more of their rights than they do of their women kind – they condemned me to death.

LEA *(gaily)*: And you're still alive to tell the tale. *(She pours out more champagne.)*

GENERAL *(with a bestial smile)*: And ready to love a pretty woman – here's to you, little one. *(He drinks.)*

LEA *(fingering her glass without drinking out of it)*: Chin! Chin!

GENERAL: But you're not drinking!

LEA: Yes, yes, I am ... What happened then when they condemned you to death?

GENERAL: Luckily I was able to get hold of the ringleader ... Only the worst part of it was I had no proofs against him and I couldn't get him to speak.

LEA: What did you do?

GENERAL *(snorts – a pause as if he recollects the affair)*: When they brought him to me I happened to be smoking a very excellent

Havannah and as I pressed my questions on him I pressed the
burning end of my cigar on his hands and face. (*He makes
gestures as if doing it, laughing brutally.*) He was securely
bound of course ... I didn't have long to wait.

LEA   (*with a shudder*): What happened?

GENERAL   (*laughing*): What do you expect? How he bellowed! I got the
names of all his accomplices though, but there was such a lot
I was forced to light another cigar.

LEA: Well ... You have got some funny ideas! I wonder where you
get them from? I wonder if you would ever treat me like that?

GENERAL   (*giving her a kiss*): You delicious little person ... (*A knock
on the door. Enter* Victor *and the* Waiter. Victor *places a
fresh bottle of champagne, cigars and cigarettes on the table,
whilst* Waiter *clears away. They exit rapidly.*)

GENERAL   (*as soon as they have gone*): Ah! If everyone had shown the
same energy as myself and followed my example these dogs
would have been muzzled long ago.

LEA: You let them see that you are the master.

GENERAL: Bah! I'd shoot 'em all down like a lot of cattle.

LEA: Oh! What a bloodthirsty person!

GENERAL: Ah! Now I've made you feel frightened of me ... Yes, I have,
my little Lea.

LEA   (*looking at him in admiration*): No ... you haven't
really ... it's extraordinary ... I can't explain to you, but
you're just the type of man I love.

GENERAL   (*getting nearer to her*): You mean that?

LEA: It's a mad thing to say but you fascinated me the moment I
saw your photograph.

GENERAL: And you'd be really sorry for me if ever I should be
assassinated?

LEA: Oh, I say, stop that ... Do you want to make me feel
miserable? Come on, drink up. (*pours him out more
champagne*) You're getting morbid.

GENERAL: Ah you think I'm joking, but I tell you I'm always in danger
of being knocked down and murdered in cold blood. I
generally get the better of them though ... There was Ivan
Michaelwitz for instance –

LEA   (*helping herself to fruit*): Another one who wanted to do you
in?

GENERAL: There was quite a lot about it in the papers.

LEA   (*with indifference*): I didn't see it.

GENERAL: He was sent to Siberia but he died under the knout before he
got there.

LEA: Special instructions from you I suppose.

GENERAL   (*laughing*): Naturally.

LEA: And yet you still think of him?

GENERAL: Often ... When he was leaving on the convict ship, he turned around towards me and threatened me with his fist and shrieked out 'Béréquise'!

LEA: What does that mean?

GENERAL: It means ... (*as if trying to find the exact words*) It means – it's difficult to translate it properly – 'may a curse fall upon you' is about as near as you can get.

LEA: Oh, I shouldn't let that worry you ... don't think about it. Have another glass of wine – it will buck you up. (*pours him out more wine*)

GENERAL: Ah! Yes, women and wine ... That's what makes life worth living. To feel a soft fresh young thing like you by my side, to crush her in my arms. (*He catches hold of her and throws her back on the divan and kisses her brutally.*)

LEA   (*struggles and her dress is torn*): Stop it, stop it, you're hurting me.

GENERAL: Ah! Your skin drives me mad ... It's so soft and velvety as a peach ... I should love to bite it.

LEA: Ah! You brute! You filthy brute!

GENERAL   (*furious and ugly*): What d'ye mean ... You mustn't call me names like that.

LEA   (*lowering her head*): It's quite true though ... (*She half falls and half sits on the divan*)

GENERAL: Good gracious! There's a fuss to make about nothing ... I was just showing you how much I loved you.

LEA: You've hurt me.

GENERAL   (*bending over her*): All the better ... I like to see you like this ... all pale and trembling. You look even more beautiful.

LEA   (*pushing him back with disgust*): No, let me be, I don't want you ...

GENERAL   (*taking hold of her brutally*): You don't want me? You don't want me–? I pay you ... I suppose I can do with you what I like? I won't be made a fool of ... D'yer hear? (*very hard*) Now then, are you going to be a good little girl or not?

LEA   (*submitting after a pause*): Yes.

GENERAL   (*leering*): Ah! That's better ... I don't like little girls who sulk.

LEA   (*making an effort*): Oh, I'm alright now.

GENERAL   (*sitting her on his knee*): That's right, ... Come and sit on my knee.

LEA: You do get in a bad temper when you've had a drop to drink, you know.

GENERAL   (*very enamoured*): I? Not at all ... you don't know what
                 you're talking about ... why, the more I drink the more
                 amorous I become.

LEA: Then I should like to see you very drunk.

GENERAL: Well, look at me now, sweetheart.

LEA: Oh, but much worse than that. (*She hands him her glass.*)

GENERAL: But I promised I would be good tonight.

LEA   (*forcing him to drink*): I suppose you're allowed to do what
                 you like.

GENERAL: Of course I am. (*He drinks.*) Oh, my head's strong
                 enough ... It's my legs which play me up. What about
                 you ... you're not drinking. Go on, you must take something.

LEA: No I'm not used to it – Makes me ill ... I wonder how much
                 champagne it would take to make you absolutely blind?

GENERAL   (*laughing*): More than you'd care to pay for. But I like
                 liqueurs best – there's more fire in them.

LEA: Especially Kummel – eh?

GENERAL   (*laughing*): Ah yes! Kummel!

LEA: Is it true that the other day you drink a big glassful of it
                 – one like that – at one go ... like a man would a glass of
                 beer? (*She shows him a claret glass.*)

GENERAL: Is it true? Ask the Count ... it was he who dared me.

LEA   (*shrugging her shoulders*): I don't believe it. It isn't possible.

GENERAL: That's what he said, and it cost him five hundred louis.

LEA   (*with admiration*): What! You really did it and won the bet?

GENERAL: Course I did ... You ought to have seen the Count's
                 face ... Five hundred louis ... But I didn't feel too good
                 afterwards either.

LEA: It couldn't have been good Kummel like this – it must have
                 been some cheap diluted stuff. (*She takes the bottle which is
                 on the table.*)

GENERAL: No, no ... same mark as this exactly.

LEA: What! You're going to make me believe that you could drink
                 – well – even so much? (*She pours him out a tumblerful.*)

GENERAL: Go on! Fill it right up, right up to the brim ... you'll
                 see ... what do you bet me? (Lea *looks at him smiling then
                 lowering her eyes.*) Good! Right you are! No backing out if
                 you lose.

LEA   (*very provokingly*): I shouldn't want to.

GENERAL: Here goes! (*He drinks slowly and with a great effort the
                 tumbler of Kummel in a single draught, putting glass down
                 on table.*) I've won!

LEA: Wonderful!! (*She rises.*) What a capacity!

GENERAL   (*speech thickened after liqueur*): Now then, little one, come and pay your debt of honour.

LEA (*moving back towards sideboard*): Certainly, but you must come and fetch me.

GENERAL (*after having tried to rise*): It's no good ... I can't move. Come along, my little Lea, come along quickly.

LEA (*laughing*): No, get up.

GENERAL (*showing signs of real drunkenness*): I can't ... You know very well when I'm drunk my beastly legs.

LEA: Come along, try, you never know what you can do till you try. (*She goes over to him and helps lift him up.*)

GENERAL (*after having risen and falling in a mass on the divan*): Damn it, I can't – I can't, I tell you. (*very drunk*) I'm done in – damn it!

LEA: Are you really drunk?

GENERAL (*with a drunken laugh*): Can't you see I am, you pretty little devil!

LEA (*with a quick change of voice and manner*): Don't laugh, Alexander Alexanderwitch.

GENERAL (*amazed*): What!!!

LEA (*in tones of venomous hatred*): 'Béréguisse' ...

GENERAL: What!!! What's that you say?

LEA (*in a low tone bending over him*): Take care, Alexander Alexanderwitch. You don't recognise me. My name's not Lea – I'm Sonia.

GENERAL: Sonia! I– I– I don't understand. I – I'm drunk I tell you.

LEA (*fixing him with her eyes*): Ah! You don't remember, of course not – the girl who came to you in Moscow and pleaded on her bended knees.

GENERAL (*half understanding*): Moscow – Moscow!

LEA: I am Ivan's sister – the man you had knouted to death.

GENERAL (*frightened*): Ivan's sister!!! What do you want here with me ... What are you doing here?

LEA: Revenge ... It's my turn now – I'm going to kill you.

GENERAL (*trying to rise, but falling back on divan*): I'll twist that little white neck of yours first.

LEA: Oh no you won't – you're helpless ... I've got you in my power.

GENERAL (*hissing between his teeth*): You she-devil!

LEA (*upright in front of sideboard*): Call me what you like but nothing will stop me avenging my brother and the other poor devils you've tortured.

GENERAL (*threatening her*): You'll pay for this – curse you – you white faced Jezebel!

LEA: Ah! You thought you were running after me, but it was I – I

who followed you about ... I've been waiting for this moment
for the last eight days. You thought to buy my love – beast
that you are – you've got more than you bargained for this
time.

(*The* General *has by this time worked himself up in a drunken
rage, he attempts to throw the bottle of champagne which is in
the ice bucket, at* Lea, *but the ice bucket falls to the ground
and the bottle slips out of his hand.* Lea *recoils to the middle
of the stage near window*)

GENERAL: You filthy cat! I'll have you arrested ... You'll see. (*Falling
back on the divan, his hand comes near the bell pull. He
pulls hold of it and rings violently – Cord breaks and he
rolls on to the floor into the middle of the room with the
bell push in his hand.* Lea *seeing him ring gives a cry of rage
and disappointment – she steps back to the other end of the
room.*) I'll have you knouted till every bone in your body is
broken ... You shall die the same death as your brother Ivan,
my fine lady.

(*As soon as the* General *has rung, noises of a bell off is heard,
the voices. The door opens and* Victor, *the* Count *and* Alice
enter. Victor *and the* Count *at once see to the* General *on the
floor –* Alice *passes round the table between the latter and the
sideboard, very upset. The waiter has also come but remains
on the threshold of the door*)

VICTOR: Is your Excellency ill?
COUNT: Whatever's the matter? You're kicking up a nice row here.
ALICE: Oh, I heard someone shriek – whatever is it?

(*These lines should be spoken almost simultaneously*)

GENERAL   (*pointing to* Lea *who has moved away to the back of stage
– standing quite motionless*): Take her – take that woman
away – she wants to murder me.
COUNT   (*aghast*): What!
ALICE: Lea ... ! You must be joking!
GENERAL: Arrest her, I say – she wants to assassinate me. (*They all look
at* Lea.)
LEA   (*very calmly*): I don't know what's the matter with him. He's
dead drunk.
COUNT: So it seems. (*to* Victor) Here ... give me a hand. (*They lift
him up.* Lea *takes an armchair and moves it near the table.*)
LEA: Put him here.
GENERAL   (*while the* Count *and* Victor *are helping him, shaking his fist*

at Lea): She's a liar – a damned little liar. Don't listen to her – She wants to kill me ... She's a liar.

COUNT (*to* Victor – *as soon as they have seated the* General): All right ... You can leave us. (Victor *makes a sign to the* Waiter *and they both exeunt rapidly*)

ALICE (*to the* Count, *pointing to the* General): A repetition of last week's affair.

GENERAL (*furious*): I'm not drunk, I tell you – damnation!

ALICE (*going over to* Lea): You've let him drink again ... I warned you.

LEA: I couldn't stop him!

GENERAL: Liar!

LEA: He became violent all of a sudden and rushed at me.

GENERAL: She's lying I tell you – it was she who came for me.

LEA: Look! (*She shows her shoulder and torn dress.*)

ALICE: My poor kiddie.

GENERAL (*shouting*): Go down and fetch the detectives up from outside.

COUNT (*by his side*): You can't drag the police in while you're in this condition ... Think of the scandal.

GENERAL: I'm perfectly sober I tell you. (*trying to get up*) It's only my damned legs playing me up again.

ALICE (*laughing*): Go on – you're blind-o –

GENERAL (*more and more furious*): I'm not – I know what I'm talking about – my head's as clear as anything. Don't you believe me? (*pointing to them with his fingers*) I know who you are – you're Henry and you're Alice.

COUNT (*pointing to* Lea): Quite so, quite so, and there's Lea.

GENERAL: No! That's Sonia.

COUNT: Poor chap, you're very drunk –

GENERAL (*shrieking*): It's Sonia – ask her yourself – it's Sonia!

COUNT: For Heaven's sake, calm yourself.

GENERAL: It's Ivan's sister –

COUNT: Ivan's dead ... for Heaven's sake, let him rest in peace.

LEA (*makes towards* General – *speaking quite kindly*): Why, whatever's the matter with you, old dear? Don't you know me any more?

COUNT: You see very well she doesn't wish you any harm.

GENERAL: If you weren't here she'd kill me. (*threatening her with his fist*) I'll have you sent to Siberia – the mines are the only fit place for a person like you.

ALICE (*aside to* Lea): You've got some pluck, my dear, to stop with a brute like that.

GENERAL (*almost worn out by his last speech and hardly able to*

articulate in his rage): I'll knout you myself, same as I did
your brother.

ALICE   (*to* Lea): Leave him and come with us.

LEA: No, I'd better stop and see him through it ... don't you
worry ... I know how to tackle him – besides he's promised
me some money.

ALICE   (*beckoning to the* Count): All right my dear, I suppose you
know your own business best. Come along Henry.

COUNT: Yes, we'd better be off.

(Alice *makes towards the door* – Lea *as if to hasten their
departure has gone to the door and put her hand on handle
of same*)

GENERAL   (*seizing the* Count *by the arm*): No, no, don't leave me alone
with her ... Take me with you. Take me with you.

COUNT   (*to Alice and* Lea): We can't possibly take him out in this
state.

LEA   (*very sweetly*): Don't you worry. You can leave him to me.
I'll get him round alright.

GENERAL   (*clutching desperately at the* Count): No, no, I won't be left
alone with her. Take me with you, for God's sake.

COUNT: Don't make a fool of yourself – as soon as you're in a fit
condition you shall go home alright.

GENERAL   (*supplicating*): Don't leave me, Count ... Stay here.

COUNT: You don't want me ... Besides Lea's here. (*At this moment
Lea has opened the door.*) She'll look after you.

LEA   (*anxious for them to go*): Of course I will.

ALICE   (*to the* Count): Yes – come along. (*to* Lea) Wish you luck
kiddie – take care of yourself.

GENERAL   (*shouting*): Don't leave me, Count, don't go!

COUNT   (*going out*): He's perfectly disgusting when he's drunk like
this.

(*He joins* Alice *in the corridor and their voices are heard
gradually dying away.* Lea *listens till they are out of earshot
– she then locks the door and fixing the* General *with her eyes
she bursts into laughter and speaks very loudly as if to make
anyone outside hear.*)

LEA: Ah! Ah! Whatever's come over you ... it's too funny ... you
frightened of me you silly old thing ... frightened of Lea
– Your little Lea.

GENERAL: Humph!

LEA   (*in an undertone*): It's my turn now.

GENERAL   (*looking at her with understanding*): What do you mean?

LEA   (*same business as before, speaking loudly*): I think it's
           disgusting the way you drink.

GENERAL   (*muttering*): Yes – I know I've had too much.

LEA   (*still speaking loudly and laughing*): Oh you're a wicked old
           devil, when you're drunk too.

GENERAL   (*still following her with his eyes*): Be careful – I've still got
           some strength left.

LEA   (*negligently taking her muff from sideboard*): Oh, yes, I
           know you're strong, very strong indeed. (*She takes a revolver
           out of muff.*) But I'm going to kill you all the same.

GENERAL   (*terrified*): Put it away – put it away. Don't shoot, for God's
           sake!! Lea – Sonia – For God's sake, don't shoot!

LEA   (*after long pause*): All right, I won't shoot if you'll be
           reasonable.

GENERAL: I'll do anything … anything you like … only spare me.

LEA   (*after another pause*): I want money.

GENERAL: Ah! So that's it, is it – money? Very well then … You shall
           have all I've got on me.

LEA   (*coldly*): How much is that?

GENERAL: I don't know. Two or three thousand francs.

LEA: That's not enough. It's a life you've got to pay for, and I'll
           make you pay dearly. Have you got your cheque book on
           you?

GENERAL: Yes.

LEA   (*commanding*): You are going to write me out one for fifty
           thousand francs. (*She looks towards side-board for pen and
           ink.*)

GENERAL: Very well, then … You've got me, you little devil. Give me
           pen and ink. (Lea *takes blotting paper and pen and ink with
           left hand and puts them on the table.*)

GENERAL   (*taking out cheque book*): Push the table nearer. (General
           before writing looks at revolver which Lea *still holds in her
           right hand.*)

LEA   (*following his look*): Don't be frightened. I'll put it down
           here while you're writing. (*She puts it on sideboard and after
           slight pause carelessly takes up her gloves and toys with
           them while speaking.*) Hurry up! (*She comes down stage
           behind* General.) Write clearly, very clearly, fifty thousand
           francs – That's right – Don't forget the date. Now sign it
           – (*She bends over him a little then with a quick movement
           puts her glove round his neck and strangles him – the
           General struggles –* Lea *puts her foot on back of armchair
           to give her more strength – A long struggle – during the
           last convulsions of* General's *body, she shouts and laughs to*

deafen his groans.) Don't struggle, my darling! Don't struggle
so much! You'll soon be all right!

(*When all is finished and the body no longer moves, she takes
a long look at the* General's *face – seeing that he is dead, she
draws gloves away with left hand making them slip along his
neck, still keeping her eyes on the corpse she takes cheque
and hides it in her corset, she takes pen, ink and paper to
sideboard – puts gloves and revolver in muff, then comes back
to* General – *She takes his head in her right hand and passing
her left hand under his arm, pushes him forward so that his
head rests on table in a position as if he had fainted. She then
looks round to see if there is anything which will incriminate
her – then running to door unlocks it opens it and shrieks out
in corridor*)

LEA: Waiter! Waiter! Help! Help! Oh my God, come quick. Help!
Help!

VICTOR   (*in corridor*): What is it? What's the matter?

LEA   (*coming back from door, followed by* Victor *and* Waiter,
pointing to General): I don't know what's happened to him.
He collapsed all of a sudden – He's unconscious.

VICTOR   (*running to* General): His Excellency has fainted and his
friends have just gone. (*to* Waiter) Quick – quick – go and
fetch a doctor, and tell the two detectives who are outside
what has happened. (Waiter *exits.* Victor *holds the* General's
head up and the General *is stretched on chair – he goes
quickly to window.*) We'd better have some air in. (Lea *opens
window and leans out visibly making signs to someone
outside – sounds of fete are heard.*) How did it happen? Give
me a serviette and some water. Let's try and get him to.

LEA   (*bringing him a serviette soaked in ice bucket*): We were
having supper and all of a sudden he had a kind of a fit.
I'm suffocating he said. Before I had time to do anything he
fainted.

VICTOR   (*after having bathed* General's *face*): He's not coming to. It's
a bit awkward for you, you know. Do you know who he is?

LEA: Yes, a real swell. A duke I believe. My luck's dead out. He
promised me fifty louis.

VICTOR: It was bound to happen sooner or later. He drank too much.

(*The two Detectives enter hurriedly*)

VICTOR: Ah, the detectives!

FIRST DETECTIVE: What's wrong? What's the matter? (*seeing* General *and
going to him*) His Excellency! (Second Detective *shuts*

the door.)

VICTOR: He's just had an attack.

FIRST DETECTIVE   (*looking at* Lea): An attack of what? What do you mean?

VICTOR: We've just sent for a doctor.

FIRST DETECTIVE: Good! In the meantime we'll phone to the Russian Embassy.

LEA   (*very humbly*): And I gentlemen? What had I better do? Can I go?

FIRST DETECTIVE   (*to* Lea *suspiciously*): Wait a minute. Do you think you can slip off like that – after what's happened here?

LEA   (*raising her voice and putting on a tone and manner of a cocotte*): Do you think it's my fault then? You always try and lay the blame on us girls.

FIRST DETECTIVE   (*brutally and raising his voice also*): It's not a question of what you think. You'll have to answer a few questions at the police station. We don't know who you are. (*to* Victor) Go and send for a cab.

SECOND DETECTIVE   (*opening door – to* Victor *and he exits*): Hurry up! Don't lose any time. (Victor *exits*)

LEA   (*continuing to shout*): You know very well it's nothing to do with me. I haven't done anything ... I haven't done anything.

FIRST DETECTIVE   (*shouting also*): Oh haven't you ... haven't you? We'll see about that. Hurry up – put your things on. You're coming with us. (*At this moment the* Second Detective *has carefully shut the door and listens behind it, makes them a sign.*)

SECOND DETECTIVE: He's gone ... Coast's clear.

FIRST DETECTIVE   (*suddenly changing tone of voice, speaking in an undertone after taking a long look at* General): You've done it Sonia.

LEA   (*looking at corpse – in tones of hatred*): Yes, this time I've done it.

SECOND DETECTIVE   (*going towards* General – *shaking his fist at the corpse*): At last! (*to* Lea) How did you do it?

LEA   (*quickly in undertone*): Strangled him with my gloves. He was writing me out a cheque and while he was doing it I– (*She makes gestures of strangling.*)

FIRST DETECTIVE: Bravo!

LEA   (*coming between the two*): And how did you manage? How about his two bloodhounds?

SECOND DETECTIVE: We made them drunk.

FIRST DETECTIVE: And took their places.

SECOND DETECTIVE: So you see we were quite ready in case of any emergency and you wanted any help.

LEA   (*making sign to* Second Detective *for her cloak*): We'd better clear off before the doctor arrives. (*She puts on cloak helped by the two Detectives.*) Hurry up, my muff. (Second Detective *gives it to her.*) Be careful of the revolver. (Second Detective *takes revolver out of muff and puts it in his pocket.*) Let's go. (*She makes a move towards door.*)

FIRST DETECTIVE   (*holding her back*): Like that? You must be mad ...

SECOND DETECTIVE   (*pulling out handcuffs*): The handcuffs.

LEA   (*holding out her wrists*): Oh! (*laughing*) Ah yes, I had forgotten.

SECOND DETECTIVE   (*putting on cuffs*): We mustn't give ourselves away.

FIRST DETECTIVE: In a few hours we shall have passed the frontier and shall be safe.

SECOND DETECTIVE: The train starts in an hour. (*noise heard off*) So, be careful.

FIRST DETECTIVE   (*starting to shout again*): Come along to the police station.

LEA   (*shouting also*): No, I won't go ... I won't go. I haven't done anything – you shan't take me.

FIRST DETECTIVE   (*brutally*): Will you keep quiet? Come along now. (*At the moment* Victor *enters – The two Detectives are struggling with* Lea.)

SECOND DETECTIVE: Are you going to be obstinate ... Are you, you little devil?

(*The two Detectives are dragging her towards the door whilst she is shouting 'Let me go! Let me go! I tell you I've done nothing!'*)

VICTOR   (*to* Lea *as she is dragged away*): Keep quiet, will you? We don't want to make a scene in the place.

LEA   (*still struggling exeunts with the 2 detectives*): Let me go! You brutes! You brutes!

(*Victor exits behind them closing the door – slow curtain on dead body of* General. *Lea's shrieks are heard gradually dying away and the noise of the fete coming through the window*)

CURTAIN

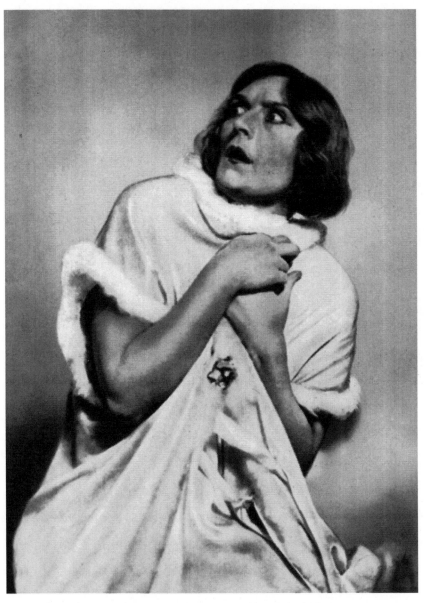

Figure 15. Daisy (Sybil Thorndike) in *The Person Unknown,* 1921

The Person Unknown

by
H.F. Maltby

Preface

H.F. Maltby's *The Person Unknown* was submitted to the Lord Chamberlain under its original title *Her Promise*, and it was approved for performance as part of the Second Series in January 1921. The play was a late addition to the Second Series, along with George E. Morrison's comic sketch *The Shortest Story of All*. The Second Series had opened in December 1920 and *The Person Unknown* and *The Shortest Story of All* were introduced to replace another Maltby play *What Did Her Husband Say?* As the title of the latter piece suggests, this was a comedy while *The Person Unknown* is an example of Grand Guignol horror. The reason *What Did Her Husband Say?* was replaced is primarily because it had had a long run, having been introduced in the First Series (replacing Pierre Veber's comedy *How to be Happy*). At over 150 performances *What Did Her Husband Say?* enjoyed more performances than any other play in the entire repertoire of London's Grand Guignol. Another reason it was dropped was probably because Gladys Unger's *A Man in Mary's Room* was receiving very good reviews and was a comedy of manners and gentle satire in a similar ilk to *What Did Her Husband Say?* The revised programme featured a showcase of six well-balanced plays: three comedies and three horror plays. The comedies were Unger's aforementioned *A Man in Mary's Room*, Morrison's sketch *The Shortest Story of All and* Reginald Arkell and Russell Thorndike's *The Tragedy of Mr Punch*, a play in the tradition of pantomime and Punch and Judy. As an un-sourced press cutting in the Theatre Museum Archives reveals, the play showed its audience the possibly unsavoury truths surrounding Mr Punch, a favourite icon of children's theatre:

> Mr Punch was the first Bolshevik, a man of shameful morals, a cruel husband, an unnatural father, and a murderer many times over, and yet, we all love the rogue.

The French 'Guignol' is that culture's equivalent of Punch and Judy, and it is interesting to note that *The Tragedy of Mr Punch* – a Punch and Judy show for adults – is thus more literally 'Grand Guignol' than any play in the French repertoire.

Along with the comedies, the three horror plays were Reginald Berkeley's *Eight O'Clock*, José Levy's translation of André de Lorde and Pierre Chaine's *Private Room Number 6* and *The Person Unknown*. This package offered an impressive diversity of Grand Guignol terror from the self-proclaimed 'sordid' realism of *Eight O'Clock* to the high melodrama of *Private Room Number 6*. As for *The Person Unknown*, this horror play is one of the masterpieces of the British Grand Guignol repertoire. In Maltby's play, a hideously disfigured veteran from the First World War confronts the female singer who led him and many others to enlist in jingoistic fervour. The woman dies of fright. The play, like *Eight O'Clock*, is distinguished by its concision and a sense of unity of time, place and action, while it has moments of heightened melodrama like *Private Room Number 6*. Maltby's play is fascinating as an example of explicitly anti-war drama. In his autobiography, Maltby explains why he wrote the piece. He despised Paul Rubens's patriotic song 'We Don't Want to Lose You, But We Think You Ought to Go' – a song synonymous with recruitment drives in the early stages of the war – and the publicity stunts of young women singing it to encourage men to enlist. For Maltby, the bitterest irony is that the jingoistic fervour conveniently involved the following proviso:

> Forgetting all about the promise contained in the last line of that dreadful chorus: 'We will love you, hug you, kiss you, when you come back home again.' (Maltby, 1950, 130)

The play has distinct echoes of Maurice Level's 1912 *The Final Kiss* (see Hand and Wilson, 2002, 180–94): in both plays a hideously injured man exacts revenge on the woman who is held to blame for the disfigurement. The plays are both grotesquely erotic in their gendered conflict: just as Henri makes his sexually loaded demand for a 'final kiss', Dick Hobbs insists on Daisy making good on her promise to 'hug and kiss' him. In both plays, the climax to the drama comes when the men tear off the bandages and the women see, in gruesome detail, the results of their original crimes before, in the French play, receiving a taste of her own medicine while in Maltby's play a much more melodramatic (and more likely to be granted a licence) climax comes with Daisy dying of fright (a mode of demise for the heroine which will also be used in the Fourth Series' *The Vigil* later in the same year). In Level's play, Jeanne committed a *crime passionel* – throwing sulphuric acid at Henri in a fit of jealousy – while Maltby's play is more blatantly satirical and politicised: Daisy's crime is a crime of the state. Indeed, this explains the change in title: *Her Promise* was perhaps regarded as too personalised, while *The Person Unknown* is a title which makes a blatant allusion to the 'Unknown Soldier' who was interred in Westminster Abbey just a few weeks before (November 11, 1920). Moreover, the choice of 'Person' makes the figure even more universal – ostensibly genderless and maybe even representative of all victims of an atrocious war.

The Person Unknown

A Drama in One Act
by
H.F. Maltby

First Performed: 17 January 1921

The Person
Daisy
Mary
Tom
The Charwoman

SCENE: *Drawing room of Daisy's flat.*

The curtain rises in the dark and it is difficult to distinguish anything except that the scene is a room and that somebody is moving about in it. After a slight pause a key is heard fitted in a lock off and an outer door is heard to open. The Person on the stage rushes up stage bumping against furniture etc. in doing so. Voices are now heard off.

DAISY   *(off)*: Well, you'll come in for a minute anyhow?
MARY   *(off)*: No, really!
DAISY   *(off)*: Don't be so silly.
TOM   *(off)*: But old thing, think of the time.
DAISY   *(off)*: Time was made for slaves
TOM   *(off)*: Oh, I know all about that, but I have to work tomorrow.
DAISY   *(off)*: You're not the only one. Don't argue about it – be sporty – come in for a minute or two.
MARY   *(off)*: Come along, Tom, we might just as well be hanged for a sheep as a lamb.
TOM   *(off)*: Just what you say. *(Door opens and a shaft of light from the hall floods the room – A second later the electric lights are switched on, revealing an elegantly furnished drawing room – There are two recessed windows at the*

*back, both heavily curtained. The curtains of the window
on right are shaking slightly just as if someone had recently
passed through them –* Daisy *stands by door hand on switch
showing others in – She is a pretty girl of about 25 – She is
in the costume of a Columbine –* Mary *enters – She is about
the same age as Daisy and is attired in 18ᵗʰ century dress
– She is followed by* Tom *who is dressed as Mephistopheles
–* Daisy *closes door.*)

DAISY: It's awfully good of you to see me home and to come in for a
minute.

MARY: It is only for a minute though.

DAISY: One feels so jolly miserable getting home by oneself after all
the fun.

TOM: Reaction, old bean.

DAISY: Yes, I suppose that is what it is.

MARY: I say, Tom, I hope that taxi chap will wait for us all right
and not clear off and leave us in the lurch.

TOM: Not he. I haven't paid him yet.

MARY: My poor old mother will be having the fit of her life if I'm
not home before breakfast.

TOM: Breakfast is one of the topics that are barred just now.

DAISY: Talking of breakfast, there is some champagne in that
cupboard, Tom, be a sport and trot them out and get some
glasses.

TOM: Your lightest wish shall be obeyed. (*goes to cupboard*)

DAISY: I'm so tired, I simply can't move. (*is sitting back*)

TOM (*is getting champagne etc. out*): I don't wonder. It's half past
four.

MARY (*to* Daisy): You've got a matinee today, haven't you?

DAISY: My dear, don't talk of it. I had two shows yesterday as well.
If they spring any more matinees on us I shall kick.

TOM (*opening bottle*): Don't you do enough kicking on the stage
as it is.

DAISY: Only four songs, three concerteds and three dances. This
child doesn't do any work – oh dear no!

MARY: I bet you'd kick up a dust if they tried to cut any of your
numbers out though.

DAISY: No fear of that – they're always trying to push fresh stuff
in for me – my dear, I'm fed up. (Tom *hands her glass.*) Ta,
you're a Christian.

TOM: Not much compliment to my make-up.

MARY (*raising glass*): Cheerio, old thing.

DAISY: Hurray!

TOM: Tootle-too! (*They drink.*)

MARY: Well, I think it was quite a success, don't you?

TOM: Oh, the Bohemian Ball always is a success.

DAISY: I don't wonder, everything was beautifully organized.

TOM: Hope it isn't followed by any fatality this year.

MARY: What do you mean?

TOM: Well, it has been for the last two years – last year some fellow died in his car going home – and the year before there was that veronal business – what was her name?

MARY: You're a nice, cheerful companion, aren't you?

TOM   (*continuing his thoughts*): She was a well known society beauty – funny I can't think –

DAISY: Oh, shut up, Tom – (*breaking off*) Well, we're all going to be in the 'Mirror' tomorrow.

TOM: Today, old dear, you mean.

MARY: You will, anyhow, My dear, I hadn't the faintest idea they were going to take us, that wretched flash thing frightened me out of my life.

TOM: She clung to me and ejaculated 'Oh, God!' just as if she were going to pass away.

DAISY: It will be a scream if you come out in the papers locked in each other's arms.

MARY: Cue for mother to ask what your intentions are.

TOM: Cue for me to ask what your intentions are. Mary! Will you marry me?

MARY: No.

TOM   (*to* Daisy): There, you see. You can't say I'm to blame.

DAISY: Don't you get married, my dear, you remain like me. When you are single you get taken out – when you are married you get left at home. This child knows.

TOM: She talks like a married woman who has been divorced.

MARY: Your maid has gone to bed long ago, I suppose?

DAISY: My dear, I haven't got a maid now.

MARY: Never!

DAISY: She's in hospital with gastritis – or neuritis – or whatever maids get!

MARY: Then however do you manage?

DAISY: Manage on my lonesome, darling. Oh, I've got a woman who comes in and does for me. She gets here at eight – and clears out goodness knows when – the old cat. She always takes jolly good care that she is washing up or doing something when I go to the theatre, so that I have to leave her in possession. I bet she has some bean feasts in here when I'm out. (*Pauses, suddenly looking at occasional table upon which is the photo of a man in a silver frame.*)

TOM: I wouldn't be surprised. (Daisy *has risen and gone to table.*)

DAISY: Now look at this.

MARY: What about it?

TOM: Dear old Bobby – heard from him lately?

DAISY: He writes me every mail, God bless him. (*kisses photograph*) But that's not the point.

MARY: What is the point?

DAISY: I want to know how he got on to that table – his place is in the centre of the mantelpiece – that's where he always sits.

MARY: What a shame – dethroning the only boy in the world.

TOM: If I remember rightly, the only boys in the world are always placed in the centre of the mantelpiece. George I was there – then Fred – then Percy – then George II –

DAISY: Oh, stow it, try to talk sense. (*to* Mary) When I left here yesterday that photo was on the mantelpiece – now I find it here. I don't like my things being shifted about – I – (*is going to mantelpiece with photo and stops dead*) Now isn't this the limit?

MARY: What?

DAISY (*pointing to a small army conscript photograph in tin frame*): Now, how did *that* get there I'd like to know.

TOM: What's that? (Daisy *holds photo up disgustedly.*) One of the former only boys resurrected himself?

DAISY: Don't be so funny.

MARY: Who is it?

DAISY: How should I know? (*looks at it*) A common soldier in a tin frame. One of that old cat's relations, I suppose. They've had a little jazz in here by themselves while I was out – that's what they have done.

TOM: Don't you know him?

DAISY: Know that? Not much! Never set eyes on him in my life. Well, she can damned well pick him up when she comes to clean the room. (*Throws photo on floor – it drops at foot of curtain right window – unseen by those on stage* The Person's *hand comes through curtain and picks it up. She puts Bobby's photo on mantelpiece.*)

TOM (*looking at wrist watch*): Well, old peach, what about it?

MARY (*almost rising*): I think so –

DAISY: No, don't go yet – have another drink – be sociable.

TOM (*pouring out wine*): The woman tempted me – and I fell.

DAISY: My dear, I don't know how those old Columbines ever managed to dance in these things – you don't wear corsets, do you Tom?

TOM: No, but I know how to take them off.

DAISY: Chance is a fine thing! I positively must get out of these
        – they seem to be –

TOM: Go on! I'm deaf, dumb and blind.

MARY: It's not good for him to hear – he's not married yet.

TOM: Nothing to miss.

DAISY: Just sit down like a couple of angels, will you, while I slip
        into something loose.

TOM: Ah, I love something loose.

DAISY: He's talking about you, darling.

MARY: If he dare!

DAISY: I shan't be a minute, really, good people, let me get out of my
        misery.

TOM: Right-o!

DAISY: Help yourself to what you want.

TOM   (*referring to Mary*): She won't let me.

MARY: I like that!

DAISY: I won't have you in here again if you can't behave yourself.
        (*goes out – pause – they sip wine*)

TOM: Well, this is very nice, but it's damned near five o'clock and I
        have to be in the City at ten.

MARY: That's the worst of Daisy – you can't get away from her.

TOM: Oh, she's one of the best – and success doesn't seem to have
        spoilt her.

MARY: Yes, she's just the same as she was when she was only playing
        small parts.

TOM: She's made a big enough hit now in all conscience she's got
        all the other musical comedy girls skinned.

MARY: They want her to go to America.

TOM: What, with the same piece?

MARY: Yes.

TOM: She'll go, of course?

MARY   (*rising and crossing stage*): Don't know – depends upon
        Bobby.

TOM: Funny the influence he's got on her.

MARY: I don't know where the 'funny' comes in – he'd marry
        her tomorrow if he hadn't got a wife. (*She stops by piano
        – Upon music stool of same is a torn and dirty piece of
        music such as might have been cut out of a Sunday paper
        – Quite unconsciously Mary stands and plays with one hand
        – the air is 'We don't want to lose you'.*)

TOM   (*singing*): 'But we feel you ought to go. For your King and
        your Country, Both need you so.' – Oh, help! (*She plays on.*)
        'We'll love you, kiss you, hug you, when you come back home
        again.' What cheery music Daisy keeps in the house, doesn't

she?

MARY: I'd almost forgotten that old thing.

TOM: About time everyone had forgotten it – Lord, it takes me back to the dark ages (*reciting*) – 'We don't want to lose you but we think you ought to go.'

MARY: You didn't go very far, did you?

TOM: As far as I wanted to – but I was held up at Whitehall, where my glossy Sam Browne and scarlet tabs were the envy of everyone who came home on leave. (Daisy *enters – she is in a very fetching negligee – laces, ribbons etc.*)

DAISY: Whoever has been playing that awful old tune?

MARY: Guilty mi'lord!

DAISY: Whatever made you think of it?

MARY: I didn't. (*points to piano*) It was there waiting to be played. (Daisy *goes to piano and snatches up music.*)

DAISY: Now that proves that that old cat has been having a musical evening in here. (*crumples up music and throws it on floor – it falls at foot of curtains and* The Person's *hand come out and picks it up*) Damn her! My dear that song! If anything ever got on my nerves that song did. I used to sing it every night – twice every night, my dear – when I was doing a tour on the halls – I always loathed it – but things looked very black then and one felt one simply *had* to do *something* for one's country. My dear, I got quite a lot recruits. When I had finished the manager used to come forward and ask who would join up, and we'd have them all on the stage, and I'd give them all a 'good luck' kiss. My dear, you don't know *what* I have kissed – it was dreadful – really – I should have been made a dame or something, and often I thought I was in the running for the V.C.

TOM: Ah, well, our efforts have been crowned in victory, and victory has been celebrated by the Bohemians of Grosvenor Square, and we are what is left over from the night before. (*Looks at watch.*) Five-fifteen! (*goes up to left windows and opens them, letting in the grey morning light*) And a dull and rainy morning! Soon the wily milkman will be wending his weary way. (*to Mary*) And Mama will be watching for the return of her erring daughter – and my man will have drunk all my whiskey – and my taxi driver will have about £2,500 on his clock – so what about it?

MARY: I agree with you. (*turns to Daisy*) Well, night-night, old thing. See you sometime soon.

DAISY: Hope so. (*They kiss.*)

TOM (*holding up face*): Remember the gent what saw you home.

DAISY: You don't deserve it. (*kisses him*)

TOM: Blessed are they who don't deserve for they generally get the pickings. (Daisy *opens door for them.*)

MARY: Oh, don't trouble to come out.

DAISY: My dear, I'm going to bed now, I'm not coming back here again.

> (*They go out and she switches out light and follows them – The room is in darkness save for the grey early morning light that comes through L. window – They are heard saying goodbye, etc.* The Person *comes out from window right and goes down stage – Outer door heard to close – Pause – then room door opens – shaft of light from hall illuminates part of room –* Daisy *enters and goes to small table centre and picks up trinket she has left there – she turns and is about to go when the person closes door with a bang – The room is now in darkness save for morning light in window –* Daisy *and* The Person *are now in room alone together –* Daisy *gives a little involuntary cry – pause.*)

THE PERSON: You ain't got nothing to be afraid of – it's only me.

DAISY: And who are you?

THE PERSON: Dick.

DAISY: Dick?

THE PERSON: Dick 'Obbs.

DAISY: But who are you? I don't know you.

THE PERSON: Yes, you do – but you've forgotten me, maybe. You met so many blokes at the time you met me that you'll have overlooked Dick – poor Dick 'Obbs. (*pause*)

DAISY   (*nervously*): I dare say I'd know you at once if I saw you – but it is so dark – (*makes movement forward towards switch but he bars the way*)

THE PERSON: Don't touch the light! It don't suit my purpose to 'ave a light on – just you an' me an' the dark! (*She makes movement to telephone but he again bars the way.*) Nor the telephone neither – none of your friends won't be up at this time, and we don't want to be interrupted, do we? (*Pause. It can be just seen that* The Person's *face is covered in something white – it might be a mask or it might be bandages.*)

DAISY: And – and – what do you want?

THE PERSON: You. (*She gives a little start.*) Don't take on – I've always wanted you. Years and years ago when I used to buy your picture postcards and put them on my mantelpiece in my digs. I was a foreman in the engraving works in West Bromwich then – but I loved you – and I always felt I'd like to – (*pause*) And then the war broke out and I was going to join up – to fight for the women – you was all the women in my mind – but my boss wouldn't let me – he said I was more useful to the country where I was.

DAISY   (*trying to conceal her fright*): Quite so – a skilled engineer – I daresay he was quite right. (*pause*) You needn't think I should think any the worse of you for not serving – a lot of my friends – (*He gives a little laugh.*) Really, you are a little unreasonable coming here at this time – I'm sure I don't know how you got in – if you want my autograph –

THE PERSON: No – I don't want that – I want you – I got in through that window for you.

DAISY   (*making a movement to window*): That window – (*He bars the way.*)

THE PERSON: No, you don't. (*pause*)

DAISY   (*suddenly – bursting out hysterically*): Help! Help!

THE PERSON   (*forcefully*): Stop it! (*She stops shouting but sobs hysterically.*)

DAISY: Oh, my God! Oh, help me!

THE PERSON: There ain't no need to make such a fuss – I've only come to hold you to your promise.

DAISY: My promise?

THE PERSON: To me.

DAISY: To you? What promise?

THE PERSON: Do you remember singing at the music hall at Birmingham?

DAISY: I've sung there several times.

THE PERSON: I know – but in 1915, I mean.

DAISY: I don't remember particularly –

THE PERSON: No, it's slipped your mind – it was nothing to you – but it was everything to me. Do you remember what you sung?

DAISY: I –

THE PERSON: I'll tell you – you sung a recruiting son – 'Your King and Country need you.'

DAISY: Yes, I believe I did.

THE PERSON: Do you remember the words?

DAISY: It is so long ago, I –

THE PERSON: No, they've slipped your memory too. I thought they would – that's why I put that bit of music there to remind you. But they were nothing to you – I see that now – they were only a part you had learnt off – but to us poor blokes – (*repeats*) Them's the words, ain't they?

DAISY: Yes, yes, I think so.

THE PERSON: I heard you sing them first house, that Monday night. The manager made a speech inviting any blokes who would join up to come on the stage – and saying that you would give them a good luck kiss. I could have stopped in my engineering job all through the war – and made good money too – but I couldn't bear to see you kissing them other chaps – I wanted to feel those sweet lips of yours that I had kissed so often on your photos – I came on the stage and you kissed me in front of all the people – it was like 'eaven – that moment was – to me. But it meant nothing to you – you went home and laughed over it – as you laughed just now with your pals. I went back with the recruiting sergeant and joined up that night.

DAISY: Well, I'm very glad to see that you've got back safe and sound – I'm sure if I saw you I'd recognise you at once – I –

THE PERSON: No, you wouldn't. You saw my likeness on the mantelpiece just now – but you threw it away –

DAISY: Was that you? I must – have –

THE PERSON: But I don't look the same as that now – I've changed

DAISY: Yes – it's wonderful what a change the army –

THE PERSON: I was wounded in the face – end of 1916 – and I've been in dock ever since. A bit of H.E. did it – I ain't got much face left – not the lower part anyway. They've patched me up with bits of wax – and that, but I ain't much to look at – that's why I always wear these. (*It is lighter now and the bandages on his face can be seen.*) I don't want to shock the people in the streets. (*pause*) They was all like me in my ward – but I was the worst – that's why they wouldn't allow no woman in there – or leave a looking glass about – we could only sit and watch the others when they was being dressed and wonder if – Oh, God! (*pause*) They've patched some of them up fine – but they didn't seem to have no luck with me. They've turned me adrift now – hopeless – incurable – something they can't do nothing with. I'm an outcast – that's what I am – I've got to keep in the shadow – Men want to spew when they see me – Women – (*pause*) But I'm a man just the same, and 'as feelings same as other men – and I might 'ave been in my job at Bromwich now – but for you – and your promise – which you're going to keep ... (*approaching her*)

DAISY: Oh lord! Oh lord!

THE PERSON: There were eight of us came on the stage same house as I did – and how many more during your tour? You don't know – you don't care. What's happened to them – have you taken the trouble to find out? Perhaps they have buried one of them in Westminster Abbey – My word, if they had and you knew it, wouldn't you be cock-a-hoop? You'd have something to talk about at your next jazz – 'My boy has been buried in the Abbey!' Your boy! Well, one of your boys is here now – holding you to your promise –

DAISY: My promise, but –

THE PERSON: 'We will love you, hug you, kiss you, when you come back home again.' No one else isn't keen on it with my face all blown to hell; I've longed for a woman's bare arms round my neck, and a woman's soft face next to mine – what's left of it; I've longed for the feel of a woman's breath and her warm body close to me; but I shan't get that no more – that has been taken from me – I don't expect it now – but with you it's different, 'cause you've *promised*. 'We will love you, hug you, kiss you, when you come back home again.' (*snatches bandages off – the audience does not see his face – but she does*)

DAISY (*screaming*): Oh, God! Oh, Christ! Take it away!

THE PERSON: Ah, ha! I ain't so pretty as I was – but that is what you 'ave got to love and hug and kiss – 'cause I've *got* back home again. (*takes her by the throat and kisses her – she screams*) Ha, ha, ha, ha, ha! You can make promises you can, but you don't like to keep them. But you ain't hugged me yet – (*takes her arms and puts them round his neck – she struggles*) Hug me – hug me! (*She struggles – and then he throws her down – she falls limp on to ground.*) And so now you kept your promise after all. (*Stands for a second looking at her – then goes to door and goes out – outer door heard to open and close.*)

(Daisy *lies motionless – gradually the light goes up – still she does not move – Birds heard chirping off – Outer door heard to open and close – A Charwoman enters – Business – sees Daisy and rushes to her – Business.*)

CHARWOMAN: Miss Dolland! Miss Dolland! (*suddenly realising that she is dead and rushes to telephone*) Give me the police! Quick! Quick! There's a murder been done 'ere and ...

CURTAIN

Latitude 15° South

by
Victor MacClure

Preface

Latitude 15° South, which was originally titled *On the Fringe*, was Victor MacClure's only piece for London's Grand Guignol and was premièred at the Little Theatre on 29 June 1921 as part of Levy's Fourth Series, sharing the bill with the notorious *The Old Women* and another de Lorde translation, *The Vigil*. It ran for 117 performances until October of that year. MacClure (1887–1963) did not really establish himself as a playwright, but made a living as a minor novelist and architect, and *Latitude 15° South* is, in fact, a relatively short play. It is nevertheless interesting for a number of reasons.

The play takes place on board 'a small steamer' that is caught in the doldrums and unable to move in the stifling heat, and essentially concerns itself with the effects on the crew of a growing sense of claustrophobia. The theme is not an uncommon one in the Grand Guignol and, in this sense, is probably most comparable to Paul Autier and Paul Cloquemin's *The Lighthouse Keepers* (Hand and Wilson, 2002, 109–120), which had played at the Grand Guignol in Paris as early as 1905 and had been reprised on two occasions during the following decade. *The Lighthouse Keepers* concerns Bréhan and his son, Yvon, who have just begun their tour of duty at a remote lighthouse only to learn that the son has contracted rabies. Bréhan commits filicide as an act of mercy, but faces the prospect of spending the next month alone in the lighthouse with his son's corpse.

In the same way that *The Lighthouse Keepers* has three key moments of horror (the murder of the son, the imagined isolation of the father, and the realisation that a ship is heading for the rocks), *Latitude 15° South* also has three principal points around which the tension is located. The first is the stabbing of Bill by Farquhar and the subsequent shooting of Farquhar by the Mate. The second is the seeming approach of the ghostly ship which spells doom for all on board. As with the approaching ship in *The Lighthouse Keepers* this turns out to be a false alarm. Just as Bréhan manages to switch on the light just in time to avert disaster, so the ghostly bell turns out to be a floating bell-buoy. However, the real horror lies in the imagined terror that awaits the protagonists, and their inability to escape from it. It is not just that the lighthouse and the steamer are claustrophobic settings, but they are also prisons and their warder is nature itself – Bréhan cannot escape the lighthouse because of the tempestuous weather conditions, and the sailors cannot escape because of the eerie *lack* of wind. As with so much Grand Guignol drama, the enacted violence acts as a release of tension and is much less horrific than the unseen violence.

The significance of plays such as *Latitude 15° South* and *The Lighthouse Keepers* lies in the particular challenges that the plays present for the actor. These are not plays that demand sleight-of-hand trickery or special effects, but rather an *intensity of acting* designed 'to achieve a mood of claustrophobic terror' (Hand and Wilson, 2002, 109). Fortunately, *Latitude 15° South* is one of the plays performed at the Little Theatre for which we have photographic documentation, which is revealing in its own way. Lewis Casson and Russell Thorndike are shown in a pose which is quite melodramatic in tone. Thorndike's body is tightly closed, his hand in his mouth, in contrast to his eyes which are wide with fear. Casson's body, by contrast, is more open, pleading, his eyes betraying a more desperate resignation. In both cases, though, these are examples of the body *in extremis* and they are sculpted by a strong muscular tension. The intensity of the acting is enhanced by heavy make-up, and in this way it seems to differ from the photographic evidence of other productions at London's Grand Guignol. In fact the photograph is more redolent of the image of Paulais performing in René Berton's *Euthanasia* (Hand and Wilson, 2000, 269) at the impasse Chaptal.

One of the most striking aspects of the script is the way that MacClure uses language in the play, particularly to denote class and the all-male environment of the ship. The dropping of aitches, the representation of a kind of working-class cockney and use of vernacular expressions is common in the banter between the sailors. But this is not an attempt at realism, as such – or if it is, it is a rather clumsy attempt – but is a stylized stage cockney, as is evident in words such as 'Gawd!', 'Lumme!' and 'nothink'. This is a tactic used by a number of other British Grand Guignol writers, most notably H.F. Maltby in *The Person Unknown* who contrasts the speech of the characters to denote their social class.

The play is interesting for its handling of the stifling masculine atmosphere of the ship and its crew. As such, it is reminiscent of the first act of Eugene O'Neill's *The Hairy Ape* (1922), a consciously expressionist work but one which also explores dialect in detail. The presentation of religion, especially in relation to desperation, provides an ironic treatment not dissimilar to 'Matrosen Tango' in Bertolt Brecht and Kurt Weill's *Happy End* (1929), which is a narrative of the machismo of sailors and its evaporation (to be replaced with a sudden devout faith) in the face of danger. The fact that the supernatural element in MacClure's play – the 'Flying Dutchman' – proves to be bogus is a device which will be similarly explored in Arnold Ridley's comedy-thriller *Ghost Train* (1925). Aside from drama, *Latitude 15° South*, and the irony of its plot, is reminiscent of Joseph Conrad's fiction, not least *Typhoon* (1903) which animates a similar crisis on board a ship and the psychological impact of it. Indeed, MacClure's bleak exploration of the crew's psychological journey is distinctly Conradian in the tradition of *Heart of Darkness* (1900), like another classic offering from the French Grand Guignol repertoire, de Lorde and Morel's *The Ultimate Torture* (Hand and Wilson, 2002, 93–108).

Latitude 15° South was granted a licence with little controversy, but not without some interference from the infamous blue pencil. Not surprisingly, the Lord Chamberlain took exception to the occasional use of 'bloody' as a swear word, and the usual tactic of substituting it for 'ruddy' or 'bloomin'' was used. More interestingly, the censor also objected to some of the sexual references in the sailors' conversation. For example, the following speech by Bill was singled out for censure:

> I remember once at
> Rosario seein' 'im go off with three dago wimmen one
> night, an' 'e slep' with them all that same night!
> Dago wimmen!

The position of the blue pencil cross here would seem to indicate that the objection is to the reference to the four-in-a-bed scenario, rather than the racist slur. Likewise in the following speech by Bill, we can assume that the censor is responding to the reference to the nakedness of the woman, rather than the racism or the misogyny implicit in the line:

> 'E was playin' casino with a low
> greaser, an' they was usin' a naked dago woman for a
> card table!

Similarly, the Lord Chamberlain insists on the removal of what seems to be an implied reference to homosexual practices:

> They say 'e gave up wimmen – used to go to the other
> shops – you know ...

Of course, such lines and the censor's responses to them merely betray the social attitudes of the British establishment in the 1920s, and it is partly what renders them interesting as historical documents.

Latitude 15° South

A Drama of the Sea
by
Victor MacClure

First Performed: 29 June 1921

Nobby
Bill
Ollsen
Joe
Mate
Farquhar
The Skipper

SCENE: *The main deck of a small steamer, of cargo-carrying type, about 2,000 tons. In the centre of the scene is the forward hatch, aft of which rises the mast with a derrick. A steam winch cuddles the mast foot. Two seamen are sitting on the hatch cover. They are lightly dressed in dungaree trousers and thin cotton vests with sweat rags round their necks. One wears a dilapidated bowler and the other a deep-sea cap, very greasy and worn. It is obviously a stifling morning in the South Seas. The sky is brazen, and the seas, which can be seen now and then over the gunwale, is of a leaden colour, and the waves are oily hummocks. The men are almost gasping for breath, and every now and then one or the other will wipe his face with his neck-rag. One is called* Nobby, *for the reason that he is entered on the ship's books as 'Clark, A.B.' The other is simply* Bill.

As the curtain rises, 'Six Bells' is struck.

NOBBY: Six bells! Coo! Wish we c'd rig a hawnin' for them dog watches – this 'eat!

BILL: Crool, I call it. There's a bit o' wind, but it don't do no good. Makes the 'eat wusser if anythink!

NOBBY: Coo! Couldn't I do with 'arf a pint, drawed mild, with an
          'ead on it. Watcher say to walkin' down the Mile End Road
          in shore-goin' togs, stoppin' at any pub you fancies –

BILL: Ow, chuck it Nobby! You make me thirsty, an' I don't want
          to move forrard for some perishin' water – Smoke ain't no
          good to you neither – just makes you thirstier. Tell you wot it
          is, Nobby, you ain't never been down in them seas afore?

NOBBY: No. An' if I ever gets outer them, you don't find me back
          again. That's wot!

BILL: I don't blame you. But I'll tell you wot it is, Nobby, a
          hawnin' wouldn't stand a dog's chance! Last night the old
          man was worried about the barrow-meter. Pumpin' up an'
          down it was, somethink fierce –

NOBBY: Well, wot abaht it? I don't 'old with them barrow-meters.

BILL: That's just ignorance, Nobby. The old man knows them
          seas, an' 'e knows what a pumpin' glass means. Means an
          'urricane, it does. We're in for a blow –

NOBBY: Coo! An' them engines broke down – lumme! Ne'mind, that
          jib we rigged'll give us way enough.

BILL   (solemnly): The blow that's coming', if it do come, will
          blow that jib sky-hootin'. Shouldn't be surprised if we loses
          all the deck-gear. I remember it was a day like this before
          the Minnei was piled up on the Low Islands. Gawd! That
          was a blow! It blew enough to scalp a man. Never see such
          a wind!

NOBBY: You are a cheerful bloke an' no mistake, Bill. I've been in a
          few blows north o' the Line, an' I ain't afraid o' anythink
          that can 'appen down 'ere.

BILL: That's just ignorance again, Nobby. W'y, I've seen the ships
          boats 'eld straight out like by the falls, just as if they was
          that much buntin' – an' blowed away, too, at the last. I tell
          you, if prayin's in your line, you pray for them engines to
          turn.

NOBBY: Well, you are a cheerful bloke, Bill, an' no mistake. Wot with
          you an' old Farquhar, this ship is an 'appy 'ome! Coupla prize
          croakers, you are!

BILL: I ain't no croaker, Nobby. I just warns you. We're 'eadin' into
          an 'urricane, with engines broke down. Gawd knows wot'll
          'appen if we don't get a bit o' way in the ship!

NOBBY: I 'eard the Chief promise the old man steam up by noon.
          Listen, the black squad's workin' away like thunder ... (*There
          is a pause in which can be heard the faint clinking of
          hammers and the sound of a ratchet at work*) Poor perishin'
          blighters – down in that 'eat! (*There is another pause.*)

BILL: Funny, ain't it, old Farquhar getting' religion! An' 'im such a rip before – boosin' an' wimmen, an' scrappin', an' gamblin'. Chee! 'E was an' 'oly terror!

NOBBY: That's the kind that gets religion wust – don't do their dee-bauches by 'arf, an' go the 'ole 'og in 'oliness. I've seen it time an' time again at sea.

BILL: You said an' earful then, Nobby. You're right! But Sam Farquhar was the quickest liver I ever saw. The blindoes! An' the wimmen! I remember once at Rosario seein' 'im go off with three dago wimmen one night, an' 'e slep' with them all that same night! Dago wimmen! 'E broke ship, an' we went to look for 'im. We found 'im in a wine shop – an' wot d'ye think 'e was doin'?

NOBBY: I dunno – some 'ellishness, I'll bet.

BILL: You're right! 'E was playin' casino with a low greaser, an' they was usin' a naked dago woman for a card table!

NOBBY (easily): Ow, that's nothink! I've seen it done myself!

BILL: I dessay, but not with a man that took to religion. Sam could get round a woman quicker than anybody I ever see. I'm a sailor-man, I am – an' I've seen some things in my time, but Sam –

NOBBY: They say 'e gave up wimmen – used to go to the other shops – you know –

BILL: I believe you. An' now 'e's got religion– (Another man joins them. He drops on the hatch cover exhausted.) Wotcher, Ollsen? Ain't this 'eat somethink perishin'?

OLLSEN: Yaes. Too much heat altogether, I think. How them engines go, have you heard?

NOBBY: Steam up by eight bells, the Chief says.

OLLSEN: Good t'ing, too. Presently he blow big guns. Glass is falling too quick. Down in the fo'c'sle it is too hot altogether. An' Sam Farquhar reads his good book out loud. Too much holiness down there for me. I t'ink he has bats in the belfry, as they say – his eye is too wild – like Fokke of the phantom ship, the Flying Dutchman.

BILL: Wotcher mean, the Flying Dutchman?

OLLSEN: They say the Flying Dutchman was a wild man like Sam Farquhar – and so was condemned to sail the sea for ever. (a pause)

NOBBY: You think old Sam's gone off his rocker?

OLLSEN: Yes. Sam had a wild eye. It is not good to be in a small fo'c'sle with him – it stifles me! I come up for air, but there is no air.

BILL: You'll have all the air you want in an hour or two, Ollsen.

Too much.

NOBBY: I wish I was back in the Mile End Road –

BILL: Oh, stow it, Nobby!

OLLSEN: When the blow comes, it won't be cold. It will be dam' hot! I wish I could hear them engines! (*A pause – The group is joined by another seaman.*)

BILL: Wotcher, Joe?

JOE: D'you believe in'ell, Bill?

BILL: Wot's that? (*He sits up.*)

JOE: D'you believe in 'ell?

BILL: I dunno. W'y?

JOE: It's old Sam down there.

NOBBY: Talkin' 'Ell, is 'e? – old perisher!

JOE: Ses we're doomed – every sailor-man's doomed!

BILL (*philosophically*): I shouldn't be surprised!

JOE: Ses little babies is born doomed –

NOBBY: Wot? Babies?

JOE: Yus! Even babies before their mother 'as them.

BILL: Wot? Unborned babies?

JOE: Yus!

BILL: Where does 'e get the noos from?

JOE: Ses the Bible ses it. (*He gets more sullen every reply.*)

BILL: An' wot does 'e say about stoppin' bein' doomed?

JOE: Nuthink! Only somethink we can't get. 'E calls it 'grice'.

NOBBY: Well, 'e is an old perisher! Wot I ses is this; if old Sam –

OLLSEN: Half a minute, Nobby – lissen! (*He holds up a warning finger.*) Can't you not hear it?

BILL: 'Ear wot, Nils?

OLLSEN: A bell. Can't you not hear it? (*There is a pause – Everybody listens intently.*)

BILL: I can't 'ear nothink! Can you, Nobby?

NOBBY: Quiet a bit. Naw! I can't 'ear no bell. Did you, Joe?

JOE: Naw!

BILL: Musta been somethink in the engine-room, Nils. There ain't no ships in these waters. Off the beaten track.

OLLSEN: I must have been mistaken. Somet'ing in my ear –

BILL: Imagination, Nils. (Ollsen *shakes his great fair head, and sits listening still.*) I bet it is. Wot was it you said about babies, Joe?

JOE: It wasn't me that said it, it was that perisher, Sam Farquhar. Everybody's doomed to hell fire, 'e ses. Right from the beginnin' of bein' born.

NOBBY: Ow, rats! Don't you believe 'im, Joe.

JOE: But 'e read out bits from 'is book. Not the Bible – the other.

NOBBY: Was it in print?

JOE: (*sullenly*): Yus! That book 'e 'as – the 'Doctryne of Pre-predestitution', or somethink!

NOBBY: Well, wot's the use of old Sam gettin' religion? If 'e's goin' to 'ell anyway, 'e might as well 'ave stopped a rip –

OLLSEN: Lissen, now! Don't you hear the bell now? (*a strained pause*)

NOBBY: Ow, chuck it, Nils! You've got a bell on the brain!

BILL: There ain't no bell, Nils old man. The 'eat's makin' your 'ead sing. Go an' 'ave a swig o' water, chum. (*Still they listen.*)

NOBBY: I believe – I believe I can 'ear somethink! Naw! I can't!

JOE: I don't 'ear no bell.

BILL: Look at it sensible, Nils. 'Ow can there be a bell? We're off the track of ships, an' even if there was one, Jim Sparkes'd see it. Quickest eyes on the ship 'e 'as. Go an' 'ave a swig o' water, Mate. That's wot you want. (Ollsen *gets up heavily, shaking his head.*)

OLLSEN: There is a bell – I can hear it. (*He goes forward. The others look at one another, a trifle stealthily.*)

NOBBY (*shaking his head*): Poor old Nils is off colour. It's the 'eat! 'Earin' bells! Everybody knows them Scans ain't got no ear-sight. They can 'ear but not quick-like. But their eyes is good –

BILL: That's a fact! I never met a Scan with good ear-sight yet –

NOBBY: Stop a bit! Either I've got 'em, or – I believe I 'ear a bell!

BILL: Ow, chuck it, Nobby!

JOE: I can 'ear a bell allright! (*There is a silence.*)

BILL: I believe – I believe I 'ear it, too! (*Another pause which is broken by the voice of the* Mate *on the bridge.*)

MATE: Any of you men down there hear a bell?

BILL: Yessir! We all seem to hear it now – faintlike.

MATE: Where d'you make out it comes from?

BILL: Down the wind, sir!

NOBBY: No it ain't, Bill. It's to starboard ahead.

JOE: If you ask me, *I* ses to windward.

MATE: Quiet there a minute! (Ollsen *rejoins the group – He is shaken.*)

OLLSEN (*in a low voice*): What you t'ink now, fellers? A bell allright, I fancy?

BILL: You were right, Nils. It's a bell allright! (*A sense of awe is on the sailors, They walk to either side of the ship and gaze to sea.*)

MATE: Anyone see a sail – or smoke?

CHORUS: No, sir!

MATE: Nip aloft one of you – you, Ollsen – and see if there's anything in sight.

OLLSEN: Aye, aye, sir! (*He swings on to the ratlines and ascends.*)

BILL: Nip up on the fo'c'sle, Joe, an' 'ave a look! (Joe *runs forward. The light is failing into a dun red. The wind is rising.*)

NOBBY: That little bit o' rag forrard's fair drivin' 'er, Bill.

BILL: You're right, it is, Nobby. Twenty-odd knot wind, I should say. Be about ninety knots in 'arf an hour.

NOBBY: Cheese it, Bill – ninety knots!

BILL: An' undred – two 'undred! I'll betcha! I wish I could 'ear them engines! (*a pause*)

MATE: Can you see anything, Ollsen?

OLLSEN   (*aloft*): No, sir – not a t'ing, sir. Too dark.

MATE: Get on deck then. Wonder what the hell it is? (*His voice is querulous.*)

BILL: First's getting' uneasy –

NOBBY: I don't blame 'im! Wi' them engines broke down– (Ollsen *is seen descending. He drops lightly on the deck. Presently* Joe *returns. Faintly, as if at a great distance, can be heard the* 'tink-a-tin' – 'tink-a-tin' *of a bell.*)

OLLSEN   (*softly*): I knew I would see no ship – it is no ship's bell!

JOE   (*scared*): Well, wot is it, Nils?

OLLSEN: It is not a real bell – it is not a real ship –

JOE: Wotcher mean?

OLLSEN: It is Falkenberg –

BILL   (*with an unsteady laugh*): D'you mean the Flying Dutchman?

OLLSEN: Yaes! It is more likely him – Falkenberg is always in the North. It will be Fokke of the Flying Dutchman.

BILL: Ow, turn it up, Nils! That's only a yarn –

OLLSEN: You t'ink so yaes? But I know better – any sailor-man from the North will tell you. My father see him. Next minute the ship is wrecked!

BILL: Ow, stow it, Nils! You don't believe that yarn?

OLLSEN: I do! My father –

BILL   (*crossly*): I never believe that sort o' bilge –

NOBBY: Steady, steady, Bill. It ain't no use tempting Providence. It's just askin' for a judgement on yourself – and the ship!

BILL: Gawd! I wisht I could 'ear them engines goin'! We'll never weather wot's comin' without them! The old man's on the bridge! Chee! 'E don't look 'arf worried!

(*They all turn and look aft in silence. It is getting darker and darker. The bell seems to be getting more distinct*)

JOE: Christ! It's 'ot! It's like a hoven – I kin 'ardly breathe!

NOBBY: I feel as if somebody was sittin' on me 'ead! Oh, for a breath o' cool air! (*The* Mate *passes the group, who gaze at him seriously.*)

MATE: It's going to blow soon, men. The bottom's right out of the glass. Stand by to reef that jib presently.

BILL: How's the engines, sir?

MATE (*over his shoulder*): They may have steam in them in time, Jones, it's a race with the weather. (*goes forward*)

JOE (*suddenly*): Damn that bloody bell!

NOBBY: Cussin' won't do us no good, Joe. It ain't chancy neither.

BILL (*hardily*): I ain't afraid on no bell – it's the 'urricane I'm dreadin'. (*He goes to the side and peers over.*)

OLLSEN (*suddenly*): It's a ghost ship's bell we hear. It is Fokke of the Flying Dutchman. And it means that this ship will be at the bottom of the sea in two – three watches. Some will be saved, maybe, but not the men who scoff. I know! I am a Norseman! And my father has told me –

NOBBY: Ow, stow it, Nils! While there's life there's 'ope! If you could only see where that bell comes from! There ain't a thing in sight –

OLLSEN: We shall see it – we shall see it! The ghost ship – a blue flame at her mast-head. Fokke will be on the poop, and the grey men will stare over the side, dead men, dead for centuries. We shall see them before we sink!

BILL (*coming back*): Quit croaking, Nils! We'll have enough to do in a minute without that. Listen to that blinkin' bell! Gawd! Ain't it dark! (*There is a sound like the cracking of an immense whip, and a heavy fluttering.*) Christ! What's that?

NOBBY: The jib's gone! I knew it would – it was old and near perished. (*The* Mate's *voice is heard.*)

MATE: Cut away that jib, some of you men! Lively now!

BILL (*on his feet*): I'll do it. (*They all rise to follow.*) One'll be enough. Come on, Nobby. (Nobby *and* Bill *run forward.* Nils *and* Joe *crouch on the hatch and look forward. The fluttering ceases. Enter* Sam Farquhar, *a dark Scot of powerful build – not gaunt and red like the Scot of tradition, but square and sturdy. Like the others he is dressed only in vest and thin trousers. In his belt is a long sheath-knife, and he carries a Bible.*)

FARQUHAR (*exulting*): They are as the beasts that perish, these men in the fo'c'sle. They play their cards and gamble away their souls in the face of their Maker. Cursed are they, for they sing obscenely in the jaws of death. Fire – eternal fire is their portion, for they laugh as fools do at the word of God. Flee ye therefore while there is yet time. Flee ye, therefore, from the terror of the wrath to come!

JOE: What's the matter, Sam?

FARQUHAR: Have you eyes? God has darkened the face of the waters with His frown. Have you ears? He hath sent a bell upon the deep to call sin-stained seamen to repentance. The peril of the wrath of God is at hand. None on the smitten earth so vile, none so steeped in iniquity as those who go down to the sea in ships. Do I not know? Before grace was given me to turn from evil, none was so vile as I, none so sunk in vice –

JOE: You cert'nly had a gay old time, Sam.

FARQUHAR: Gay! Mine was the gaiety of the devil. I found joy in the tents of Shem – I wallowed in the stews and vile places of the earth. Painted women were my companions. I wasted the light God gave me in the arms of adultresses.

JOE: You didn't ought to say them things, Sam Farquhar. It ain't decent. Is it Nils? (Ollsen *is prostrate on the hatch-cover. He groans and hides his head.*)

FARQUHAR: Repent ye! Repent ye! The hand of God is upon you! (Joe *is bewildered and a little scared at the force of the Scot. The* Mate *returns from the fo'c'sle with* Bill *and* Nobby.)

BILL: Do we 'ave another go at riggin' something, sir?

MATE: Not much good, I'm afraid, Jones. Nothing would stand – we're adrift! Let's hope the engines start soon!

BILL: That jib nipped my knife outa my mitt, an' it went overboard, as clean as a whistle – cuss it!

FARQUHAR: I heard a voice from Heaven –

MATE: You'll hear a voice from the bridge in a minute, my man. Hold your row! (*He goes aft.*)

BILL: What's got ye, Sam?

JOE: He's talkin' like 'Oly Bible, Bill. You shoulda 'eard wot 'e said just now.

FARQUHAR: Besotted in your ignorance – steeped in iniquity, call ye for forgiveness before it is too late. Once I was as you –

BILL: Once you was a damn sight more iniquitous than any here, Sam.

FARQUHAR: My sins are behind me. I have found grace –

BILL: Well, don't make such a row abaht it. Can't you sit down nice and comfortable and talk abaht it quiet-like, 'stead o' standin' there 'owlin'? you'll 'ave the old man down on you in a minute.

FARQUHAR: God moves upon the waters. He sends the storm, he darkens the sky to warn you of his wrath. Turn not a deaf ear and imperil your souls. Listen! You can hear the knell of doom!

BILL: That's a bell allright! (*Soothingly!*) I can 'ear. I can 'ear.

JOE: (*whimpering*): 'E's right! It ain't no 'uman bell! (*There is a hush. The tolling of the bell is heard above the rush of the wind.*)

NOBBY: I wisht I was back in the Mile End Road. I wish I'd never went to sea.

JOE: It ain't right! It ain't right! An' them engines bust!

BILL: I never see such sailormen. I'm ashamed to be on the same ship. I tell you there's a typhoon blowin' up, an' you're all gettin' scared because some *bloody* bell keeps ringin'. There ain't a one of you goin' to be any use when it strikes us, as it may at any minute now. You, Ollsen! Wot are you lyin' groanin' there for? Get up this minute an' see about a lamp! Go an' 'elp 'im, Nobby! I never see such sailormen!

FARQUHAR: Fool! Would you tempt God?

BILL   (*in a sudden rage*): You and your God – ain't you got no better sense than start sky-pilotin' when the men needs all their wits? You, Ollsen – an' you, Nobby – do as I tell you! (Ollsen and Nobby *get up and slouch forward.*)

FARQUHAR: Take heed, Bill Jones! Death is stalking this ship. Repent of your sins, before God's wrath descends on you. You are as a strong tree before the woodman's axe, as corn before the sickle. In the darkness death steals on us –

BILL: Blimme, Sam – if I didn't know you, I'd say you was scared!

FARQUHAR   (*with sudden repression*): I *am* scared, Bill Jones! I am scared for your soul and for the souls of the sinful men about me. Death will take you and them, all unforgiven and unrepentant to the eternal flames. Are you prepared to meet God?

BILL: Are you?

FARQUHAR: By the grace that God has given me, yes.

BILL: Well, all that I can say is, you're blooming lucky – after the life you've led. Let me get through wot's comin' to us an' do my job like a seaman, an' per'aps I'll repent. Now, I ain't got the time for religious argufyin'. I'm leadin' seaman o' the watch on deck, an' I'm goin' to be busy presently. God can wait while a man does his job, surely?

FARQUHAR: Blasphemer! Has death no terrors for you?

BILL: Not more'n usual – not more'n it used to 'ave for you when you 'adnt repented.

FARQUHAR: I was ignorant then. Now I know what waits for the unrepentant.

BILL   (*shortly*): Well, I don't. And wot's more, I don't want to know. I'm goin' to 'ave a look round an' see that all's snug,

as is my duty. An' if you asks me my opinion abaht you
– you've gone dotty. (Bill *goes aft. The bell is coming nearer,
apparently.* Joe *is huddled on the hatch-cover. He begins to
sob, he is merely a boy.*)

JOE: Sam! Sam! That bell's comin' nearer!

FARQUHAR: It is! It is! The flames of hell draw nearer.

JOE: Ow, cheese it, Sam. You don't mean that?

FARQUHAR: I mean it, Joe. Cast your sins upon the throne of grace, and
be saved!

JOE: Wotcher mean, Sam? Wot's the throne of grace?

FARQUHAR: Cast the burden of your sins upon the Lord and he will save
you –

JOE: Yer mean ter say I shan't be drownded?

FARQUHAR: Blessed are they that die in the Lord. Even if death took you,
still you would be saved.

JOE: I wish you'd talk sense, Sam. How could I be saved if I was
dead?

FARQUHAR (*sitting down beside him and talking earnestly*): You'd be
saved from hell fire, Joe. You don't want torment for ever in
hell, do you?

JOE: No blarsted fear! I say, listen to that blurry bell!

FARQUHAR (*almost in a whisper*): It is coming, Joe. It is coming. Repent
of your sins before it is too late.

JOE (*blubbering*): Wotcher do to repent, Sam?

FARQUHAR: Be conscious of the wrong you've done and be sorry for it.

JOE: I am sorry! Gee! I'm scared enough for anythink! I aint never
been in a typhoon before –

FARQUHAR: Are you convicted of sin –

JOE: I ain't never been convicted –

FARQUHAR: Are you – do you know that you've done wrong?

JOE: Blimme, yuss! There was that gal in Sund'land I led wrong
– I didn't meant to do it. It just come over me like– (*Enter
Ollsen *and* Nobby *with the lamp, which they lash to a
bracket on the mast. It burns steadily enough. They sit down
on the hatch-cover beside* Joe *and* Farquhar.)

NOBBY: Listen to that bell! It's gettin' nearer. Gawd! I wisht I'd
never seen the sea!

FARQUHAR: Your time at sea is spent, Nobby Clarke. Death is creeping
over the waters.

NOBBY: There ain't no sight of a ship anywheres. I wisht I knew wot
it came from.

OLLSEN: It is the ghost ship. By and by we see it. Then – then we
sink.

NOBBY (*fiercely*): Well, wotever's comin', let it come quick. That's

	wot I say. I can't stick this 'angin' on.
OLLSEN:	It will come – the ghost ship will come!
FARQUHAR:	God forgive you for an ignorant foreigner, Ollsen. The darkness and the bell are warnings of the peril of the wrath to come. Repent ye! Joe has cast his burden on the Lord, and awaits His coming in the faith.
NOBBY:	Wot's 'e done?
FARQUHAR:	He has repented of his sins.
NOBBY:	Pore little blighter!
FARQUHAR:	And if you are wise, you'll do the same, Nobby Clarke. And you, Nils Ollsen –
NOBBY	(interested): Wotcher 'ave to do, Joey?
JOE:	I dunno. Awsk 'im. It ain't done me no good anyway. I'm still scared – an' I don't care who knows it.
FARQUHAR:	Man is born in sin and he cannot escape from it. Not all those that repent will be saved, for many are pre-destined to destruction. The child in the womb is given to death and torment and the wrath of God is its portion. Some God will save by his grace, when He separates the sheep from the goats – (He rises to his feet and mouths.) Repent ye! Repent ye! Judgement is at hand!
NOBBY:	It ain't a fair gamble, seems to me. Mean to say some are goin' to hell whatever they do?
FARQUHAR:	Aye! Even as the beasts that perish!
NOBBY:	'Streuth! I don't see much fun in getting' religion then.
FARQUHAR:	Who are you to set yourself in judgement on the Almighty? I tell you, Dick Clarke, your only hope in eternity is to throw yourself upon the mercy of your Maker. If it is His will, he will set you on the right hand of the throne. (Bill comes into the glare of the lamp.)
BILL:	Look here, Sam Farquhar. I'm fed up with you and your sermonisin'. I'm leadin' seaman here, an' this is my watch on deck. I'll thank you to step down to the fo'c'sle and clear the decks. Watcher been doin' to young Joe?
FARQUHAR:	I have been trying to save his soul, Bill Jones.
BILL:	Seems to me you've abaht scared him stiff. You get below an' leave the men alone, or you'll answer for it.
FARQUHAR:	I'll answer at the judgement seat, Bill Jones.
BILL:	You'll answer in the lee scuppers if you don't buzz off quick. I'm fed to the teeth with you. Wot with that blinkin' bell an' the heat, an' you, I'm fit to murder you. Git!

(The bell is coming nearer and nearer every minute. It is distinct in the hush that follows Bill's speech. The two men glare at each other)

BILL: Git!

FARQUHAR (*in a choked voice*): Cursed is he that tramples his neighbour's vineyard. You, Bill Jones, hinder me in bringing these men to God. On your head is the guilt. God –

BILL: You take yourself *and* your God down the fo'c'sle, or, by God, I'll kill you– (*The Mate's voice is heard.*)

MATE: Quiet, you men down there!

FARQUHAR (*in a low tense voice*): Ye thwart the purposes of God, Bill Jones – beware the instruments of his vengeance.

(Bill *walks forward to him, threateningly. The Scot's hand steals round to his back, to the haft of his knife. As* Bill *comes round the hatch at him,* Farquhar *draws the knife*)

NOBBY: Look out, Bill! 'E's gone mad! 'E'll knife you.

(*At the warning,* Farquhar *bunches himself and springs at* Bill, *burying the knife in his breast*)

JOE: God A'mighty!

(*In the hush that follows the bell is insistent. Then comes the sound of feet. The* Mate *comes into the lamplight. He is carrying a pistol*)

MATE: Drop that knife, Farquhar, and throw up your hands!

(Farquhar *stares at him stupidly, then down at the body of* Bill, *but does not drop the knife. He raises it*)

THE SKIPPER (*off*): Shoot, Smithers, shoot! He's gone mad!

(Farquhar *moves forward. The* Mate *fires from his side, and the Scot drops on his face. There is a crash of wind and the lamp goes out. The Bell is now almost on the ship*)

NOBBY: Gawd! It's alongside!

(*The* Mate *is seen in the dimness running to the gunwale. The bell is evidently passing the ship. He flashes a torch on to the waters, and there is seen, floating past, a vagrant bell-bouy, on the rusty sides of which is faintly discernible: 'PORT OF LONDON' 346.*)

MATE: It's a bell-buoy, sir. Adrift all the way from London River!

(Joe *begins to laugh hysterically. The light is getting stronger. As the clatter of the bell fades in the distance; the 'rub-a-dub' of the engine is heard*)

THE SKIPPER: Under way, Mr. Smithers. We've been on the fringe of the typhoon. It has missed us.

MATE: On the fringe, yes. On the fringe!

(*He makes a sign towards the bodies of* Bill *and* Farquhar)

CURTAIN

The Old Women

by

Christopher Holland

Preface

The Old Women is one of the key plays in the repertoire of both the French and British Grand Guignol. In the original French language – André de Lorde and Alfred Binet's *Crime dans une maison de fous ou Les Infernales* – it is a paradigm of the French Grand Guignol form and, arguably, one of de Lorde's greatest plays, if not his quintessential masterpiece. It is intriguing to note that, according to Agnès Pierron, *Crime dans une maison de fous* was not performed at rue Chaptal until June 1925, and so the Christopher Holland translation was in fact the world première. Given its status in the

Figure 16. Aubrey Hammond: Poster for *The Old Women*, 1921

Grand Guignol as a whole, staging the première of *The Old Women* can be seen as a major coup for the Little Theatre. However, this came at a price. According to Sybil Thorndike, the audience demanded that 'each new play must be more terrifying than the one before, and we found it impossible to beat a masterpiece like *The Old Women*, which was the best of all' (Sprigge, 1971, 142). This statement reveals how *The Old Women* was a tough act to follow: the zenith of performed horror at the London Grand Guignol (staged, appropriately enough, as part of the fourth of the Little Theatre's eight seasons) after which anything else could only be an anticlimax. It was, however, not merely on aesthetic grounds that things were to go downhill. We have already seen how the Lord Chamberlain was hoodwinked into passing *The Old Women*. Whether it was because anything after *The Old Women* was disappointing – at least for Sybil Thorndike if no one else – or because after being so humiliated the censors would come to watch the Little Theatre like a hawk, the end was in sight for José Levy's experiment and the British Grand Guignol ended less than a year after the staging of this play.

The Old Women is a paradigm of Grand Guignol formula in terms of its location, its narrative and its technical strategies. The action of the play takes place in that favourite location for Grand Guignol drama, a lunatic asylum. The array of characters – from over-rational medics, overzealous nuns and over-the-top lunatics – provides *dramatis personae* ripe for dramatic interpretation. It is interesting to note that Russell Thorndike played the role of the demonic female lunatic La Borgnesse: the cross-gender performance so usually associated with British stage pantomime and comedy (especially in works such as Brandon Thomas's 1892 play *Charley's Aunt*) is here used for the purposes of horror. But the tightrope walk between horror and comedy is never far away in Grand Guignol: the review of *The Old Women* in the *Observer* (never a friend of British Grand Guignol) takes malicious delight in declaring: 'The climax of horror turned – as often happens at the Grand Guignol – into a moment of farce' (3 July 1921).

The characters in the play establish varying degrees of conflict: the ultimately gruesome violence instigated by some of the lunatics is inevitable, but perhaps more compelling is the conflict between the doctors and the nuns. The two sides have little time for each other: the doctors regard the sisters' ethos – some are 'fanatics' – as making them problematic and even mutinous. By the same token, the sisters seem to nurse a disdain for the doctors, most disastrously evident when one of the sisters refuses to stay with Louise despite the Doctor's orders. Louise's tragedy is that she falls in the gap between the two irreconcilable adversaries, science and religion. The dramatic ironies are manifold: the doctors find Louise an interesting case, while the sisters discriminate against her because of her atheistic parents, and prefer to devote their attentions to the dead: 'You know that the dead need our prayers. The dead should come before the living'. Like

Eight O'Clock, the play is critical of religion, and we seem to be firmly in the Grand Guignol's godless universe. The reviewer of the play in the *Era* (6 July 1921) regarded the play as being an example of 'cheap cynicism'. The reviewer complains that the only redeeming feature of this 'crudely written' play is the character of the 'kindly' doctor, until realising that this was merely a ruse that accentuates 'the author's contempt for the religious'.

The play works its suspense brilliantly. It is ominous from the start, and turns the screw of its narrative with foreboding lines and stark symbolism. We saw earlier how *Eight O'Clock* perhaps contains indirect allusions to *Hamlet*; *The Old Women* makes this intertext explicit, with Louise directly compared to Ophelia by the doctor. Technically, the play exploits lighting, with the effective use of lamps and moonlight, and also develops a highly effective offstage world through auditory signals: the audience hears bells and the sounds of the other lunatics, creating a depth of context.

The Old Women

by
Christopher Holland

First Performed: 29 June 1921

Louise
La Borgness
La Normande
La Bossue
Madame Robin
The Sister
Another Sister
The Doctor
The House-Surgeon

ACT I

Scene. A small white-washed room. Three beds, with a little table beside each. Doors right and left. Window to left. A cast-iron stove between second and third beds. A shelf on the wall with a statue of the Virgin. The scene is at St. Leger in Normandy.

At the rise of the curtain the Sister, *seated in a corner, is saying her rosary. A pause. A bell rings at a distance.*

Madame Robin *enters from left.*

MADAME ROBIN:	Sister?
SISTER	(*finishing her beads*): Wait a moment.
MADAME ROBIN:	I beg your pardon, Sister, I beg your pardon. I did not see you were engaged.
SISTER	(*when she has finished telling her beads, kissed her medal, and made the sign of the cross*): Well, what is it?
MADAME ROBIN:	The doctor asked me to let you know that he will be

making his rounds with me in a few minutes.

SISTER: Very well. Thank you. Have the patients left the refectory yet?

MADAME ROBIN: Not yet, Sister. I was not very hungry this evening. I left before the others.

SISTER (*putting on her spectacles*): Bring me my crochet work please. There, on the shelf.

MADAME ROBIN: Very good, Sister. I will make up the beds and get the night-light ready.

SISTER: Mind you put everything tidy. Don't leave anything lying about.

MADAME ROBIN (*arranging the beds and turning back the coverlets*): You needn't tell me that. No one is more particular than I. When I had a little house of my own I used to spend all my time putting things tidy. I enjoyed it. That was a long time ago. La, la!

SISTER (*working*): How long have you been here in the Asylum?

MADAME ROBIN: Forty years. (*reflecting*) Forty years. That was in Doctor Delbec's time. You don't remember him ... he is dead now. The house-surgeon was called M. Bernier ... he's dead too. Then there was a Sister – Sister Felicity she was called – she's dead too – everybody's dead. It's queer when you come to think of it. (*She goes to the shelf and takes out the night-light from the cupboard.*)

SISTER: Why did you stay on here after you were cured? Hadn't you any relatives?

MADAME ROBIN: Oh yes, Sister. But you know when you've been so long in an asylum, you can't get used to being outside. Your relations always look so queerly at you. They're afraid you'll go off your head again. When they know you've been in a madhouse they shrink from you as if you had the plague. So it's happier to return to St. Leger, asking only one thing, to die here. (*noise off left*)

SISTER: What is that?

MADAME ROBIN: It's nothing. It's only that Marie at it again. Ah, I'd like to be this little one.

SISTER: Who do you mean?

MADAME ROBIN (*pointing to the bed nearest the window*): Why, little Louise, who sleeps there. She has better luck than I. She's young. She can still be happy. Is it true, Sister, that she is quite cured, that she's going home soon?

SISTER (*dryly*): So they say.

MADAME ROBIN: Lucky little girl. You know, Sister, she comes of a good family. I know them quite well. I come from their part of the country.

SISTER (*rising and putting her work on the shelf; disdainfully*):
Bah! They've brought up their child in a queer fashion.
You know ...

MADAME ROBIN: Ah!

SISTER: She knows nothing whatever.

MADAME ROBIN: She can read.

SISTER: Yes, she can read, but she knows no prayers. I sometimes
doubt if she even believes in God.

MADAME ROBIN: You mustn't blame her for that, Sister. It's not her fault if
her parents brought her up like that, quite naturally.

SISTER: Without belief in God? You call that naturally!

MADAME ROBIN: Well, Sister. It's a thing you know nothing about – you
learn it from somebody else.

SISTER: She's a very obstinate little girl. She already shows signs
of evil tendencies. Twenty times I have tried to induce her
to go to chapel. But would she go? Not she. And what
sort of conduct can you expect of her when she leaves
here? People who have no religion are like beasts. (*A bell
sounds.*)

MADAME ROBIN (*goes to window*): Ah! They are coming out of the
refectory. Then I'll go. I don't want to meet those two
here.

SISTER: Whom do you mean?

MADAME ROBIN (*pointing to the two beds*): The old hags who sleep here.
Those two old women. La Bossue and La Normande,
wicked old devils.

SISTER: Come, come, Madame Robin.

MADAME ROBIN: I beg your pardon, Sister – that slipped out. But somehow
when I think of them I can't ...

SISTER: What have you against them – two poor mad old women?

MADAME ROBIN: Two very dangerous old women. They're wicked as the
devil himself.

SISTER: They never seem so to me. I have always found them very
obedient and quiet.

MADAME ROBIN: Yes, they put that on with you. Mad people are just like
everybody else. You'll find wicked brutes among them and
you'll find hypocrites among them, who think and scheme
how they can get round you. Don't you trust them. Where
do those two old witches come from?

SISTER: I don't know.

MADAME ROBIN: Is it true what they say? That they went mad from grief at
the loss of their girls?

SISTER: Yes.

MADAME ROBIN: And so they can never look at a girl now without being jealous of her, without wanting to hurt her, as if she were the cause of their trouble.

SISTER: And whom do you think they want to hurt?

MADAME ROBIN: The little girl here.

SISTER: Little Louise?

MADAME ROBIN: Yes. I've noticed a lot of things since I've been doing this dormitory. You know that old woman with one eye who sleeps in the next room the other side of that door?

SISTER: Oh yes, La Borgnesse.

MADAME ROBIN: You can't call *her* a good Catholic anyway. A woman who was condemned to death for killing children; the Ogress they called her.

SISTER: She was out of her mind – mad. The doctors all said so. That is why she was acquitted.

MADAME ROBIN: Well, even so, she's not the sort of person to put in with other patients. She ought to be shut up somewhere else in an asylum for people like her. She's dangerous.

SISTER: She has been paralysed for six years. For six years she has never left her bed. There's nothing to fear from her …

MADAME ROBIN: I'm not so sure.

SISTER: You're too easily frightened. No one can run any danger here. The asylum is too well looked after. There are ten Sisters in the woman's quarters alone.

MADAME ROBIN: Yes, in the day. But at night you leave them alone.

SISTER: That is the rule.

MADAME ROBIN: I know. You tire yourselves out all day and sleep at night.

SISTER: At night we pray. We pray for you.

MADAME ROBIN: That's all very well, but at some asylums they go the rounds at night. You don't here.

SISTER: Nothing has ever happened.

MADAME ROBIN: Not yet perhaps … but … (*noises left and right of the inmates entering the dormitories*) The inmates are coming up to bed.

SISTER: Will you stay here a moment, Madame Robin, and see after them? I must go and tell Sister Placide about the service to-night.

MADAME ROBIN: What service, Sister?

SISTER: Sister Sulpice died this morning. All the community has to watch to-night round the body in the chapel. (*She goes out to left.*)

MADAME ROBIN: Poor Sister Sulpice. She was a real good woman, she was. (*Enter from the right* La Bossue *and* La Normande, *two little shrivelled old women, with cunning, devilish faces.*)

	Here they come. Ugh! I hate them. (La Normande *enters first and looks round, then turning round, says* 'Psst'. La Bossue *enters. They speak in low tones.*)
LA NORMANDE:	Isn't she there yet?
LA BOSSUE:	She must be walking in the courtyard.
LA NORMANDE:	Yes. Let's go and see La Borgnesse.
LA BOSSUE:	She's expecting us.
LA NORMANDE:	We're only waiting for her.
LA BOSSUE:	And when she gives the signal ...
LA NORMANDE:	The death signal!
MADAME ROBIN:	What are you mumbling there, you two? (La Normande *laughs.*) What are you laughing at?
LA NORMANDE:	And he said, 'You're the brat from Cambourcy, aren't you?'
LA BOSSUE:	He'd given a tip to the cemetery-keeper too, but the keeper said, 'It is closed from nine to eight. By my mother's cross ... Be it so then.'
LA NORMANDE:	Amen. (*They cross themselves.*)
MADAME ROBIN	(*shrugs her shoulders and laughs in spite of herself*): The old wretches; one can't help laughing at them sometimes.
LA NORMANDE	(*crosses the room and stops before* Louise's *bed*): Look!
LA BOSSUE:	The head there ...
LA NORMANDE:	The feet there ...
LA BOSSUE	(*laughing*): Ha! Ha!
LA NORMANDE	(*laughing*): Ha! Ha!
MADAME ROBIN:	Have you nearly done there? Why don't you go to bed? Why can't you let that girl alone? What has she done to you?
LA NORMANDE:	There are some things one must not say out loud, you know.
LA BOSSUE:	If one said them out loud they'd bring bad luck.
MADAME ROBIN:	Oh yes, I know all about that. Now look here, if you go on frightening and tormenting her with these monkey tricks of yours ... Oh, I saw you the other day trying to trip her up ... Well, I shall tell the doctor, and he'll put you both into strait-jackets, as he did another day with *you*. (*to* La Normande)
LA NORMANDE	(*frightened*): Curse you, be quiet, can't you? (*She goes off to the left.*)
LA BOSSUE	(*following her*): Toad. Filthy toad. (*goes off to left*)
MADAME ROBIN:	That scares you, doesn't it? Where have they gone? (*She looks through the open door.*) There they are, by La Borgnesse's bed. What can those three have to cackle about! They're looking this way and making horrible

faces ... They'll frighten me before they've done. I wouldn't like to sleep in the same room with them. (Louise *enters; she is a young girl of sixteen, pretty, shy, delicate, fair hair. She sees* Madame Robin *from the threshold.*)

LOUISE: Ah, Madame Robin. I'm so glad to see you. You're still here then?

MADAME ROBIN: I'm waiting for the Sister, she's coming back in a minute. Well, you look happy to-night, little one!

LOUISE: I should think so.

MADAME ROBIN: It's true then that you're leaving here? That you're going quite soon?

LOUISE: I believe so. I'm quite cured.

MADAME ROBIN: You're glad, eh?

LOUISE: Of course. There is only one person here I shall miss, and that's you. You've been so kind.

MADAME ROBIN: Have I? Well, that's the least one can do. And you've been so good and sweet to me. You've never had anything sent you without sharing it with me.

LOUISE: There's so much sadness here, we must try to give each other what happiness we can. (*She looks round.*)

MADAME ROBIN: What is it?

LOUISE: They haven't come up yet?

MADAME ROBIN: Yes. They're in there with La Borgnesse.

LOUISE (*frightened*): Oh!

MADAME ROBIN: What's the matter?

LOUISE: Nothing.

MADAME ROBIN: They're hatching some mischief or other. They're always together.

LOUISE: Yes. Listen, Madame Robin. I can tell *you*. Those three women make me afraid. Whenever I pass them they stare at me, stare at me, especially La Borgnesse. They make me cold all over. I hardly dare cross the dormitory now. What is the matter with them? What have I done?

MADAME ROBIN: Nothing – they're mad – don't take any notice of them.

LOUISE: I can't help it, Madame Robin. They frighten me.

MADAME ROBIN: Why don't you speak to the Sister if it upsets you as much as all that?

LOUISE: She won't listen to me. We don't get on well together.

MADAME ROBIN: About religion, I suppose. Yes, I know. Then why not see the doctor? You can speak to him, can't you? He's so nice and kind.

LOUISE: Yes, but I daren't. You see ...

MADAME ROBIN: Sh! There's Sister. (*They are both silent.*)

SISTER   (*entering by the left – sees* Louise): Ah! It's you. They tell me the doctor says you may leave here soon.

LOUISE: Yes, Sister. I think so.

SISTER: You must see that all your things are in order before you go.

LOUISE: Yes, Sister.

MADAME ROBIN: I'll give you a hand.

LOUISE: Thank you so much.

SISTER   (*to* Louise): I did not see you at chapel yesterday. It was Sunday. How was that? (*silence*) There was no reason, was there? I met the Chaplain just now and he said, 'Sister, there is only one inmate in the whole asylum who has not made her confession – and she is in your charge.' Do you think it's pleasant for me to receive a reproof like that?

LOUISE: No, Sister.

SISTER: You have been very ill. Twice you nearly died.

LOUISE: I know.

SISTER: Next time perhaps you will not escape. And when death comes and knocks at the door, to bear away your soul, you will be afraid, you will want then to make your confession, and perhaps it will be too late.

LOUISE: Don't. Don't.

MADAME ROBIN   (*aside to* Louise): Come, come! Never mind! Sister has to say all that, it's part of her life. Good-night, little one. There, there, it's only a little while now – it will soon be over. Good-night, Sister.

SISTER: Good-night. (*A bell tolls in the distance.*)

MADAME ROBIN   (*as she goes out right*): Listen, there's the bell tolling for poor Sister Sulpice.

LOUISE   (*shivering as she listens to the bell*): Oh, those gloomy mournful bells! (*The* Doctor *enters left with the* House-Surgeon.)

DOCTOR: What is that bell tolling for? Is someone dead?

SISTER: Yes, doctor. Sister Sulpice passed away at eleven o'clock this morning during High Mass. All the community gathered round her bed.

DOCTOR   (*with irony*): And meanwhile what became of the inmates? Who took care of them?

SISTER: We were not away very long.

DOCTOR: I should hope not. Is there anything to report here?

SISTER: No, doctor, everything is quite quiet as usual.

DOCTOR: No fever, nerve storms or attacks?

SISTER: No doctor, nothing at all.

DOCTOR: Good. (*to the* House-Surgeon) Coming Lebrun. (*He is going out.*)

LOUISE: Sister!

SISTER: What is it?

LOUISE: I would like to speak to the doctor, please.

SISTER: He hasn't time.

DOCTOR   (*coming back*): Oh yes, I have, Sister. You want to ask me something, my dear?

LOUISE: Yes, doctor. Yes please.

HOUSE-SURGEON   (*to* Doctor *aside*): A pretty little girl, isn't she?

DOCTOR: Yes. Isn't she?

HOUSE-SURGEON: Reminds me of Ophelia. With her fair hair and pathetic look, doesn't she, Sister?

SISTER   (*dryly*): I don't know.

DOCTOR: Well, come along, my dear, what can I do for you? Sister, do you mind bringing us two chairs? You want to talk about your leaving here, eh? I'm sure that's it.

LOUISE: Yes, doctor.

DOCTOR   (*smiling*): What ingratitude! And why do you want to leave us?

LOUISE: Because I'm cured. You have cured me.

DOCTOR: Yes – I hope so. You certainly look much better. (*to the* House-Surgeon) Her eye is much clearer and brighter isn't it?

HOUSE-SURGEON: The whole face looks more alert and intelligent ...

DOCTOR: You see! I put her down as a melancholic of the Kraeplen type,[1] whilst you ...

HOUSE-SURGEON: Yes. I saw her rather as a case of dementia precox.[2]

DOCTOR: If she had been, she'd never have arrived at the state you see her in now.

HOUSE-SURGEON: There are some cases of recovery.

DOCTOR: Not so complete as this. (*The door opens and a woman's head appears and says to the* Sister *in a low voice.*)

VOICE: Sister. They're putting her in the coffin.

SISTER: Very well. I'll come. (*The* Sister *goes out left. The bell continues in the distance.*)

DOCTOR   (*to* Louise): Then you've had no more of those nightmares, no more of those hallucinations?

---

[1]   This spelling – which is the same in the original de Lorde and Binet script – evidently alludes to Emil Kraepelin (1856–1926), who is sometimes seen as the father of modern psychiatry. He discovered schizophrenia and manic-depression and was the co-discoverer of Alzheimer's Disease.

[2]   This was Kraepelin's early definition of schizophrenia.

LOUISE: I –

DOCTOR: You don't even remember them now? Well, so much the better.

LOUISE: No, doctor, I'm sure I'm quite well now, I feel it. I feel as if I'd come back to life somehow. And I long to get back home.

DOCTOR: I understand ... but we must go carefully. (*to the* House-Surgeon) Where does she come from?

HOUSE-SURGEON: From Fecamp, I think.

LOUISE: Yes, all my relations live down there.

DOCTOR: Were you at home when this trouble came?

LOUISE: No, I was working. I have always worked since I was ten. I was in a situation.

DOCTOR: And your employers noticed that your head had gone wrong, eh?

LOUISE: Yes.

DOCTOR: Do you think they'll take you back again after this?

LOUISE: I don't know.

DOCTOR: Everybody down there will know that you have been at Saint Leger. It is going to be difficult for you to find another place. You see, life is rather hard for people who have been in an asylum.

LOUISE: Yes, I know. It is hard, but still, now I'm cured I can't be kept in an asylum for always. It would be no life at all.

DOCTOR: Surely. But wait here just a little.

LOUISE: Wait?

DOCTOR: Yes. Stay on a little longer. It may not be very exciting here. But that's all the better for you.

LOUISE: Oh! No ...

DOCTOR: Yes, yes. And that will give us time to see what we can do for you.

LOUISE: No. You see I *must* go.

DOCTOR: And where do you mean to go when you leave here? Have you thought at all?

LOUISE: I shall go to Paris.

DOCTOR: To Paris?

LOUISE: It's a big town. I shall always find work there.

DOCTOR: Do you know anyone there?

LOUISE: No. But that doesn't matter. I shall manage somehow.

DOCTOR: I'm afraid you don't understand. Paris. Paris. A pretty girl like you. You'll be lost down there. And you'll have so many trials and disappointments that your trouble would soon reappear. It's impossible.

LOUISE: Doctor!

DOCTOR:	No, no. It's out of the question.
LOUISE:	Then you do not want me to leave?
DOCTOR:	Not immediately. You know you're a very interesting case. I want to keep an eye on you. (*to the* House-Surgeon) You know, you've set me thinking by what you said just now. (*to* Louise) And till we can find a good place for you to go to –
LOUISE:	When?
DOCTOR:	When? Oh, I don't know. Say in a fortnight, a week perhaps.
LOUISE	(*strongly*): I don't want to.
DOCTOR:	Why?
LOUISE:	Another week here! No, I won't! I won't!
DOCTOR:	Come! Come!
LOUISE:	I tell you I don't want to stay here any longer. I want to go away. (*lowering her voice*) I don't want to sleep any more in this room.
DOCTOR	(*struck by her tone*): What's this? Come now, this is a different matter. You've never mentioned this before. (*seeing* Louise *glancing quickly round the room*) Why do you look round there?
LOUISE:	I don't want the Sister to hear.
DOCTOR:	Have you been having trouble with her? (Louise *lowers her head, without replying.*) I'm not surprised. She is a fanatic. What has she been worrying you about? Was it because you have not been to Mass?
LOUISE:	Yes. But it's not that.
DOCTOR:	Well then, what is it … ? You can tell me surely … Now. Just between ourselves … Is it something that has happened here?
LOUISE:	Yes. In this room.
DOCTOR:	When?
LOUISE:	At night. When everybody has gone.
DOCTOR:	How do you mean everybody? There are the other patients.
LOUISE:	Yes, but all the Sisters have gone. Then …
DOCTOR:	Then … Come, you mustn't tremble like that. (*He takes her hand paternally.*) Tell me …
LOUISE:	Oh, I don't know how to tell you. Just to think of it sends my head all funny.
DOCTOR:	Yes, yes. We'll see to all that. Now, quietly …
LOUISE:	Well, when the Sister has gone, the lights are all out, everything seems to change in the dormitory.
DOCTOR:	Why, what changes?

LOUISE: All sorts of things happen that I don't understand. First
– that door there ...

DOCTOR: Well?

LOUISE: The Sister shuts it when she goes out. Last night, in the
middle of the night, I saw it open, at first a little, then
more and then more again – silently, and when I see that
– for I am always watching for it – I say to myself – Now
the door's opening. Now *that's* going to begin ...

DOCTOR: You saw someone open the door?

LOUISE: It opened of itself, and then as if it had been a
signal ... the two old women who sleep there – you know
them?

DOCTOR: Yes – go on.

LOUISE: They got up.

DOCTOR: What? They got up?

LOUISE: Yes. There was no one here to stop them.

DOCTOR: Wait a moment. I had one of the two women, La
Normande, put in a strait-jacket last night.

LOUISE: I know, but the other let her loose.

DOCTOR: But you can't do that without a key.

LOUISE: She *has* a key. She has everything she wants for –

DOCTOR: For ...

LOUISE: Why are you both looking at me like that?

DOCTOR: (*to the* House-Surgeon) I'm afraid she's still suffering
from over-excitement.

HOUSE-SURGEON: It looks like it.

LOUISE: My God! Do you think I'm lying, or that I'm still mad?

DOCTOR: No, no, my child ... Then when they had got up what did
they do?

LOUISE: They came silently up to my bed, and leant over me,
staring at me, as if they meant to do me some harm.

DOCTOR: Some harm?

LOUISE: But they did not dare. They looked round through the
doorway, and shook their heads and said, 'No, no,' as if
they were afraid of something. They seemed to be talking
to somebody. And there *was* somebody there.

DOCTOR: Who was it?

LOUISE: La Borgnesse. She was making signs to them.

DOCTOR: You say it was ...

LOUISE: I knew it was she by the black shade over her eye. She
was making signs.

DOCTOR: But it's impossible.

LOUISE: Doctor, I saw her.

DOCTOR: I tell you it's quite impossible. You may have seen the other two women, they can walk. But the one you call La Borgnesse is paralysed in both legs and completely bedridden. She can neither rise nor stand.

LOUISE: I tell you I saw her, Doctor. She was standing there in the doorway.

DOCTOR: You see, my child, that you are not yet quite cured.

LOUISE: I am. I know I am.

DOCTOR: I'm afraid not, for the things you assert are quite impossible.

LOUISE: I don't know how to convince you, doctor, but I saw her. It wasn't a dream. I was wide awake and I saw her, making signs to the others, and they were afraid and wouldn't do what she wanted. I tell you I saw her.

HOUSE-SURGEON: She has had these hallucinations before.

DOCTOR: I'm afraid that is what it is.

HOUSE-SURGEON: It's quite possible that these fancies ...

DOCTOR: Are the preliminary symptoms of another attack. Poor girl!

LOUISE: No, no doctor. (*to* House-Surgeon) No, sir, I tell you I saw it all.

DOCTOR: Yes, yes, of course. You saw. You think you saw it just as if ... (*aside to* House-Surgeon) I'm sure of it.

HOUSE-SURGEON: So am I.

DOCTOR: Those hallucinations again.

LOUISE: No, no, no, doctor. I'm not mad any more, Doctor. You must see that I'm perfectly well now. I swear I am.

DOCTOR: Now, now. You mustn't distress yourself like this.

LOUISE: I know I'm excited but I'm not mad really. I'm not talking nonsense. (*to* House-Surgeon) That's true, isn't it, sir, I'm not talking nonsense. Do, please, believe me.

DOCTOR (*trying to calm her*) Yes, yes. I believe you. But I'm afraid we must keep you under observation for a few days longer.

LOUISE: A few days! But if that begins again ...

DOCTOR: You must let me know.

LOUISE: But you're not going to leave me here! If you can't send me away at once, at least put me in another room.

DOCTOR: I'm afraid all the beds are full just now.

LOUISE: Oh do.

DOCTOR: Very well, to-morrow you shall change your room, I promise.

LOUISE: But to-night! I'm so afraid! I'm so afraid!

HOUSE-SURGEON: What a state she's in!

DOCTOR: Tonight the Sister shall not leave you.

LOUISE: She won't stay.

DOCTOR: I will give her definite orders.

LOUISE: She will go away.

DOCTOR: We'll see about that.

LOUISE: As soon as you're out, she'll – she'll go away.

DOCTOR: Come now, that will do. If you go on like this we shall know you are not cured, and in that case I shall still have to keep you here for a long time too.

LOUISE: My God! (*The* Sister *enters from the left.*)

DOCTOR   (*calling her*): Sister!

SISTER: Doctor!

DOCTOR: I have been scolding our little friend here for being so unreasonable. She still seems very nervous and full of fears that seem to me quite groundless. But still they are bad for her and I want to spare her unnecessary suffering. To-night you will sit up with her.

SISTER: But doctor ...

DOCTOR: I insist. Your presence will ward off these nightmares.

SISTER: Nightmares are not of very great importance.

DOCTOR: Quite enough to require your attention.

SISTER: If she gets too restless I will give her two spoonfuls of chloral.

DOCTOR: No. I prefer that you should remain with her.

SISTER: That is going to be rather difficult to-night.

DOCTOR: Why?

SISTER: There is a service we have to attend.

DOCTOR: What service?

SISTER: For Sister Sulpice.

DOCTOR: Oh yes. I know.

SISTER: We are to watch by her body all night and sing the office for the dead. All the Sisterhood will be there.

DOCTOR: They must find someone to take your place.

SISTER: That is not possible.

DOCTOR: It is quite possible if you show a little good will.

SISTER: The Mother Superior does not allow any of us to neglect the service of the sanctuary.

DOCTOR: I must point out to you that the claims of humanity are of more importance than the service of the sanctuary.

SISTER: I don't know ... That is a matter of opinion.

DOCTOR: I am surprised that you still hesitate when I tell you that your duty is to remain here.

SISTER: My duty is to obey the Mother Superior.

DOCTOR: Watching the dead is all very well. But surely care for the living should come before it.

SISTER: My duty is to obey the Mother Superior.

DOCTOR: Your first duty is to obey me. The doctor, not the Mother Superior, gives orders in the wards of the asylum. Do you understand?

SISTER: Yes, doctor.

DOCTOR: Very well. I order you to pass the night, the whole night, in this room. Are you going to obey, or not?

SISTER: I am only a servant. My duty is to obey. (*She murmurs a few words under her breath.*)

DOCTOR: What did you say?

SISTER: Nothing, doctor. I have nothing to say.

DOCTOR: (*severely*): Very good. (*to* Louise *affectionately*) There now, you feel reassured I hope? (Louise *does not reply.*) Good-night, my dear – good-night. (*to the* House-Surgeon) Oh these Sisters, these Sisters. They're very worthy people, quiet, earnest and devoted, but when you come up against a question of religion it is almost impossible to do anything with them. It is a sort of organised rebellion against authority.

HOUSE-SURGEON: Why don't you replace this one?

DOCTOR: They're all the same. (*They go out right, followed by the* Sister.)

LOUISE: (*alone, seating herself on her bed*): They wouldn't believe me. (*Crying.*) My God! My God! (*Enter* La Normande *and* La Bossue *from left. They can scarcely be seen, for night is falling. They advance quietly, close to* Louise. *She turns at the noise, frightened and cries out.*)

LOUISE: Ah!

LA NORMANDE: Don't be afraid, my little darling.

LA BOSSUE: You shouldn't cry out before you're hurt.

LA NORMANDE: Wait a little.

LA BOSSUE: Just a little.

LA NORMANDE: The night is long.

LA BOSSUE: Ah, the night is good, very good.

LOUISE: Why do you look at me like that?

LA NORMANDE: We mustn't look at her now.

LA BOSSUE: You're so pretty.

LA NORMANDE: Especially your eyes.

LA BOSSUE: They're not yours, you know.

LA NORMANDE: I know, I know.

LA BOSSUE: The old woman said so. She has an owl inside her.

LA NORMANDE: And one day it will fly away.

LA BOSSUE: (*with a gesture of flying*): Pfft! Pfft!

LOUISE: Go away. Don't come near me. (*calling*) Sister!

La Normande:	It will never be caught again. (*They laugh and approach her again.*)
Sister	(*reappearing at door right. The two old women silently withdraw to their beds*): What's the matter? Who called me? You again?
Louise	(*still very frightened*): Yes, Sister.
Sister:	I don't like people who are always complaining. What is it now?
Louise	(*pointing to the two women*): They are there.
Sister:	Of course they are there, since they sleep in the same room as you. Now get into bed quickly, all three of you. (*She strikes a match and lights the night-light. She glances round the room. There is a noise of voices in the next room.*) Now, now, you in there. (*She takes the night-light, opens the door right and looks into the room.*) Silence there. No more noise. It's time to go sleep. Do you hear? (*The noise subsides gradually, then there is a deep silence. She shuts and locks the door. The two old women prepare for bed.* Louise *remains seated on her bed. The* Sister *puts the night-light back on the shelf and kneels before the Virgin saying, 'Ave Maria gratia plena etc.'* La Normande *and* La Bossue *are heard indistinctly murmuring* 'Ave Maria gratia plena etc. Amen.') Amen. (*She gets up and stands listening. The bell tolls again at a distance. The* Sister *listens, hesitates, then making up her mind she approaches* Louise; *in a soft voice.*) Louise.
Louise:	Sister.
Sister:	Aren't you going to bed, my child?
Louise	(*after a hesitation*): Yes, Sister.
Sister:	You're not afraid any more, are you? I hope not. You see everything is quite quiet. You'll have a good night, won't you?
Louise:	Yes, Sister. (*The bell tolls again.*)
Sister:	Listen. There's the bell calling for me. I must do my duty to the dead.
Louise:	But, Sister –
Sister:	You know I can't stay here. You're not selfish, are you? You've a kind heart, haven't you? You know that the dead need our prayers. The dead should come before the living.
Louise:	But the doctor ...
Sister:	The doctor will know nothing about it if you don't tell him. If you told him you would get me into trouble, and look at the scandal that would cause. You know what the doctor is. He makes such a fuss about everything. He

would report it to the governors. He would want a report, and the Mother Superior doesn't like that at all. And one mustn't do anything to vex her. After all, she is in charge here, isn't she? Do you see what I mean?

LOUISE   (*resigned*) Yes, Sister.

SISTER: Come now. You be reasonable. We'll be good friends, won't we, we two? It's for your good I assure you. I can do a lot to help your going away from here. That's right. I was sure you'd be reasonable. Good-night. (*She goes to the door right as the curtain falls. The bell continues in the distance.*)

ACT II

Scene. The same. It is now late at night. The moon is shining through the window and falls on Louise's *bed. The night-light flickers in the glass on the shelf. Deep silence. A clock in the distance strikes ten.* La Bossue *and* La Normande *begin moving quietly in their beds.*

LA NORMANDE   (*in a low voice*): Psst!

LA BOSSUE: What is it?

LA NORMANDE: Is she asleep?

LA BOSSUE: I think so.

LA NORMANDE: We must be sure.

LA BOSSUE: I'm going to see.

LA NORMANDE: Wait. I think there's someone coming along the corridor.

LA BOSSUE: Is the Sister coming back?

LA NORMANDE: I daresay. (*They lie down again. Another silence. The noise dies away. They sit up again.*) They're not coming here.

LA BOSSUE: No, they're going down the staircase.

LA NORMANDE: So they are. (*a pause*)

LA BOSSUE: Then it is to be to-night?

LA NORMANDE: She says so.

LA BOSSUE: We must obey her ... if we don't ...

LA NORMANDE: She'll do us some mischief.

LA BOSSUE: As she did to the girl.

LA NORMANDE: You haven't forgotten what she asked for?

LA BOSSUE: What was it?

LA NORMANDE: A linen towel.

LA BOSSUE: I haven't got one.

LA NORMANDE: Tear off a piece of the sheet with your teeth.

La Bossue:	That's a good idea. (*A sound of tearing is heard.*)
Louise	(*wakes and sits up*): What's that?
La Bossue:	She's waking.
La Normande:	Quiet! (*A pause. They remain quite still.*)
Louise:	I heard something. I'm sure. It was in here … (*She looks round the room.*)
La Bossue	(*who has pushed the piece of sheet under her pillow*): There it is.
La Normande:	Now let's wait for the signal.
La Bossue:	The signal!
Louise:	They're talking! They're not asleep! (*She cranes her neck to see better.*)
La Bossue:	Look. She's awake.
La Normande:	She's listening. (*They are seated on their beds.*)
Louise:	Why do they keep so still? (*aloud*) What is it? What do you want?
La Normande:	Don't be afraid, little darling.
La Bossue:	It's all right.
La Normande:	Was it the owl's cry that waked her?
La Bossue:	That's the death signal. (*They laugh.*)
Louise:	Be quiet! Oh, it's awful to be here with these madwomen.
La Normande:	You're madder than we are! (*laughing*)
La Bossue:	She thinks she's not mad any more! (*laughing*)
La Normande:	That she's soon to leave the asylum.
La Bossue:	You'll never go out.
La Normande:	If you ever go out, it will be feet foremost. (*They laugh.*)
Louise:	I'm afraid. I'm afraid. I don't want to stay here all alone. I don't want to …
La Normande:	You are not all alone.
La Bossue:	We're both here. (*They rise*)
Louise:	Leave me alone. Leave me alone. Leave … (*At this moment a sort of long whistle is heard from the room on the left. Louise stops. The two old women remain motionless.*)
La Normande:	Be quiet. It is she.
La Bossue:	Make no noise. She'll hear you.
La Normande:	If she hears you she'll be angry.
La Bossue:	If she's angry look out for yourself.
La Normande:	Yes, look out for yourself.
La Bossue	(*as at prayer*) Miserere.
La Normande:	Miserere nobis.
La Bossue:	When you go out –
La Normande:	You'll go feet foremost.
La Bossue	(*pointing to the door left*): She's coming! Look!

LOUISE (*who is standing glued to the window*): The door is opening of itself. Help! Help! (La Borgnesse *has entered by the door on the left. She shuts the door silently.*)

LA BORGNESSE: Bossue, bring the light here.

LA BOSSUE: Good.

LA BORGNESSE: It's too dark.

LA BOSSUE (*bringing the night-light and lighting up* Louise): Here it is.

LA NORMANDE: She holds her well.

LA BOSSUE: Yes. Yes. Doesn't she?

LA NORMANDE: What is she going to do?

LA BOSSUE: She knows. She knows.

LA BORGNESSE: Normande, have you the linen?

LA NORMANDE: Here it is.

LA BORGNESSE (*to* La Normande): Hold her hands. Have you a large needle?

LA BOSSUE: A needle?

LA NORMANDE: I know, the Sister's needle.

LA BOSSUE (*going to fetch it*): Oh yes, on the shelf.

LA NORMANDE: Before the Virgin.

LA BOSSUE: Here it is.

LA BORGNESSE: I can't see properly.

LA NORMANDE: You want more light.

LA BORGNESSE: Bring the night-light nearer.

LA BOSSUE: Will that do?

LA BORGNESSE: Nearer. (La Bossue *brings the light quite close.*)

LA NORMANDE: You'd think she was dead. She looks dead.

LA BORGNESSE: No. I have only squeezed her neck a little. She'll soon come round.

LOUISE (*struggling*): Ah!

LA BORGNESSE: What did I tell you?

LOUISE: Where am I?

LA BORGNESSE: Don't struggle so.

LOUISE (*seeing them*): Ah. What are you going to do to me?

LA BORGNESSE: Don't cry so. I'm not going to do anything to you. It's those two there.

LA BOSSUE: Ha! Ha! (*laughing*)

LA NORMANDE: Ha! Ha! (*laughing*)

LA BORGNESSE: Quiet! Listen, little one. We're going to do you a service. You've been mad, haven't you? Do you remember?

LA NORMANDE: Of course she does.

LA BOSSUE: She remembers.

LA BORGNESSE: While you were mad an animal took possession of you – an owl. It is still within you. There! If you cry out I shall have to squeeze your neck again. Now listen while I explain. I am going to drive the owl away.

LOUISE: No. Mercy! Mercy!

LA BORGNESSE: Don't you understand?

LOUISE: I beg of you ... !

LA BORGNESSE: It is for your good.

LOUISE: Mercy! You'll kill me.

LA BORGNESSE: This won't kill you.

LOUISE: Help! Help!

LA BORGNESSE: Will you be quiet? We must be quick. She mustn't cry out any more.

LOUISE: Ah!

LA BORGNESSE: Keep still! It will soon be over. I know where they are, but it's not so easy to find them now. (*She stabs her.*) Ah! There it is. It is warm. It is good. Just like the children long ago. (*There is a noise of footsteps off to the right.*)

LA BORGNESSE: Hush!

LA NORMANDE: Listen!

LA BOSSUE: Someone's coming. (La Borgnesse *puts out the light. The room is plunged in darkness. The moon only lights up the body of* Louise.)

LA NORMANDE: Look out. (*They stoop down and hide behind the beds. A pause. Footsteps and a voice.*)

A SISTER (*off*): I tell you, Sister, I'm sure I heard a noise. (*She enters.*) What's the matter? Did anyone call? (*She stops on the threshold. A pause.*)

SISTER: You must have been mistaken.

A SISTER: Everything seems quite quiet.

SISTER: Come on then. It's all right. You know the Mother Superior does not like us to leave the chapel. (*An Alleluiah sung very sweetly by women's voices is heard in the distance.*)

A SISTER: Yes, I was mistaken. You're quite right, Sister. Let us get back to the chapel.

(*They go out as the curtain falls slowly*)

CURTAIN

The Nutcracker Suite

by

Eliot Crawshay-Williams

Preface

When *The Nutcracker Suite* was submitted to the Lord Chamberlain's Office in late February 1922, Eliot Crawshay-Williams was already an established writer at London's Grand Guignol, having enjoyed critical success with other plays, most notably the comedy *E. & O. E.* in the previous year. This was in fact Crawshay-Williams's fifth play for Levy in less than a year and he had become a regular feature at the Little Theatre. It was not received with any great enthusiasm by the censor – Street described it as an 'unpleasant play', but conceded that it was 'less horrible than others passed at this theatre' (Reader's Report, 25 February

Figure 17. Rosalie (Sybil Thorndike) and Max (Ian Fleming) in *The Nutcracker Suite*, 1922

1922), and it was, therefore, passed without amendments on 2 March and was scheduled to be part of the penultimate Seventh Series which opened on 3 April.[1] Although the play does involve marital infidelity (and there are times when the Lord Chamberlain might have objected to that), it is clear that the character of Rosalie, played by Sybil Thorndike, is trapped in an abusive marriage. Furthermore, Rosalie and Max's affair is hardly endorsed, since they come to a sticky end at the hands of the cuckolded bully, Nicolas.[2]

The Nutcracker Suite is unusual in the repertoire of the London Grand Guignol in that it potentially makes great technical demands upon the production team – a descending ceiling is no mean feat. This is perhaps what Crawshay-Williams had in mind when he wrote to Levy as early as 10 May 1921 stating, 'I should like your opinion about an idea I have, which involves some novelties in scenery and lighting which, I think, would be quite simple, and yet produce a new "thrill"! But I'm not sure that the plot would get past the censor …' By the time he came to write the script, however (presumably after his discussions with Levy), the issue of the descending ceiling had been resolved in a way that is technically simple – the ceiling is represented by the curtain which slowly descends upon the stage. This also has the effect of ensuring that all violence takes place behind the curtain and is invisible to the audience – something that would certainly have reassured the Lord Chamberlain.

In relieving the technical designer of a problem, however, it transfers the responsibility to the actor. It takes a performance of great accuracy and timing to keep exact pace with the descending curtain in anything like a believable manner. It is a clear example of Levy making use of the extraordinary talents of his company of actors in order to meet the demands of the form and to compensate for the restrictions imposed by the Lord Chamberlain.

When Crawshay-Williams wrote to Levy on 10 May 1921, he was principally thanking Levy for tickets to see the Third Series. A fortnight earlier Levy had written to Crawshay-Williams informing him that *Rounding the Triangle* had finally been licensed and that it was to be included in the next series (with *The Old Women* and *Latitude 15° South*). Crawshay-Williams was understandably enthusiastic about the project and heaped

---

[1]   In the published version of the play, however, it states that the play was first performed at the Little Theatre on 22 May 1922. This would seem unlikely, as the series itself ended on 27 May, and we can assume that the earlier date is the correct one.

[2]   Crawshay-Williams himself was no stranger to illicit love affairs. He was forced to resign as Liberal MP for Leicester in 1911 after being named in the divorce proceedings of a fellow MP. He later went on to marry his lover. Writing was very much his third career (after politics and a spell as an officer in the First World War).

praise upon Levy and the show he had just seen, which he undoubtedly considered as innovative:

> Your staging and effects are so much ahead of other places, apart from the programme itself. And there wasn't a dull moment in the whole programme. It is very plain that you have come to stay.

Crawshay-Williams could not have been more wrong, of course. Just as he was about to make his debut at the Little Theatre, Levy's Grand Guignol experiment had little more than a year left to run, and with its demise went a useful source of income for the writer.

Crawshay-Williams's play obviously owes a great deal to Wilkie Collins's 1852 short story 'A Terribly Strange Bed', a classic of horror fiction, in which a victim is crushed to death in a deviously designed four-poster bed. This diabolical invention can be found elsewhere in fiction, including in Joseph Conrad's 'The Inn of the Two Witches: A Find' (1913), a particularly Grand Guinolesque tale of two terrifying landladies who kill unfortunate travellers in a similarly lethal four-poster bed.[3] As well as reoccurring in fiction, the gruesome inventiveness of this horror story lends itself supremely well to radio interpretation and there have been numerous versions of 'A Terribly Strange Bed' over the years. The classic BBC horror drama series *Appointment with Fear* broadcast a radio version of *The Nutcracker Suite* on 26 March 1946. The play was adapted by J. Leslie Dodd and follows Crawshay-Williams's original very loyally, maintaining the same characters (including their names and their precise ages). The thirty-minute radio form obliges a streamlining of the script, and it is not surprising that the 'dumb but not deaf' Balthazar is omitted. Even a radio adaptation can possibly throw light on aspects of Grand Guignol practice: J. Leslie Dodd's adaptation of the play locates a key moment – when Rosalie notices the ceiling move – as a point when the pace of performance should accelerate, as the following note in the BBC script emphasises:

> *From this point the tempo of the production should be quickened. Rosalie's voice should adopt a harsh, strained tone, and everything possible should be done to instil into the listeners a sense of impending horror.*

Interestingly, the role of Nicholas in the original stage version was played by Franklin Dyall, the father of Valentine Dyall who would become 'The

---

[3]   Although the literary antecedent seems clear, Conrad insisted that he had never read the Collins story and based his short story on a true incident of a mechanical bed that was found in an inn on the highway between Naples and Rome in the eighteenth century.

Man in Black', the host synonymous with *Appointment with Fear*. On a couple of occasions in the 1940s, when Valentine Dyall was unable to play 'The Man in Black', he was actually replaced by his father: one likes to think that apart from 'keeping it in the family', Franklin Dyall's experience in a play such as *The Nutcracker Suite* at the London Grand Guignol equipped him most suitably to play the role of British radio's greatest horror host.

The text of *The Nutcracker Suite* by Eliot Crawshay-Williams is published by permission of Samuel French Ltd on behalf of the Estate of Eliot Crawshay-Williams.

The Nutcracker Suite

by
Eliot Crawshay-Williams

First Performed: 3 April 1922

Rosalie (aged 26)
Max (aged 30)
Nicolas (aged 40)
Marie (aged 19)
Balthazar (aged 70)

Scene 1

Rosalie *and* Max *are in a small boudoir-sitting room in the chateau of* Rosalie's *husband,* Nicolas. *The room is furnished in a light and intimate style – couch, easy-chairs, and curtains, all upholstered in a flowered cretonne; a few small tables and chairs; and a piano. At the back is a large window looking over a park. Left and right are doors – one leading into a main passage, one into a back passage. A fireplace is between the right door and the audience. The piano is at the back, on the left.* Rosalie, *who is in a tea-gown, is just finishing playing a number from Tschaikowski's 'Casse Noisette' suite.* Max, *in ordinary country day clothes, is sitting in an easy-chair, half-listening, half-reading a book.* Rosalie *is a charming young woman of twenty-six;* Max *a good-looking man of thirty.*

MAX   (*as* Rosalie *ends; getting up and going over to her*):
Thank you, darling. I do love that 'Casse Noisette' music, Tschaikowski never did anything better than his 'Nutcracker Suite'; not even in an opera.

ROSALIE   (*turning to him*): Yes, it's perfect, isn't it? I'm so glad you gave it to me. (*with a smile*) And I'm getting to play it better, too, aren't I?

MAX: You play it beautifully, Rosalie. (*He puts his hand on her shoulder.*)

ROSALIE: Already! And by the time we're – we're together – (*She is looking up at him, and at this point he stops her saying any more by bending down and kissing her on the lips. The kiss, however, is rudely interrupted by the sudden and unceremonious entry of* Marie, *a pretty minx-like servant girl, of about nineteen, who comes in without knocking, through the door on the other side of the stage.*)

MARIE   (*stopping at the sight of the lovers*): Oh! (*then impetuously*) Madame! Madame! The Master!

ROSALIE   (*jumping up*): What?

MARIE: He's here – coming up the drive! (Rosalie *and* Max *rush to the window, and look out.*)

ROSALIE   (*in panic*): Good God! – Yes. There he is. But – he should be still in Paris! (*to* Max) Max! – go. (*hustling him*) Go – quick! Marie, fetch his things. (Marie *runs out.*) You must get out the back way. (*stamping*) Oh! Where is that girl?

MAX   (*upset but with more composure than* Rosalie; *putting his arm round her soothingly*): It's all right, darling. There's plenty of time.

ROSALIE   (*tearfully*): Oh, there isn't! We shall be caught! Why has he come back? (*throwing her arms round* Max) And I can't let you go, my own darling.

MAX   (*kissing her*): You must, darling. It's only for a little, you know; in a month– (*He is interrupted by* Marie's *breathless return with his hat, coat and stick.*)

ROSALIE   (*snatching them from* Marie): Thank you, Marie. You may go. (Marie *goes out. Dressing* Max.) There! now, quick! Be off!

MAX   (*kissing her*): Good-bye, my Rosalie – for a little.

NICOLAS: For a very little. Good-bye. (*She hurries him out through the door on the left. Then she sinks into a chair, disordered and panting. There is the sound of a door slamming outside on the right.* Rosalie *starts, pulls herself together, and after a moment's bewildered hesitation, goes to the piano, sits down, and starts playing the 'Casse Noisette' suite again. Before she has played more than a few bars the door opens and* Nicolas *comes in. At the sound of his entry* Rosalie *gives a start, partly feigned, partly genuine, and turns quickly round.*) Nicolas! (Nicolas *is a handsome but somewhat grim man of forty. A tyrant; ardent in his passions; primitive in his nature. There is an air of dominance about him. He has day clothes on, with an overcoat, and his hat is in his hand.*)

NICOLAS   (*standing in the doorway*): Yes, it's me. (*after a little pause*) You don't seem very pleased at the surprise.

ROSALIE   (*jumping up and coming to him, as he enters and shuts the door behind him*): Oh, my dear, don't be foolish. (*She is palpably nervous – on edge.*) Why – why, you gave me such a start, coming in like that. Of course I'm glad. Ever so glad. (*Mustering up her delight she puts her hands on his shoulders and kisses his cheek.*)

NICOLAS   (*brusquely*): Thanks! (*He takes off his coat and throws it on to the back of a chair, putting his hat on the seat.*) You'll forgive my coming straight in like this, won't you? (*with a curious touch of sarcastic bitterness*) I couldn't wait.

ROSALIE   (*uncertainly*): Because you – you wanted to get back to me so?

NICOLAS   (*laughing*): What else? You know I always want to get back to you. More, sometimes, I think, than you want me to get back.

ROSALIE   (*with an effort at a laugh*): Don't be silly, Nick. Why are you so horrid to-day? Sit down and be good.

NICOLAS   (*wandering over to the piano*): And how have you been amusing yourself at this time while I've been away? Been practising, like a good little girl?

ROSALIE   (*following him*): Yes, dear. Quite a lot. I was playing when you came in.

NICOLAS: So I heard. (*taking the open music off the piano-rack*) What's this? (*closing it to see, and reading*) Tschaikowski! The Nutcracker Suite! I'm not a musical man – like some of your friends; but you're becoming quite ambitious, aren't you?

ROSALIE   (*tremulously*): Yes, aren't I? (*stretching out for the music*) Give it me a minute, I want to show you –

NICOLAS   (*withdrawing it, as she tries to get it*): Wait a moment. (*Looking closer.*) What's this? (*reading*) 'My Favourite'!

ROSALIE   (*feverishly*): Yes – it is my favourite. I like it best of –

NICOLAS   (*interrupting*): This isn't your handwriting.

ROSALIE: No – no. it isn't my handwriting.

NICOLAS: Whose is it?

ROSALIE: It's-it's Max's. He gave it me, you know.

NICOLAS   (*scowling*): Max? Has that fellow been here while I've been away.

ROSALIE   (*very quickly*): Oh no! He gave it to me months ago. (*continuing rapidly, partly to avoid further questions, partly to make a counter attack*) And surely there's nothing wrong in his giving me a bit of music?

NICOLAS   (*disregarding*): You've never played it to me before.

ROSALIE: Oh no – it takes a lot of learning.

NICOLAS: You've never practised it before I went away this time.

ROSALIE   (*desperate*): Oh yes, I have, when you haven't been about. I – I wanted it to be a little surprise for you.

NICOLAS   (*grimly; putting down the music and turning away*): It has been a little surprise for me – in a way.

ROSALIE   (*passionately*): Oh, Nick, what's the matter? Why are you so unkind, so cold? You-you don't mind my knowing Max, do you? You don't mind my taking that piece of music?

NICOLAS   (*still with a curious tinge of sarcasm*): Oh no, Rosalie; of course not. It's your favourite, isn't it? The 'Nutcracker Suite'. And his, too.

ROSALIE   (*tearfully*): Oh – if you're going to be so beastly, I – I'll go. (*She goes towards the door.*)

NICOLAS   (*after a moment's hesitation; assuming a kindlier air, and going over to her*): Forgive me if I've been harsh. I'm a queer chap, you know. (*getting back to his old mood; with a curious laugh*) A queer chap, Rosalie. Occasionally I have queer fancies!

ROSALIE   (*tremulously*): You – you frighten me. Sometimes I think you're – almost mad.

NICOLAS: Oh no! Just queer. Fantastic, perhaps. A fellow with queer fads: queer whims. I've always been like that. You mustn't mind. My queer fancies are usually harmless. There's no need to mind them – unless – (*he looks at her*) – unless – (*he laughs*) – well, unless there might happen to be any reason why one should! Then perhaps their queerness might be – (*he snarls*) – unpleasant.

ROSALIE   (*frightened*): Nicolas! What –

NICOLAS   (*interrupting, and again adopting a more gentle tone*): But there, I'm frightening you. And I don't want to do that. Forgive me. I'm tired. And a bit worried.

ROSALIE   (*looking at him steadfastly*): Not about anything much, dear?

NICOLAS: Oh no – not about anything much. (*He pauses, looking at her, for a couple of seconds; then bends and kisses her almost violently.*) Now, run away and dress for dinner.

ROSALIE   (*reassured*): All right, darling. I'm glad it's nothing much. You'll be all right when you've had something to eat and drink. (*She goes out through the door on the right. Left alone, Nicolas wanders over to the piano.*)

NICOLAS   (*taking up the music of the 'Casse Noisette' Suite; to himself in a tone of infinite irony*): Nothing much! (*bitterly*) No – she's nothing much. (*He crosses to the bell-push and presses* it. *then he goes over to a chair and sits down, waiting moodily. In a few moments* Marie *enters.*)

MARIE   (*standing at the open door*): Did you ring, sir?

NICOLAS: Yes, Marie. Come in! And shut the door. (Marie *comes in, a trifle nervously; shuts the door, and stands by it.*) Come over here and stand by the table. (Marie *comes timidly over and stands a few feet away from him. Looking at her intently.*) Now, Marie, I want to know what's been going on in this house while I've been away.

MARIE   (*with the air of utmost surprise*): What's been going on, sir? (*after a very slight pause*) Oh, the usual things, sir.

NICOLAS   (*with a faint smile, half to himself*): The usual things! (*to* Marie) I mean, not merely when I've been away this time, but all the other times I've been away. What's been happening?

MARIE   (*fidgeting a little*): Well-sir-just the usual things; the place has been very quiet. There've been one or two callers –

NICOLAS   (*interrupting*): Now, Marie, you know exactly what I mean. You must know. And there's no harm in telling you, *I* know. I've heard. I only want to know a little more. A little more in detail. I want you to tell me what, exactly, has been happening these times when I've been away.

MARIE   (*still obdurate*): I'm sure I don't know what you mean, sir.

NICOLAS   (*with a touch of anger*): You do know what I mean. I suppose you've been bribed by my wife and this – this fellow. (*resuming persuasion, as the girl looks frightened*) Now look here, Marie, what's the good of trying to pretend. You do know – all abut it. And if you've been given anything – from time to time – by your mistress or – or anyone else, I'll give you twice as much to be perfectly frank with me – and keep your mouth shut afterwards.

MARIE   (*unpersuaded but not quite so firm*): I – I'm sure I don't know anything, sir – I haven't been given anything.

NICOLAS   (*trying another tack*): Look here, Marie, how long have you been in my service?

MARIE: Nearly six years, sir.

NICOLAS: Do you remember how you came into my service – when you were thirteen?

MARIE   (*shuddering*): Yes, sir.

NICOLAS: I took you from – from unutterable horrors, unmentionable dangers, and gave you a home.

MARIE   (*shaken*): Yes, sir.

NICOLAS: And now – do you think it fair – kind – to be false to me?

MARIE   (*miserably*): N-no, sir. (*half-heartedly*) I'm not being false to you, sir.

NICOLAS   (*playing his last card*): Marie, come here. (*He beckons to her.*)

MARIE   (*coming reluctantly up to him and standing within a couple of feet of him, as he sits in his chair*): Yes, sir?

NICOLAS   (*putting his arm round her and drawing her to sit on his knee*): Do you know why I took you away to come and live here?

MARIE   (*much embarrassed, but liking it; for in truth, her early surroundings might not have suited her so badly in the end*): No, sir.

NICOLAS: Because you were so pretty. (*He draws her closer to him. She makes a panting, half-hearted attempt to shrink away, and then gives in. Going on.*) And I've watched you ever since growing prettier and prettier – more and more lovely. (*She hangs her head; and he cuddles it to his shoulder.*) You see, Marie, I'm telling *you* everything. And if – if my wife has had her passions, don't think I haven't had mine. But I've controlled them. I've stamped them down. I've been – been what the world calls honourable. Now I know that she hasn't been honourable. And so – well, Marie, things are different, now. (*Marie gives a start and raises her head.* Nicolas *presses it down again, and goes on.*) Now, wait a minute. Don't jump to conclusions. I know you're a decent girl. And after what I've told you, you ought to know I'm a decent man. I'm not suggesting that I should – should do as she's done. (*He waits, but* Marie *remains mute.*) I'm not suggesting you should become my mistress, as she's become the mistress of another man. No, I swear that. With you, I know, it must be all – or nothing. And it *shall* be all or nothing.

MARIE   (*starting up*): What do you mean?

NICOLAS: If my wife – (*breaking off*) – since my wife is false – well, that's an end to it.

MARIE: To what?

NICOLAS: To our marriage.

MARIE   (*breathlessly*): Yes?

NICOLAS: And then – well, I don't think life alone would appeal to me. Life alone, here, in the country, with few friends – no real friends. I'm a lonely sort of fellow, Marie; and yet, I need company, affection, love. I'd have to marry again.

MARIE   (*incredulous*): You'd marry *me*?

NICOLAS: Why not?

MARIE: But – but I'm a servant.

NICOLAS: You're beautiful, you're sweet, you're some one I love. You would love me, you would look after me – this place – better than some senseless ninny from Paris.

MARIE   (*half aloud*): Look after you! – This place!

NICOLAS: But there – what's the use of talking. If my wife hasn't been untrue to me – and you must know if she has – why, then, we go on. Go on as we were.

MARIE   (*starting up, and jumping off his knee*): She *has* been untrue.

NICOLAS   (*almost involuntarily; with a triumphant smile*): Ah!

MARIE   (*going on excitedly, and unheeding*): For months – nearly a year. Always, when you went away, he used to come here –

NICOLAS   (*interrupting*): He? Mr. Max –

MARIE   (*cutting in and going on rapidly*): Yes – of course. At first he just came to call, or for a walk. Then he used to spend the whole day here.

NICOLAS: Here? In here?

MARIE: Yes, in here. With her. I used to have to keep every one away. And then, just lately, he's slept here.

NICOLAS   (*violently*): Slept here?

MARIE: I used to let him in through the back door, when every one else had gone to bed, and let him out again early in the morning. (Nicolas *gets up and goes over to the fireplace*; Marie *still stands in the middle of the floor, declaiming her confession.*) And now – they're going to run away together.   •

NICOLAS   (*turning quickly*): Run away? When?

MARIE: In a month.

NICOLAS: Where?

MARIE: Oh – far away. I don't know. She hasn't told me. But the first night they're going to sleep at a little inn, up in the hills, where no one will think of looking for them, and no one will give them away. You see, it's kept by a cousin of mine. They –

NICOLAS   (*suddenly interrupting her in a strange voice*): Be quiet a minute! (Marie *stands silent*, Nicolas *turns, folds his arms, rests them on the mantelpiece, and sinks his head upon them. He remains perhaps thirty seconds in silence, presumably in thought. Then he turns again and looks at Marie. The girl is still standing there, breathless and excited; but motionless. In a controlled and even voice.*) That inn is kept by your cousin, you say, Marie?

MARIE: Yes – sir.

NICOLAS   (*with a peculiar smile*): You needn't call me 'sir' now – when we're alone. Do you think your cousin could take a holiday for a few weeks?

MARIE: What do you mean, s–? (*She stops the 'sir' half-way.*)

NICOLAS: I mean, if I made it worth your cousin's while, could she go away from her inn for, say, a month – with whatever servants she has, and let me take it over? And ask no questions, before or afterwards?

MARIE   (*seeing light*): Oh! I – I don't know. (*in trepidation*) You, you don't mean to –

NICOLAS   (*cutting in*): Never mind what I mean to do, Marie. All that matters to you, or to me, is that my wife and her lover are going to go far away – very far away. Right out of *our* lives, at all events. I promise you that. And that – *that*, Marie (*coming over to her and putting his arm around her*), is what matters to us. Isn't it? (*He draws her to him, and stands looking down into her eyes.*)

MARIE   (*half mesmerized*): I – I don't know. What are you going to do?

NICOLAS: Nothing that you need trouble about, Marie. But you must help me. Help me to do justice. Help me – clear the way – for us. Will you?

MARIE   (*in a low voice*): What do you want me to do?

NICOLAS: I want you first to go to your cousin and tell her that a wealthy gentleman has a sudden fancy to run her inn for a few weeks. You can tell what tale you like. You might say I – I want to run away with someone's wife, if you like. (*He laughs, unmirthfully.*) But what you *can* say is that she shall be given ten times as much each week as she has ever made in a week in her life. And what you *must* say is, that she is to swear never to ask, or answer any questions, or make any inquiries. She must swear that. And if she breaks her oath – well, you know what that will mean to you – to us.

MARIE   (*very low*): Yes.

NICOLAS: Will you do that? Can you do that?

MARIE: Yes.

NICOLAS: Very well. Go to-morrow. And now – we go back to the old world – the world of half an hour ago. And keep our secrets till we can reach the world of – a month to come! (*He lets her loose. She stands looking at him, her hands on his arms.*)

MARIE.   And you do love me? You will marry me? (Nicolas *does not answer, but suddenly takes her in his arms and passionately kisses her lips. Then he sets her free, and she walks slowly and unsteadily to the door, looking downward, one hand to her forehead, as if half dazed. Nicolas watches her go out. Then he breathes a deep sigh, walks quickly over to the fireplace, spits into it, and wipes his mouth violently on his hand, with an air of disgust. Next he crosses to the piano, takes up the 'Casse Noisette' music, and holds it in front*

of him, looking at Max's *writing on it. He appears to find
something humorous in the sight, for he smiles evilly.*)

NICOLAS   (*chuckling to himself*): A queer fancy! A very queer fancy!

The CURTAIN *falls*

Scene 2

A sitting-room at the inn in the hills.

*The room is a curious one for such a small and primitive
place. It is daintily furnished with the flimsiest of furniture.
The most part is wicker, and what wood there is, is of a fragile
description. The room is on the ground floor, and at the back
is a window, across which is a lattice-work of iron bars. There
are two doors, the one on the left into a passage, the one on
the right into a bedroom. The walls are clean, and distempered
in a light shade of green. Along their top is painted a frieze of
squirrels cracking nuts. Over each door are painted two pairs
of nutcrackers, sideways, their handles outwards, with, over
the centre, where they meet, in each case one huge nut. When
the curtain goes up there is no one in the room; but almost
immediately* Balthazar *enters through the left door, conducting*
Rosalie *and* Max.

Balthazar *is an aged man with toothless gums and a bald head.
He stoops as he walks, and his voice is quavering and almost
falsetto. He is afflicted with a dry, husky cough. His laughter
is a cackle. He is dumb; but not deaf.*

Rosalie *and* Max *are in travelling dress.* Balthazar *is carrying
a suit-case and a dressing-case, which he places on the floor,
after entering; standing by them in silence. There is something
horrible about* Balthazar – *about the whole place, despite its
delicate decoration.*

It is evening; but still daylight.

ROSALIE   (*looking round*): What a charming little room! (*to* Balthazar)
Why, however–? (*breaking off*) Oh, I forgot, he's dumb.
(*to* Balthazar) You can take those things into the bedroom.
We'll come and look at it in a moment. (Balthazar *takes the
two cases in silence, and goes into the bedroom. To* Max,
who has been looking round.) Oh, Max, there's something
horrible about that old man. He's so grim; so glum! And he

hears all you say, and can never say a word back.

MAX: Poor old chap; it's not his fault he's dumb. And he seems very obliging.

ROSALIE (*continuing*): And he's the only living soul we've seen here, in this great gloomy place. Oh, Max (*going to him*), I'm frightened.

MAX (*putting his arm round her*): There's no need to be frightened, darling. You're only a little overwrought with the strain of our escaping. And, really, I think you're unfair about the place. You can scarcely call this room gloomy!

ROSALIE: No. This room's bright enough. But the rest of the place! The grey building! The great dark rooms! The long dank passages! And even in the very brightness of this room there's something uncanny.

MAX: It *is* queer to find a quaint little place like this in such a wild spot. Like a jewel set in iron. We'll ask the old man how it came about. He can write a little, you know, even if he is dumb; and help out with signs. (*going to the door*) Hi! (Balthazar *comes to the bedroom door and stands there, silent.*) Balthazar, this place looks newly done up. (Balthazar *slowly nods his head.*) Can you tell me why? (Balthazar *fumbles in his pocket, and eventually finds the stump of a pencil and a grubby piece of paper. Holding these in his shaking hands he goes over to the table, and leaning over it, begins clumsily to write.* Max *and* Rosalie *come round and stand by him, looking over him.*)

ROSALIE: What's he writing? P ... – p-a-i-n. Pain? No, he's going on. (*with enlightenment*) Painter! A painter stayed here and decorated the walls? Is that it, Balthazar? (Balthazar *nods; and then goes on writing.*) He's going on. Look. Max! M-u-s-i-c. Music! What does he mean? (*to Balthazar*) The painter was a musician, too? (Balthazar *shakes his head, and slowly waves his arm round to indicate the frieze and the signs over the door.* Rosalie *and* Max *follow with their eyes.*) Oh look! Squirrels! And nuts. And nutcrackers!

MAX: H'm! Thought they were skulls and crossbones at first. (Balthazar *quietly cackles to himself.*)

ROSALIE: Oh, don't be so creepy, Max. It's all delightful and delicate. (*with revelation*) The Nutcracker Suite, don't you see? Isn't that just too nice for words! This is 'The Nutcracker Suite'! That painter was a real artist – and a humorist. (*to Balthazar*) That's it, Balthazar, isn't it? 'The Nutcracker Suite'? (Balthazar *nods, folds up the paper, and puts it and the pencil away in his pocket.*)

MAX   (*kissing her, as* Balthazar *turns his back*): You clever little girl!

ROSALIE   (*to* Max *in a half-voice, protesting mockingly*): Be quiet! We mustn't upset Balthazar. He may have feelings. (*out loud*) What a perfectly charming coincidence! We're going to spend the first day of our honeymoon in the Nutcracker Suite! (*She goes to the bedroom door and looks in.*) And the bedroom's just as nice. It's all light and fragile, like Tschaikowski's music.

MAX   (*who has followed, and stands by her, looking in*): Yes – very jolly. But I shall be glad when we're further away, darling. Far away.

ROSALIE   (*looking up at him*): Oh! That'll come soon enough, Max.

MAX   (*noticing the barred windows, and indicating them to* Balthazar, *who has been standing at the back, silently watching the two*): By the way, Balthazar, did your painter tenant keep wild beasts in here or anything? (Balthazar *attempts to smile, and shakes his head. Then he stoops down and indicates a height of about three feet from the floor with his hands; afterwards raising himself and looking at* Max. Max *and* Rosalie *stand perplexed, looking at one another. Then illumination comes to* Rosalie.)

ROSALIE: I know! Children! This was a nursery? Eh, Balthazar? (Balthazar *nods.*)

MAX   (*chaffingly*): Really, darling, I think you must have mistaken your profession. You ought to have been an interpreter, or a detective, or something of that kind. But I don't see why he should want bars, even for his children. We're on the ground floor.

ROSALIE   (*shutting him up*): Never you mind, Balthazar says I'm right, and that's enough for me! Consider yourself taken down a peg by your little wife. (Balthazar *is making sounds and noises.* Rosalie *and* Max *look at him. He indicates the door into the passage, with a query in his look.*)

MAX: He wants to know if he can go! There now! I got *that.* (*to* Balthazar) All right, you can be off. We shan't want anything more just now. But we'll be wanting dinner in here at eight o'clock. (Balthazar *looks at them both curiously. Then, with a grim and toothless smile, he hobbles out. Crustily.*) The old fool seems amused at something.

ROSALIE: Oh, he's half dotty, he's so old. But he's quite an obliging old thing.

MAX: Queer that he's the only person we've seen in this deserted spot. I hope the others aren't like him.

ROSALIE (*going up to* Max *and kissing him*): Now don't begin
grumbling, you old curmudgeon. You ought to be just full of
joy that you've got me alone, all to yourself, yours altogether,
at last.

MAX (*kissing her tenderly*): I am, darling. You know I am.

ROSALIE (*going to a chair and sitting down*): How long we've waited
for this! Now come and talk to your little wife like the real
husband you are now.

MAX (*drawing a chair up beside her*): I'm afraid I've talked to you
like a real husband for a long time past.

ROSALIE: But not – like this. You and I –free; belonging to one another
for always.

MAX (*taking her hand*): For always. (*looking round*) How dark it's
getting. We'll want a lamp in a minute or two. I'd better tell
Methuselah.

ROSALIE (*laughing*): His name's Balthazar. And we surely don't want
lamps – you and I?

MAX: Perhaps not. Not yet. But we must have one to unpack by. I'd
better tell him in time.

ROSALIE (*with mock petulance*): Oh – very well, Mr. Methodical.
Run along! (*She pushes away his hand, which she has been
holding.* Max *gets up, goes to the door on the left, and
opens it.*)

MAX (*looking out into the passage*): Hi! (*turning to* Rosalie)
What's the old fellow's name? Melchisedek?

ROSALIE (*smiling*): Balthazar.

MAX (*calling*): Balthazar! (*after a moment's pause*) *Balthazar!*

ROSALIE: I expect he's deaf. He's old enough to be deaf and dumb and
blind and everything else.

MAX (*going just outside the door*): I never saw such a tomblike
place. Not a sound anywhere. I'd better go and find some
one.

ROSALIE (*jumping up*): No, *no*. I won't be left all alone. You just stay
here with me, darling; we don't want a light yet, and it'll be
quite time enough to go and make a fuss when we do. (*She
pulls him back into the room.*)

MAX (*with mock sulkiness*): Oh, very well; very well.

ROSALIE (*dragging him to a chair*): Now you sit down there (*pushing
him down*) and I'll sit on your knee (*she seats herself there*),
and you can tell me a fairy story, and I'll – I'll just lie back
and look up at the ceiling and see all you tell me about,
there.

MAX (*humouring her tenderly*): All right, baby! (*He settles her on
his lap, and she leans back comfily. He begins.*) Once upon a

time there was a little boy. And he was all alone in the world
– all alone. And –

ROSALIE (*interrupting and sitting up*): I know! There was a little girl.

MAX: Now, who's telling this story – your or I? You lie down and
be good. (*She does so.* Max *resumes.*) As I was just about to
say, there was also a little girl. And she too, was all alone,
although she lived in a big castle, with a big man and lots of
servants. And one day –

ROSALIE (*looking at the ceiling; startled*): Max!

MAX: What?

ROSALIE: I thought I saw the ceiling move!

MAX (*laughing*): Silly little darling. You mustn't interrupt my fairy
stories with nonsense of your own.

ROSALIE: I really thought it did. (*snuggling down, but still looking up*)
But go on. I'm sorry.

MAX: Where was I? Oh yes – and one day the little lonely boy
happened to be passing the big castle and –

ROSALIE (*shrieking*): Max! Max! It did move! I saw it.

MAX (*looking up*): Look here, my baby, how am I ever to tell you
a fairy story if you go on seeing things that don't happen,
and shouting about them. Just because it's dusk, you must
imagine absurdities! Why, you *are* no better than a baby!
(*He goes on; but this time they are both looking up.*) He
was passing by the big castle, and looking up he saw – (*He
stops short and leaps to his feet, throwing* Rosalie *off his
knee. She half falls, recovers herself, and stand with him,
looking up, paralysed, at the ceiling. Regaining command
over himself.*) It – it certainly did *seem* to move. But – it's
absurd. It's the light. I'll go and tell that old man to bring a
lamp. (*He makes a step towards the door. As he does so the
ceiling suddenly drops a foot or so, until it is below the level
of the tops of the doors. For a moment* Max *and* Rosalie
stand motionless, petrified. Then Rosalie *gives a loud shriek.
Turning to her, in a voice not quite under control.*) Hush,
darling. (*a pause*) There's something queer here. I'll go and
see. (*He runs over to the door and tries to open it; but of
course it will not open. Turning to* Rosalie.) My God!

ROSALIE (*rushing to him*): Max! What is it? Oh! What *is* it? (*She
cowers down, looking up at the ceiling.*)

MAX (*bravely*): I dare say it's nothing, darling – perhaps – (*There
is a slight noise outside the window, and he stops to look
in that direction. What he sees is the face of* Nicolas *on the
other side of the bars.*)

NICOLAS (*urbanely*): Good evening.

ROSALIE   (*shrieking*): Nicolas!

NICOLAS   (*imperturbably*): I trust you like your accommodation? The Nutcracker Suite. Your favourite! (*to* Max) And yours, too, I believe?

MAX   (*holding* Rosalie *in his arms, somewhat incoherently*): What – what do you want?

NICOLAS: Nothing – *now.* And you, surely you, too, can't want anything? You have your mistress – my wife; you have your charming little Nutcracker Suite –

ROSALIE: Nicolas! For God's sake –

NICOLAS   (*interrupting, to continue*): And you have the night before you. Not merely the night. You have the rest of time before you.

ROSALIE: Nicolas, what do you mean?

NICOLAS: I should have thought that by now a quick mind like yours, my dear Rosalie, would have jumped to my meaning. But if you will have me go into details, the accommodation you occupy might perhaps be called not so much a nutcracker suite, as an actual nutcracker. I have been at considerable pains to contrive it, and I hope it may – at any rate, eventually – meet with your approval.

MAX   (*hoarsely*): Do you mean you are going to kill us?

NICOLAS: A coarse way to put it, my dear Max, a brutal way. Say rather that I am going to give a delicate performance of the 'Nutcracker Suite,' in which you will fill the delightful role of the nuts. (Rosalie *shrieks.*) My dear, that note was surely a little discordant? A little harsh, I think, for such a light and melodious trifle as the Nutcracker Suite, my little Sugar Plum Fairy.

MAX   (*in a shaking voice*): What do you want, to let us out?

NICOLAS: To let you out? Oh, but I'm not going to let you out! I've had too much trouble to get you in. The difficulties I've had to surmount! The planning! The bribing! The dirty tricks! Why, if I hadn't had a few really trusty servants – such as Balthazar there, and some others, all of whom have an interest one way or another in the outcome of this performance – I don't know that I should ever have carried it through. But now – here we are! Or rather, here am I; and there are you; and all is going as merry as a marriage bell.

MAX: You'll be hung for this.

NICOLAS: Oh dear no – oh *dear* no, my good Max. *You've* taken care I shan't be hung. That little letter that Rosalie left – 'We have gone for ever. Do not try to trace us, you will not succeed!' – That thoughtful, admirable letter, will perfectly explain why you will never be seen again. And my servants – my few trusty servants will do the rest. I fear it won't be altogether a pleasant job – some of it; but – oh, they'll do it.

ROSALIE   (*in excited triumph*): But Marie! She knows. She'll give you away.

NICOLAS   (*with a smile*): Oh no! Marie won't give me away. She would never have given me away. And now, she's dead.

ROSALIE   (*in horror*): Dead? But she was with us this morning.

NICOLAS: And now she's with the angels – or the less congenial supernaturals. It's curious to think that, isn't it? 'In the midst of life we are in death' as some one put it.

MAX: Marie dead? But –

NICOLAS   (*cutting in; taking out his watch*): At least, I think so. (*looking at the watch*) Ah no, pardon me, I was anticipating a little. To be perfectly correct, she *will* be dead in about ten minutes, I should judge.

ROSALIE: You're going to kill her?

NICOLAS   (*shocked*): My dear Rosalie, how *can* you suggest such a thing! Of course not. No. She will most unfortunately meet with an accident on her way up here – she was coming up after you – (Rosalie *and* Max *look at one another*) – you didn't know? No, you wouldn't. She was coming to meet *me*, you see. But, as I was saying, an unfortunate accident will occur. At that dangerous corner where there is literally nothing to prevent one's carriage slipping over the cliff, and down a thousand feet. I've *always* said they ought to put a wall or something up – but these councils! – Ah well, the whole carriage will go over, and I hope this last accident – there have been a number before – will make them realize something must be done. My servant, the driver, will be safe – he will be able to jump in time; but poor Marie, who will be inside, and the poor horses –

MAX   (*breaking in*): You foul creature! You –

NICOLAS   (*stopping him*): Now, please. Let us restrain ourselves. Do not let us spoil the situation by coarseness.

ROSALIE   (*violently*): Why couldn't you kill *us* like that?

NICOLAS: Oh no. that wouldn't have suited me at all. I should have lost the pleasure of this little conversation. And think how commonplace! A mere fall over a cliff! Whereas here – in all this, there is art! And we are all artists. Perhaps I am a queer one – you remember you always said I was queer, Rosalie. But in my way I am an artist, too. It would have been easy to gain my end in other ways. But I've been to considerable trouble to do the thing delicately – artistically. Oh yes! I think we may say we are all artists – in our different ways.

ROSALIE: You are a devil! A madman!

NICOLAS: Really, Rosalie, I am surprised at your lack of appreciation of all I have done to please your taste in art. But we wander. Let us return to the point. My little nutcracker! Pray let me call your attention to the exquisite delicacy of my little nutcracker. Really it is worthy of the suite, and I pride myself on having contrived it out of my own knowledge of engineering – with a little help. A minimum of help. In these matters, the less help the better. So (*with a smile*) the credit is almost entirely my own. (*He stoops a little, but still looks in through the window.*) Observe! in addition to the main mechanism, I have provided this little subsidiary lever, which I hold in my hand now. A slight turn (*He turns it.*) and the ceiling – perhaps I ought to say the upper claw of the nutcracker – rises an inch. (*The ceiling rises a little. Max springs towards the door. Continuing quickly.*) But with another slight turn, it falls again. (*He laughs and looks in.*) Very disappointing, that other slight turn, I'm afraid. But life's *like* that, isn't it?

MAX: You fiend!

NICOLAS: Oh no, not a fiend: just a disappointed, unmusical husband, trying to please his musical wife and the musical young gentleman she prefers, by a performance of the 'Nutcracker Suite'.

ROSALIE (*raising herself; faintly*): Nicolas! For the sake of old times –

NICOLAS (*going into fits of mirthless laughter*): Old times! Very old times! Now watch the ceiling come a little lower – for the sake of new times! (*He turns the lever and the ceiling drops a few inches.*)

MAX (*taking Rosalie in his arms, as she shrieks*): God!

NICOLAS: I'm afraid God won't interfere, Max. Why should he? No, I've got the field to myself. (*After an almost imperceptible pause, he goes on smoothly.*) I think I need elaborate no further on my little invention. I will merely add that there is two tons weight on top of the ceiling, and a stone floor underneath you. Your imaginations will, no doubt, supply the rest. And now I'll leave you. Leave you to your own meditations, and oh! I've still one little surprise for you. A little aesthetic surprise! Not very choice, perhaps; but then I'm not a musical man – like Max. (*As he sees Max start.*) Oh! don't be impatient! You'll see what my other little surprise is in a very short time. (*He turns to go.*) Well, good-bye; or perhaps only au revoir. I may meet you both again sometime – somewhere. meanwhile, let me wish you a very good night. No; that's a little inadequate under the circumstances. I wish you – a very good Eternity. (*He bows, smiles, and goes. For a moment* Max *and* Rosalie *look at one another in silence. Then* Rosalie *jumps up, runs to the window and, looking out through it, cries despairingly after* Nicolas.)

ROSALIE: Nicolas! Nicolas! (*But there is no answer.* Rosalie *listens for a moment, and then returns, horror in her eyes, to* Max.)

MAX   (*in a hushed voice*): Another surprise! He said another surprise! (*The ceiling commences to descend again slowly.*)

ROSALIE   (*seeing it fall; shrieking*): Oh! I can't stand it! I can't stand it! (*cowering; to* Max) I shall go mad! Blind me! Oh, Max, kill me!

MAX   (*soothing her*): No, no; be brave. One must be able to meet death with one's eyes open.

ROSALIE   (*sobbing*): Oh, I can't – I can't. Kill me! (*The sound of a gramophone playing the 'Casse Noisette' Suite is heard outside.*)

MAX: Listen! What's that? (*They listen.*) His other surprise. (*violently*) Hell's humour! (Rosalie *again leaps up and rushes to the window.*)

ROSALIE   (*desperately*): Nicolas! Oh! Nicolas! (*She waits a moment listening; but there is only the sound of the gramophone. It is nearly dark. The ceiling continues to descend. Returning to* Max, *in a low voice.*) It's no use. There's no hope. (*looking up*) Oh God! it's coming quicker! (*clinging to him*) Kill me! Kill me!

MAX   (*also looking up, and instinctively cowering; in a hoarse, hushed voice*): Be brave! (*He clasps* Rosalie *in his arms.*)

ROSALIE   (*hiding her face*): Listen! The music's ending! (*At the last few bars of the piece, the ceiling begins to drop with a sudden swiftness and a dull grinding noise. Looking up, shrieking.*) Oh! (*Still clinging together the two lovers throw themselves down before the rapidly descending surface. It inexorably moves down; hovers over the prostrate forms; touches them. There is the terrible agonized cry of two voices, a crunching sound, and the heavy crash of a great weight coming to rest. Then silence. In representation, the curtain keeps pace with the descending ceiling till just before the latter touches the bodies of* Max *and* Rosalie, *when it precedes it, by a fraction of a second, to the ground.*)

THE END

The Sisters' Tragedy

by

Richard Hughes

Preface

At the time of writing *The Sisters' Tragedy*, the aspiring young poet and playwright was only twenty-one years of age and still an Oxford undergraduate, although he had already made some influential acquaintances. In the autumn of 1921 Hughes handed his play to his friend John Masefield who was so enthusiastic about it that he arranged for a private performance of the play at his own house in January 1922, in which Hughes himself played the part of Owen, and then sent a copy, without Hughes's knowledge, along with his recommendation, directly to Sybil Thorndike.

The play was soon scheduled to be performed as part of the eighth Grand Guignol series. The chance to have a play performed in the West End by the likes of Sybil Thorndike was an enormous opportunity for Hughes. The play, however, has become inextricably linked with the endgame that was being played out between the Little Theatre and the censor.

There is little to object to in the play, even by 1922 standards, and, although Street declared in his reader's report that he felt 'the purpose of the play is merely to horrify' and that 'a young girl trying to strangle her brother, a dumb mute making inarticulate noises is a picture audiences might well be spared' (9 May 1922), only a small number of blasphemies were excised. More famously, a demand from the Lord Chamberlain that there be 'No screams from the rabbit' in the opening scene received the response from Casson that 'As a matter of fact, there never were any' (letter from Casson to H. Trendall at the Lord Chamberlain's Office, 16 May 1922).

Although the play did finally receive a licence it was not a smooth passage. Street initially recommended refusal, but Casson, who commanded significant respect in the establishment, secured an interview with the Duke of Atholl, who had taken over from Sandhurst in November 1921 as Lord Chamberlain, and was able to fashion a compromise. They met on the same day as Street was compiling his report, and Casson drew special attention to *The Sisters' Tragedy*, 'which was sent in to us with a special recommendation from John Masefield' (letter from Casson to Atholl, 10

THE MOST GRUESOME PIECE IN THE NEW GRAND GUIGNOL PRO-
GRAMME : MISS ELIZABETH ARKELL AND MR. BREMBER WILLS IN
"THE SISTERS' TRAGEDY."
" The Sisters' Tragedy," by Richard Hughes, is a peculiarly creepy Grand
Guignol horror.   Lowrie (Elizabeth Arkell), the abnormal little sister, thinks
it is her duty to murder Owen, the afflicted brother who stands in the way
of freedom and marriage for her sisters.   Our photograph shows her contem-
plating an attempt to suffocate him with a sofa cushion.—[Photo. S. and G.]

Figure 18. Lowrie (Elizabeth Arkell) and Owen (Brember Wills) in *The Sisters'
Tragedy* (*The Sketch*, 14 June 1922)

May 1922). He added, 'I feel sure that on the old standard you applied to
us the play would be passed. But in the new *tighter* standard I have some
qualms.' Atholl refused to accept that the standards being applied were any
different from what they had always been, and warned Casson that the
Little Theatre was sailing very closely to the wind. In the end, as a result
of their meeting (and no doubt the notorious charm that Casson was able
to exercise), the play received a licence on condition that certain changes
were made. The crisis was over temporarily, but Casson had to assure Atholl
that 'as soon as Mr. Levy returns to town I will strongly urge upon him the
necessity of seeking an interview so that he can give you an outline of his
future policy at this theatre' (letter from Casson to Atholl, 16 May 1922). In
a letter to Hughes, Casson recounted that the play had been passed '"most
unwillingly" & only after I had gone on my knees to him' (letter quoted in
Graves, 1994, 76).

Hughes was outraged by some of the changes Casson himself made to the script, and wrote an eight-page letter of complaint to that effect (Graves, 1994, 75). No doubt Casson made the changes in good faith, experienced as he was in producing plays for the London audience, and we can perhaps put Hughes's outburst down to youthful arrogance. Certainly Casson would seem to have been vindicated in the matter, since the play received enthusiastic reviews. *The Times* called it 'incomparably the best play of the evening' and the *Evening Standard* declared it 'one of the most discussed plays that have been seen at the Little Theatre'.

Nevertheless, in spite of the play's critical success, Hughes was left rather stung by the experience, and when the play was first published in 1924, he denounced the Grand Guignol in the preface:

> ... this is not essentially a Grand Guignol play, and should not be acted in the Grand Guignol manner; and unless it is well acted it will be a complete failure. (Hughes, 1928, 3)

Clearly Casson's production had been the opposite of a complete failure, but the young playwright had learned a harsh first lesson in professional theatre. What must have made matters worse for Hughes was that the production had distracted him from the revision for his finals exams at the time, and a few weeks after the season closed at the Little Theatre, he received his degree results. Rather than the hoped-for First Class degree, he was awarded a Fourth (Graves, 1994, 77).

According to his biographer Richard Perceval Graves, in *The Sisters' Tragedy* Richard Hughes explores 'the relationship between Christian precepts and "true" morality' (Graves, 1994, 70–71). Hughes also seems determined to explore class relationships and morality: this is especially the case with regard to the aspirant suitor John, who is *'quite obviously of a lower social class than the sisters'*, a quality which is revealed by what Hughes describes as his *'vulgarity'* at the end of the play. Hughes also dissects what he regards as *'the prevalent Welsh piety of the neighbourhood'* in a play which brings religion and euthanasia into dramatic conflict: once again, we see the British Grand Guignol tackling issues of religion, this time to a supremely effective degree. In October 1921, the Lord Chamberlain's Office refused a licence to a play entitled *Euthanasia* – not to be confused with René Berton's French Grand Guignol play about a terminal cancer victim who pleads for release (Hand and Wilson, 2002, 231–43) – in which an aristocratic family plan an act of euthanasia on their 'imbecile' son to prevent his inheriting the family estate. Hughes's play in some ways explores the same territory but does so in a more subtle and yet, ultimately, a more profoundly unsettling manner. In the play it is seen as an act of kindness to put a suffering animal out of its misery even though it will not go to heaven. When Lowrie extends this logic to her disabled brother

– with the proviso that he undoubtedly *will* go to heaven – Lowrie believes she is doing her family a favour by causing Owen's death. However, the naïve girl besmirches the family by the murder: it is the *sisters'* (not the *sister's*) tragedy, and the well-intentioned crime is a curse. Moreover, the tragic resonance is then taken a stage further, with the play ending with Lowrie's descent into madness, imagining Owen to still be alive: an ending not dissimilar to Osvald's descent into insanity at the conclusion of Ibsen's *Ghosts*. *The Sisters' Tragedy* offers rich potential in performance: the play exhibits excellent techniques of suspense, with Lowrie's faltering attempt to murder Owen and the shift from Owen's perceived compliance to his *'animal terror'*.

The text of *The Sisters' Tragedy* by Richard Hughes was first published in *Plays*, by Richard Hughes, London, Phoenix Library, 1928, and is republished here by permission of David Higham Associates Ltd.

The Sisters' Tragedy

by
Richard Hughes

First Performed: 31 May 1922

Characters: *They are all rather slovenly in appearance.*

Phillippa *is about 28, plain, with a rather grim mouth. She is elaborately but untidily and unfashionably dressed, in a way out of keeping with a country life: her locks of false hair are pathetic rather than attractive.*

Owen *is about 24, tall and very thin, with the vacant peevish air of a blind and deaf mute. The only sound he makes is a sort of throaty chuckle (referred to as 'Owen's noise') by which he attracts attention to his wants, which he explains in dumb-show. His jaw droops rather.*

Charlotte *is nineteen: a pretty, fair, but rather hard and characterless face: she would look very pretty if properly dressed and taught how to walk and hold herself. When she enters, she is wearing an old pair of army riding-breeches and a torn silk evening jumper: her hair is wildish.*

Lowrie *is about 13, and very small and slight. She is superficially like Charlotte, but not so pretty, and far more passionate and sensitive. All are bitten with the prevalent Welsh piety of the neighbourhood: but in Lowrie only does her imaginative power and curious trend of logic render this dangerous.*

John, *who is by way of being Charlotte's fiancé, is quite obviously of a lower social class than the sisters, though they do not appear to see it, which completes the general air of running to seed. This vulgarity only becomes quite patent under the stress of emotion at the end of the play. In the first scene with Lowrie his manner is a little bewildered, but good-natured; and he seems quite fond of her. One's first impression from their manner is that he is more in love with Charlotte than she with him.*

Scene: *The hall in the Sisters' house, in the country, used as a living room. There is a front door up R., with a window to the left of it: a fire left, with an armchair facing the audience and another below it: and a door above it: a table littered with work things etc., centre. The walls are panelled, and there are dingy oil portraits, some them torn; mostly crooked. The fur hearth-rug is moulted; a general air of past prosperity run to seed, untidiness, things put to their wrong uses. Decoration, such as it is, Victorian.*

The time: *Autumn, early afternoon.*

(Philippa *discovered at window, looking out, one arm in a half-darned stocking.*)

PHILLIPPA: Kill it, Chattie, kill it!

CHARLOTTE   (*without*): I can't.

PHILLIPPA: Put it out of its pain at once, for heaven's sake.

CHARLOTTE   (*without*): I can't do it: you come.

PHILLIPPA: Pull yourself together, Charlotte: hit it behind the ears with your shoe. Oh, be quick, it's screaming. (*sound of a blow: steps heard running*)

LOWRIE: Oh you brute, Chattie, what are you doing?

CHARLOTTE   (*off*): I've missed it.

LOWRIE   (*off*): Stop! Stop! It might live! (*another blow*) O-Oh, beast!

CHARLOTTE: It's dead now, poor little thing. (*Enter* Charlotte *by door up, dressed as above, hot but pale. She fits her shoe on in the door-way.*) It's dead now. It's a beastly business, I wish I hadn't been there and had to do it, it would have died anyhow in time. Somehow I couldn't hit straight, like in a dream. Silly of me. Cats are brutes.

PHILLIPPA   (*sitting down*): I thought you were never going to finish.

CHARLOTTE: It must have been the little Jones's rabbit got loose: Ginger could never have caught a wild one. I wish they'd look after it better, instead of letting it run about the garden and treating it like a pet. Poor little Anne though.

PHILLIPPA: It will be a lesson to her not to get so fond of brute animals. It isn't right.

CHARLOTTE: Well, you can tell her so. I've had enough of the whole business. She'll cry. Lowrie has gone silly over it too: look at her. (*Enter* Lowrie *by door up, with something in her arms. Her head is bent forward, so that her hair covers her face. She moves quickly.*)

PHILLIPPA: Don't bring it in the house, Lowrie. It must be buried.

LOWRIE   (*to Phillippa*): You brute, you told her to do it! Look at the blood in its eyes! (*to* Charlotte) Oh, you beast, Chattie, you murderer! You brute, though you are my sister, you – (*She bursts into tears and rushes as if to hit* Charlotte.)

PHILLIPPA   (*in a harsh voice*): Lowrie! (Lowrie *stops dead.*)

PHILLIPPA: Put that rabbit down! (Lowrie *does so.*) You dare hit your sister! What do you mean by behaving like this!

LOWRIE: She killed it.

PHILLIPPA: She killed it to put it out of pain.

LOWRIE: Killing's murder.

PHILLIPPA: You little fool, would you have let it go on screaming in agony?

LOWRIE: We might have nursed it.

CHARLOTTE: Its back was broken.

LOWRIE: Do you mean it can ever be right to kill?

PHILLIPPA: Of course it's right to put a thing out of its pain, you little idiot, when living is only a burden to it.

LOWRIE: I don't know. Perhaps I'm silly. I thought there wasn't any arguing about killing. I thought it was just wrong. But are you sure it is right? The commandments, I mean.

PHILLIPPA: Of course it's right, when it's done from high motives. You don't think John was wrong to shoot Germans, do you?

LOWRIE: No, of course, but Germans are different: this was a rabbit. Besides, it was his duty to do it.

CHARLOTTE: Well, you don't think I killed the little thing for pleasure, do you? Did I look as if I enjoyed it? I wish you'd be a bit more considerate of my feelings: I didn't want to do it, and then you make it all the worse for me by going on like this.

LOWRIE   (*turning to her with change of expression*): Oh, Chattie, I'm so sorry. I'm a beast. I didn't think. Do forgive me. I didn't see it like that, and I've been a brute to you. I must think about it all.

PHILLIPPA: Very well, then, now you've said you're sorry for your selfishness you'd better go away to your room till you feel better. (*Exit* Lowrie. Charlotte *picks up the rabbit and strokes its fur thoughtfully: she sits down.*)

CHARLOTTE: Thank goodness that's over.

PHILLIPPA: I don't think we shall have any more trouble from her. She has these naughty tempers, but once she has said she's sorry she calms down.

CHARLOTTE: She's got a logical sort of mind, you know: once she sees a point, like that, she goes on ruminating on it for days.

PHILLIPPA: She has no need to! She has far too many ideas of her own about right and wrong for her age, that child. She ought to be content to do what she's told. Instead of always reasoning about it.

CHARLOTTE: Oh well, I think we're through with this storm.

PHILLIPPA: I'm not sure. You can never be quite sure with her. But I expect we are. It's a pity she was by: but she has got to meet that sort of thing some time.

CHARLOTTE: Shall we get John to skin it? If he killed another too it would make a pair of slippers.

PHILLIPPA: Oh, Charlotte, *could* you?

CHARLOTTE: Why not? You're as bad as Lowrie.

PHILLIPPA: It doesn't seem right to make any *use* of a thing you have killed.

CHARLOTTE: I don't see it.

PHILLIPPA: Well, let's talk about something more cheerful.

CHARLOTTE: What?

PHILLIPPA: John.

CHARLOTTE (*in a lustreless voice*): If you like.

PHILLIPPA: When are you going to marry him?

CHARLOTTE: I don't know. Never.

PHILLIPPA: You're a goose.

CHARLOTTE (*exasperated*): Phil, how can I? How am I ever going to get away from this place?

PHILLIPPA (*coldly*): I say you are a goose. I am enough to look after Owen.

CHARLOTTE: How could I marry John, and leave you to look after him all your life? People would jolly soon make my life a misery for me, for neglecting my duty. I know them!

PHILLIPPA: Nonsense! You could go and live somewhere else.

CHARLOTTE: And what about you, anyway? Why should your life be sacrificed to him?

PHILLIPPA: It's the Lord's will.

CHARLOTTE: You haven't spent a night away from the house for three years.

PHILLIPPA: Why should I? I've got used to it. I – I should feel funny without dear old Owen. Anyhow, I don't want to get married.

CHARLOTTE: Have you never wanted to?

PHILLIPPA (*pause*): No. (*meaning 'yes'*)

CHARLOTTE: I suppose it's all right for you, then, if you're built that way. Self-sacrifice I mean. But I'm not. I intend to get away some time.

PHILLIPPA: Then go at once! Why not?

CHARLOTTE: Haven't I already told you I can't?

PHILLIPPA: Don't worry about me. I am only doing what is right. I shall never regret it; not in this world, and I shall have my reward in the next. I intend to devote my whole life to Owen, and so make an offering acceptable unto the Lord.

CHARLOTTE: I see: you would prefer to be martyred comfortably at home, than have it done by naked savages. It's not a bad idea.

PHILLIPPA: Chattie! How can you! You forget one must not think of oneself in these matters, but of the object. It is Owen I am thinking of: my duty lies at home: surely I may thank God for that small mercy without thereby forfeiting the full reward? It is wicked of you to put it like that, it's unkind, when all I am trying to do is to free you from your duty.

CHARLOTTE: It's not my duty you're trying to free me from, it's my conscience.

PHILLIPPA: Is it your conscience is troubling you? Or what people will say, and perhaps the heavenly consequences?

CHARLOTTE: Oh shut up Phil, you beast! Aren't I refusing to go? What more do you want? Besides, Owen may be taken away, and then I can marry, and your old conscience can take you to Somaliland or anywhere else horrid.

PHILLIPPA: If you like to keep John waiting until you're sixty of course –

(*Enter* Lowrie *by door left. The sisters do not notice her, but she must never let the audience forget her presence during the scene, to which she pays a sort of abstracted attention. She picks up a book, but does not read it attentively*)

CHARLOTTE (*suddenly*): Phil, it's a shame! I almost hate Owen when I see how he is wearing you out.

PHILLIPPA: You mustn't talk like that, Chattie, you don't know how you hurt me. You never knew Owen like I did, before it happened. He was only seven. I shall always love him.

CHARLOTTE: All the same, it's a shame about all of us. Why should you and I and John have our lives spoilt for the sake of Owen, whose life isn't worth living? It must be almost more awful for him than if he had been born blind and deaf, to lose them like that suddenly when he was seven years old, just through catching measles, and then to forget, actually to forget how to speak, too! Phil, it makes me go cold to say it, but can God be just and merciful when he does things like that?

PHILLIPPA: We are told that suffering is sent to chasten us.

CHARLOTTE: Told! Oh, yes, we're *told* often enough.

PHILLIPPA: Oh, do stop! You're making it harder for me to bear, and God knows it is hard enough already. But there's no need if that's how you feel, haven't I always told you you are free to go away at any time? You won't do any good to yourself or anyone else by staying in that frame of mind.

CHARLOTTE: And you?

PHILLIPPA: I can bear it. It is what I am for.

CHARLOTTE: I can't go! I know you'll say it's wicked, but I almost pray
that Owen may die. What's life to him, anyway? He isn't
really alive, and he's killing you. Surely even in God's eyes
your life is worth more than his.

PHILLIPPA: Don't talk like that!

CHARLOTTE: I can't help thinking like that.

PHILLIPPA: It's wicked; what good does it do, anyhow? Who are you
to try and alter God's will? Besides, He may already have
decided to take Owen to Him in His own way, by His own
instrument unknown and even unguessed at by us. We know
that He has never forgotten. Promise me you won't pray it.

CHARLOTTE: I can't promise.

PHILLIPPA: You must, or I'll be miserable.

CHARLOTTE: Very well then, but I'll still think about it.

PHILLIPPA: Where is he now, do you know?

CHARLOTTE: No, but I suppose he will be along presently. (Lowrie *walks
down stage carrying the books.* Phillippa's *and* Charlotte's
manner changes immediately.)

PHILLIPPA: Reading?

LOWRIE   (*wandering about aimlessly*): Mm.

PHILLIPPA: What?

LOWRIE: A tale. It was very silly.

PHILLIPPA: Why don't you read better books then?

LOWRIE: Because I don't like better books. It was about Mr. Badger.
It's a story, at any rate. Have animals got Christian souls?

PHILLIPPA: Why?

LOWRIE: I wondered. About that rabbit too: would he go to heaven?

PHILLIPPA: No, he wouldn't go anywhere; he'd just die. But being
nothing would be better for him than lingering on.

LOWRIE: It's better for Christians to go to Heaven anyhow, isn't it? I
mean, however happy they are here, they'll be happier there,
won't they? When old Mrs. Rhys died of the rheumatics you
said it was a merciful release. You told Ellen what a beautiful
place her Grannie had gone to didn't you, Phil? It's never just
dying into blackness for a Christian, is it?

PHILLIPPA: What are you asking such questions for?

LOWRIE: Is everyone who was christened Christian?

PHILLIPPA: Why, yes.

LOWRIE: You're quite sure about all this?

PHILLIPPA: Quite.

LOWRIE: I suppose you're right. You must be. (Phillippa *catches*
Charlotte's *eye.*)

CHARLOTTE: Lowrie, did you feed the bird to-day?

LOWRIE:	No.
CHARLOTTE:	Yesterday?
LOWRIE:	I don't remember.
CHARLOTTE:	Why can't you attend to your ordinary daily duties instead of worrying about things like this which don't concern you? You'd better go and see whether he's alive still, instead of arguing about people dying. (*Exit* Lowrie *by door left.*) What a little devil she is for questioning? What is she getting at?
PHILLIPPA:	I don't know: there's obviously something running in her head. The worst of her is that whenever she gets into her head that something is right she does it. It wouldn't matter otherwise.
CHARLOTTE:	Do you think *she's* going to pray for Owen to die?
PHILLIPPA:	I shouldn't think so: but you never can tell. I'll have to talk to her some time. Do you remember the time when she wouldn't eat meat, on her conscience? Why must she always be putting her twos to her twos, instead of leaving them quietly apart as the good God has put them? It's a bad habit, and makes me very worried about her sometimes. Is John coming up to-day?
CHARLOTTE:	I believe so: he's supposed to be going out riding with me this afternoon. He ought to be here by now: I had forgotten.
PHILLIPPA:	*Forgotten!*
CHARLOTTE:	Why not?
PHILLIPPA:	Oh! – aren't you going to change that jumper?
CHARLOTTE:	No. Why should I?
PHILLIPPA:	John, I mean.
CHARLOTTE:	Oh, *he* won't mind. (*Re-enter* Lowrie.) Is he still alive?
LOWRIE	(*jumping*) Who? Why?
CHARLOTTE:	The bird.
LOWRIE:	The bird? Oh yes, I had fed him after all, and forgotten.
PHILLIPPA	(*to* Charlotte) I'd change it if I were you.
CHARLOTTE:	Why? What does it matter? (*There is a sound of hoofs off, and a voice calling* 'Chattie'.)
PHILLIPPA:	Hallo! Come right in. (*Enter* John.)
CHARLOTTE:	All right, I'm coming.
PHILLIPPA	(*aside*): Well at any rate let me sew it up. (*Exeunt together,* Phillippa *and* Charlotte *left.*)
JOHN	(*warming his hands*): Well, Lowrie, how's life?
LOWRIE:	If you were driving a trap, John and the wheel rolled over something small in the road, and hurt it desperately but not so as quite to kill it, what would you do?
JOHN:	I'm tender-hearted, girl; unless I was in a hurry I'd give it a belt with the whip handle or perhaps a stone to put it out of

its pain.

LOWRIE: You're sure that's right?

JOHN: Why, of course.

LOWRIE: And yet animals don't have an after-life, do they? It's really much more killing to kill an animal than to kill a person?

JOHN: What do you mean?

LOWRIE: I don't know – John, are you going to marry Chattie?

JOHN (*sharply*): Who said?

LOWRIE: But why shouldn't you?

JOHN (*slowly*): I'm not saying I shouldn't.

LOWRIE: Then why don't you? Is it because of Owen?

JOHN: Why?

LOWRIE: I wish he was dead.

JOHN: You mustn't say that, Lowrie, it's wicked.

LOWRIE: Don't you?

JOHN: I wouldn't say so.

LOWRIE: I can't see the difference. It's no great joy to him being alive, and if he was dead he would be in heaven and you and Chattie could get married. What's wrong in that? He'd have ears and eyes in Heaven.

JOHN: I'm not saying it wouldn't be better for him.

LOWRIE: Who wouldn't it be better for, then? What's Owen for?

JOHN: Well, he makes Phil able to live a life of self-sacrifice, and that's the best life a Christian can lead.

LOWRIE: Self-sacrifice is what's right?

JOHN: Of course it is. It makes people holy.

LOWRIE: Then you mean that really he is being sacrificed to her, not her to him? It's all very muddly.

(Owen's *noise heard off left then fingers feeling on the door.* Lowrie *runs to it, opens it, takes his arm and leads him down to the chair by the fire facing the audience. This is to be done slowly and emphatically. She comes back to* John; *to* John) Let him feel your sleeve. (*does so*) He likes to know who's here. Jack, you must make her marry you soon, and put Owen into a hospital somewhere. It's all very well to say suffering makes people holy, it isn't with her and Phil, it's making them ill-tempered: that's what it does with most people, it makes them cross and ill-tempered, and perhaps she won't go to Heaven in the end at all, she's so snappy sometimes. Oh, John, I do love them. I'd do anything to make them happy, but I'll never be any use to anyone, but if only Owen would die you could marry Chattie and if Phil has a rest she'd get quite young again. (Owen's *noise, and he puts two fingers to his lips, sucking.* Lowrie *lights a cigarette and gives it to him.*)

LOWRIE: When I was older I would offer to look after Owen myself, because I really love him too, only I know Phil would never let me, so that would be no good. I'd give my life not to see Phil unhappy like this: I'd let God damn my soul to hell for her sake, that's sacrifice isn't it?

JOHN: Lowrie, you're blaspheming! You're a good girl, but there's no need for that, you stick to doing all your little every-day duties, and try and save Phil all the unhappiness you can. (*Enter* Charlotte.)

CHARLOTTE: Ready.

JOHN: Right.

LOWRIE: Yes, I'll do that. I'll save her all the unhappiness I can. Yes, I will. (*Exeunt together up* John *and* Charlotte; *goes to window.*) Mind the mill-pond, Chattie: Fly's frisky to-day, he tried to kick me when I fed him, and if he shies when you're mounting – oh, look out!

JOHN   (*off*): Go carefully, old girl!

CHARLOTTE   (*off*): All right! We must get a fence put up, it's too close to the door to be safe.

(*Sound of departing horses. L watches at the window, hesitates, looks round the room and presently picks up a cushion and goes slowly over to* Owen, *holding it in front of her with both hands. She stands in front of him, holding it near his face. He is quite unconscious of it. He whimpers: his cigarette has gone out.* Lowrie *puts down the cushion and lights it again for him: picks up the cushion and suddenly collapses with the cushion on his knees, her head on it, sobbing*)

LOWRIE: Oh, forgive me, Owen darling, you know I love you or I wouldn't be able to do it! It's for you and Phil both I'm going to do it. (Owen *strokes her hair affectionately, undisturbed.*) Do you think you'll struggle? I wonder if being smothered hurts, if it is very horrible, or just going to sleep. Oh, Owen do forgive me! (*She stands up again with the cushion: he throws away his cigarette end and whimpers for another.*) Yes I'll give you another, and then count, one, two, three and do it. (*She gives him a cigarette, he catches and strokes her hand, she kisses him.*) Owen, I believe you know what I'm saying, and you approve. Oh, you dear! You'll be able to see and hear again in the place I'm sending you to:
            perhaps you'll be a little boy again among the angels, and there'll be Christ there and all the most wonderful things: there'll be angels, and harps, and angels (*She is getting more and more hysterical.*) and golden crowns and one! Two!

(*Enter* Phillippa left.)

PHILLIPPA: Lowrie, have you seen my scissors? (Lowrie *gasps and drops the cushion.* Phillippa *rummages about, not taking much notice of her. As she passes* Owen, *stops and pats his shoulder.* Owen *takes her hand, then drops it.*) Isn't he strange? He always wants you now, Lowrie, to do everything: before I used to be the only person he would let touch him. I wonder why.

LOWRIE   (*still very agitated*): I don't know.

PHILLIPPA: Poor old chap. I'm sure he likes to feel you're by him. I can't find those scissors. (*wanders out left*)

LOWRIE   (*taking cloth off the table*): Supposing she had caught us doing it! What would you have done, Owen? This will be better. It may be good-bye for ever, because you're going to Heaven and I'm not sure God won't send me to Hell, but I don't care. I don't care – for Phil's sake – One! – Two! – No, you can finish your cigarette and then I'll do it. Oh, I wonder if I can, now I'm perfectly certain I ought to! Oh, God, help me to do it! I'm very young and weak to wilfully give my soul to be damned, but help me to have strength to do it, for Phil's sake and Chattie's, Amen. – Three! (*She twists the cloth round his head and pulls at it madly.* Owen *flings himself up from his chair and catches her wrist. The cloth falls off his head, but he is gasping, his face red and full of animal terror.* Lowrie *sinks down behind the chair, but he keeps a hold on her wrist over its back: she springs up wildly; he gropes for her and forces her down on the ground. Suddenly she slips free and lies still on the floor a moment;* Owen *whimpering excitedly goes down on hands and knees and begins groping about for her. She gets up and leans against the wall, panting.*)

LOWRIE: Oh, God, help me! I can't do it! I can't kill him, like in a dream! God help me! (Owen *finds the door and gropes for the handle, shaking with terror. It opens, and enter* Phillippa.)

PHILLIPPA: I'm sure I left them in here somewhere. Why, whatever's the matter with Owen?

LOWRIE   (*in a composed, but unnatural voice: her eyes are wide*): I don't know.

PHILLIPPA: Look at your hair! Has he been violent?

LOWRIE   (*with a laugh*): Owen violent. No! Fancy the old dear hurting anyone. (Phillippa *takes him by the shoulder, calming him.*) He fell asleep and had a bad dream or something, and jumped up suddenly in a fright. (Phillippa *leads him back to his chair. He sits down still shaking, and when he realizes*

Phillippa *is preparing to leave him begins whimpering with terror again.*)

PHILLIPPA: What on earth is he so terrified of?

LOWRIE: I can't think.

PHILLIPPA (*disengaging* Owen's *hands*): I suppose he's all right. Call me if anything happens.

LOWRIE: All right. I can't think what's the matter with him. (*Exit* Phillippa.) It's all over now, I must do it now, or you'd never trust me again and then they might guess. I must do it now, it's not the time to get weak-minded now. But I won't be so silly as to try strength again. (*She goes to front door, opens it, locks other door: suddenly throws the cloth over his head and springs back. He leaps up pulling it off, blunders to door left, finds it locked feels round the wall to the front door and staggers out.* Lowrie *slams the door behind him and goes to window.*)

LOWRIE: Pray God he may drown quickly, and not struggle like he did before. (*She kneels up at the window, silent for full fifteen seconds. Suddenly she gives a half scream and jumps back, covering her eyes. She turns towards the audience, her eyes covered, still gasping.*) I mustn't scream, I mustn't scream, I mustn't scream. (*She drops her hands and stares about her.*) I mustn't scream, or they'll rescue him. I must wait. (*She stands still a moment, then goes to door left and unlocks it: rearranges tablecloth: re-enter* Philippa.)

PHILLIPPA: They were in my basket after – Hallo, where's he gone?

LOWRIE: Out. He wanted to go, so I faced him to the paddock and let him.

PHILLIPPA: I suppose he's all right. You're sure you got him facing properly?

LOWRIE: Quite. He's all right. I know he's quite all right.

PHILLIPPA: Very well, only I'm a bit anxious about him because he seems queer to-day. – Do you think you can wear that frock another winter, dear?

LOWRIE: Frock? Yes, my frock's all right.

PHILLIPPA: It's getting very short. I think I had better cut this one of mine down for you.

LOWRIE (*keeping on glancing at the window*): Yes.

PHILLIPPA: Let me measure you. Why, what's the matter. What are you so excited about?

LOWRIE: I'm not excited – I – I think he frightened me a bit. Look, there's John and Chattie coming back already.

PHILLIPPA: Poor old thing! – I wonder what's wrong with him, he's a lamb generally.

LOWRIE: He didn't mean to. Chattie's leading Fly, and he's stumbling. They must have had a spill, and that's why they have turned back. I do hope they haven't hurt poor Fly.

PHILLIPPA   (*glancing at the window across the room*): He doesn't look very bad.

LOWRIE: No, I'm sure he's all right. I'm sure he's quite all right. (*She begins to laugh.*) Silly of me, I don't know what there is to laugh at in that: I know he's quite all right.

JOHN   (*off*): Help! Help!

LOWRIE: What's that?

PHILLIPPA: Is one of them hurt?

LOWRIE   (*quickly*): Perhaps that's it.

PHILLIPPA   (*opens door up, gives a quick cry*): Stay inside, Lowrie, and don't look out of the window! Promise me you won't look out of the window! (*Exit, closing door.* Lowrie *comes forward and stands dry-eyed. Presently shuffling steps and voices outside.*)

PHILLIPPA   (*off*): No, don't carry him inside. Lowrie's there.

JOHN   (*off*): Poor kid, she'll be terribly upset.

PHILLIPPA   (*off*): Yes, but for his sake we can't be sorry: it was a merciful release to him.

JOHN   (*off*): Amen to that.

PHILLIPPA   (*off, breaking down*): Oh Owen, Owen, my little Owen! Nobody knew him as I did, when you were a beautiful little boy in Holland overalls and we used to go exploring up the mill-stream together! I've been a bad sister to you, a cruel sister, I haven't treated you nearly as kindly as I ought, and now he's gone, and I can never do anything for him again! Oh Owen, I didn't know how much I loved you! (Lowrie *suddenly collapses on the floor, weeping loudly.*)

JOHN   (*off*): She's heard! We may as well bring him in. (*They open the door, and* Charlotte *and* John, *both quite composed, carry* Owen's *body in on a short ladder, his face covered in* John's *jacket. They bear him straight through the other door.* Philippa *comes to* Lowrie, *and kneels down beside her.*)

PHILLIPPA: You dear, you're all I've got left now: Chattie will get married and you and I will be all alone. But you mustn't cry for him: he is happy in Heaven now. It was God's kind will to take him to him from his suffering. You know, dear, we couldn't wish him to live on as he was; his life was only a misery to him, and it is God's mercy that has released him. Always trust in God, Lowrie, and don't let your own rebellious thoughts interfere with His will. God's purpose is worked out in His own time, and though He may use the weakest of us sometimes as His instruments, it is not for us to anticipate His will: He accomplishes it without any help from us. (*Re-enter* Charlotte *and* John.)

CHARLOTTE: I'm silly, but I can't help crying a bit. Yet I know it's all for the best. I wish I hadn't talked like that, though: if I'd held my tongue a little longer there'd have been no need. (*dabs her eyes*)

JOHN (*nervously*): I feel for you, of course, in your bereavement: but we must admit it's all for the best.

PHILLIPPA: Yes, John, you're right: it's the best thing for him.

LOWRIE: Phil.

PHILLIPPA: Yes, darling.

LOWRIE: I do love you (*pause*). It was the best thing, wasn't it?

PHILLIPPA: Yes.

LOWRIE: Oh, Phil, I do feel awful. Can what's right make you feel awful like that? Did Chattie feel like that?

PHILLIPPA: Like what, dear?

LOWRIE: I feel as if God hated me: I don't know why: I can't help it: Oh, I do feel so awful, Phil, I can't bear it.

PHILLIPPA: What's the matter?

LOWRIE (*with an effort*) Nothing. I can't tell you.

PHILLIPPA: Do tell me.

LOWRIE: No, I can't: God would never forgive that – I must bear it. (*Stands up.*) I will bear it. I won't tell you. (*walks down stage*)

CHARLOTTE: What is the matter with her.

PHILLIPPA: Sh! She'll tell us presently. She's too wrought up now, don't pay any attention to her.

JOHN: Shall I go now, Chattie? Is there anything else I can do?

PHILLIPPA: No, don't go, John, stay a bit.

CHARLOTTE: Phil.

PHILLIPPA: Yes?

CHARLOTTE: How did it happen? He doesn't generally go out in the afternoons, and anyhow when he's faced towards the paddock he generally goes straight there. Was he alone?

PHILLIPPA: I don't know, Chattie: he was very excited and queer this afternoon. Lowrie started him off all right, she says.

CHARLOTTE: Do you think –? (*She pauses, to suggest suicide.* Lowrie *suddenly screams.*) You'd better make her go to bed, Phil, or she'll be ill.

PHILLIPPA: I do hope it wasn't that. (Lowrie *screams again.*)

CHARLOTTE: He knew the pond was there, so he might have done it. You say he seemed very excited and queer.

PHILLIPPA: Oh, Chattie, I hope he didn't: I'd be miserable all my life if I thought that was it. Oh, my poor Owen.

JOHN: There's no need to think that, Phil: let's take the charitable view. I can't believe he would be so wicked as to take his own life violently away.

CHARLOTTE: We had better question Lowrie.

PHILLIPPA: No, don't, you'll only upset her worse.

CHARLOTTE: It can't be helped. – Lowrie. (Lowrie *moves up a little, but keeps her face to the audience.*) Did you see him start?

LOWRIE: I saw him walk straight across to the water, and he was kicking with his legs but he couldn't swim only he went round and round in circles and I couldn't look.

PHILLIPPA: Lowrie!

JOHN: You saw him fall in!

PHILLIPPA: Why didn't you call me? Why didn't you tell me? Oh, Lowrie, we might have saved him!

LOWRIE (*shaking her head*): I couldn't tell you.

PHILLIPPA: Oh, Lowrie, we might!

LOWRIE (*turning*): No, Pippy dear, you said it was for the best, didn't you? You said he was happier now, and it was God's will: so why should you want to save him?

PHILLIPPA: How can you say such wicked things?

LOWRIE: I'll tell you how I can say such wicked things, Pippy, it's because I killed him, that's why! I tried to kill him again and again, but I couldn't because he was so strong and I was such a weak little fool. If only I had thought of drowning him at first I could have done it easily, but in the end I had to frighten him so that he didn't know where he was going. I did it for you, Pippy, because I couldn't bear to see him spoiling your life, and Chattie not able to marry, and he living on in misery. I thought he would be glad to die, Pippy, but he wasn't, he hated it, he fought me. I never meant to tell, I meant to keep it secret, so as you and Chattie would be happy and free and not know: and even if God thought I was wrong and sent me to Hell perhaps you would never know. But I'm a little fool, I couldn't bear it, I had to blurt it out, and now it's all no good and you will be unhappy all the same, because you know. (John *steps towards her and deliberately knocks her down.*)

JOHN: Murderer! Murderer! You, to kill your own blind brother! (*She clings to his foot.*) Give up crawling round me! (*Heaves her off his foot.*)

LOWRIE: Phil.

PHILLIPPA: I can't speak to you yet, Lowrie. (*exit hurriedly left*)

LOWRIE: But I did it for you and Chattie, John: can't you see it was for Chattie I did it? So as – you – get married?

JOHN: And d'you think I would marry into a murderer's family? D'you think I'd marry the sister of a girl what's going to be 'ung?

LOWRIE: Hung!

JOHN: Yes, when I've told the police they'll come and hang you, Lowrie: and may God have mercy on your soul: though I doubt much if He ought to.

CHARLOTTE: Will you tell!

LOWRIE: I'll go with you, John: I'll go to the police quietly: I'd rather go than wait for them to come and fetch me.

JOHN: You will not! Do you think I want my name dragged into a business like this, a dirty, foul business? You'll stay here! Christ, I'm afraid of the lightning dropping while you're about me! (*Moves to door up*: Lowrie *follows him*.) Get inside! And don't you ever exasperate the Lord by praying to Him, you snake. (*Exit*: Lowrie *buries her face in a chair*.)

CHARLOTTE: John! (*She runs suddenly after him, calling, leaving the door open*.)

LOWRIE: It isn't true! It isn't true! I never did it, I never! Oh, I know I never did it, I couldn't do, I couldn't do it. I couldn't kill anything! Oh, Owen! He'll go telling lies and the police will come and hang me and it's all a mistake, a dream, I never did it, I only dreamt it, it's all a dream! (*kneels upright*) Oh, God, it's a dream, isn't it? Kind God, help me to wake up and I'll never dare to go to sleep again, ever, never! Oh, let me wake up! (*She bites the back of her hand and waits a moment, rigid, expectant, with her eyes shut: then suddenly opens them*.) I'm awake now, say I'm awake now, say I dreamt it all about Owen, say I'm in bed; say he's all right, oh God. I'm sure he's all right, I'm sure he's quite all right. I know he's quite all right – silly of me to laugh. (*gets up looking round the room*) Owen! Owen! Where are you? They said you'd be able to hear and see again where you've gone to: you must hear me, you haven't died into the blackness have you? (*She falls by the pool of water near the door*.) Oh, wicked water, you know you're only a dream, aren't you? I didn't really see you dripping out of him – oh wicked water, why won't you let me wake up? Owen, Owen! He's all right, only he can't hear me, and now John is telling lies when it was all a dream! Oh, Owen, come and save me! Owen! (*She stands stock still, listening: there is silence for five seconds, then* Owen's *noise is heard off left, exactly as in the earlier scene.* Lowrie *runs to the door, opens it: there is nothing there. She gives a cry of delight, and crooks her arm exactly as before: comes back as if leading him to his chair by the fire.)*

LOWRIE: Oh, I knew it was only a dream!

QUICK CURTAIN

The Better Half

by
Noël Coward

Preface

The Better Half can hardly be hailed as one of Noël Coward's more
significant plays. It merits but a passing mention, if that, in most Coward
biographies, and the playwright himself only mentions it once in his
Autobiography, describing the play as 'too flippant' in a repertoire of 'full-
blooded horrors' (1986, 115). At the time of writing *The Better Half*, the
twenty-two year old Coward was still two years away from *The Vortex*,
the play which secured his reputation and fame as a writer, and was living
a somewhat hand-to-mouth existence, surviving on the generosity and
credit provided by his friends. Coward was only four months older than
Richard Hughes, whose *The Sisters' Tragedy* appeared in the same series
as *The Better Half*, but he was already much more established than the
undergraduate Hughes. Coward had enjoyed some modest success as both
an actor and writer in the years immediately after the end of the war, but
his successes were sporadic, and a near-disastrous attempt to establish
himself in New York in the summer of 1921 had left him almost penniless,
and upon his return to England at the end of that year he found work
hard to come by. In Coward's own words, '1922 began for me in a welter
of financial embarrassment' (1986, 103). Unlike the practically unknown
Hughes, Coward was 'too well known to be able to accept little jobs, and
not well known enough to be able to command big ones' (1986, 104).

In March 1922 Athene Seyler gave Coward the use of her cottage in
Dymchurch, Kent, for two weeks, and he installed his mother in a cottage
nearby. Seyler was 'a close friend of the whole Casson family' (Devlin, 1982,
129) and a member of Levy's Grand Guignol company. Whether or not
she was responsible for encouraging him to write for the Little Theatre is
unclear, but by 9 May the play was with the Lord Chamberlain's Office for
consideration for performance at the end of the month. Coward's attitude
to the Grand Guignol is not known. When he visited Paris in 1920 with
his friend Stewart Forster, he does not mention visiting the rue Chaptal
(although he does mention the Moulin Rouge and the Folie Bergère). The

pair reportedly 'did all the things young men usually do in the evenings in Paris (Lesley, 1976, 61), and as the Grand Guignol was firmly on the tourist trail at that time, a visit to the famed theatre of horror would have been likely.

The Better Half, however, was no doubt written for more pragmatic reasons. In part it may have been a way of repaying Seyler's kindness, but more importantly it helped Coward's financial position and 'it ... served the purpose ... of keeping my name before the public' (quoted in Hoare, 1995, 105). Coward himself felt it to be a rather inconsequential piece and unable 'to compete with the terrors which preceded it on the bill' (Hoare, 1995, 105), although he may be being unduly harsh in this respect. Certainly his play, which had been praised as 'a clever, one-sided and exaggerated little satire by George Street (Reader's Report, 9 May 1922), was eclipsed by the impact made by *The Sisters' Tragedy* and the accompanying controversy. As a result, *The Better Half* remains a forgotten piece, but nonetheless of interest. Written as it was, just before Coward's breakthrough, it is a stylishly written comedy which displays much of the morality of the post-war generation so detested by St. John Ervine and which led to Coward being unfairly accused of being frivolous and 'very indifferent to the intellectual content of his work' (Pellizzi, 1935, 293).

The play deals with the *unconventional* morality of Alice, who is willing to sacrifice her *conventional* husband, David, to her best friend Marion for the sake of their mutual happiness – effectively placing personal happiness above public decency. In some ways it is surprising that the Lord Chamberlain's office did not raise any objection to the moral standpoint expressed by Alice in the play. Whilst Coward does not explicitly support her position, neither does he criticize it, and Alice is arguably the most sympathetic character in the play. She is, at least, the most articulate. In the event, though, Street only placed a blue pencil mark against one phrase, spoken by Alice:

> ... just because your endeavours are egged on by women of the Marion type who camouflage their desire for your body behind a transparently effusive admiration of your brain!

Presumably it is the suggestion that women may be driven by purely sexual desires that Street finds objectionable, but even this he qualified this with a comment that he did 'not think it goes too far in these plain-spoken days, since it is used seriously'. Ultimately he concluded, 'From the point of view of censorship I see no reason for interference. The "daringness" is confined to speech and is no more daring than any amount of dialogue in Shaw's plays' (Reader's report, 9 May 1922).

Barely a year previously, Eliot Crawshay-Williams's *Rounding the Triangle* had been initially refused a licence for its portrayal of unconventional morality in the form of a love triangle. A similar fate befell H.F. Maltby's *I Want to Go Home* in 1920 for its reference to marital infidelity. Although *Rounding the Triangle* was eventually passed, after Crawshay-Williams was able to use his political connections to secure a private interview with the Lord Chamberlain, *Collusion* (1920) by American writer George Middleton was not so lucky. Despite its having been successfully produced in the States, Levy was unable to secure a licence for the play. It is a serious social critique of the divorce laws, and concerns a man who selflessly sets himself up to be discovered with a prostitute in order that his wife can divorce him and marry the man she really loves. It was refused on the grounds of its portrayal of a married man in a prostitute's bedroom. In the case of *The Better Half*, what is perhaps significant is not the unconventional morality that is portrayed, but the confidence and matter-of-factness with which Coward deals with it.

The Better Half

A Comedy in One Act
by
Noël Coward

First Performed: 31 May 1922

Alice
Marion
David

The scene is the elaborately furnished bed-room of a house in Mayfair. There is a large dressing-table down left covered with scent bottles, cosmetics etc. A large four poster bed right hung with beautifully coloured curtains. There is also a door opening into dressing-room right, below the bed, and another door back centre. There is a white and silver ball dress laid out on the bed, also stockings and shoes etc. When the curtain rises the stage is empty. Alice Ruthven and Marion Hunt enter. Alice is in an elaborately simple tea-gown, Marion in a plain dinner frock.

ALICE: I can never come up to dress for a late party without a small inward desire to go firmly to bed instead.

MARION: It certainly does look inviting, anyhow I don't envy you going out to night – it's foully cold.

ALICE: My face feels dreadfully dry and hard. I shall give it a sort of massage before I dress. Stay and talk to me.

MARION (*fingering things on table*): All right. What's in this bottle? (*She takes it up and smells it.*)

ALICE: Some scent of Guerlain's 'Apres l'Ondee' I think.

MARION: It's lovely. You have got some divine things.

ALICE: Yes, I love a crowded dressing-table. It gives me a sort of Dubarry-Pompadourish feeling! How I should have adored living in those days, all intrigue and deceptions and hiding lovers in cupboards and things –

MARION: I don't think those habits are entirely confined to the eighteenth century.

ALICE: Perhaps not, but there seemed to be more glamour about them then. Look at the Harrison divorce case, how sordid and nasty it all sounds, I'm sure it would have been quite romantic in a picturesque and correct costume.

MARION: According to the papers, Mrs. Harrison's lack of correct costume was one of the primary reasons for the divorce.

ALICE: I wonder what I should do if David thrashed me nearly to death!

MARION (*quickly*): He never would. He's much too chivalrous.

ALICE: What do you suppose he'd do then if he discovered I'd been behaving – well – like Irene Harrison?

MARION (*wistfully*): He'd be wonderful – he'd forgive you.

ALICE: I'm not sure the thrashing wouldn't be better for me. (*She goes off into the dressing-room.*)

MARION: How can you Alice? That man Harrison was an absolute brute!

ALICE (*off*): A little primitive perhaps, but on the whole I think she deserved all she got.

MARION: I don't. I think he should have tried to understand – to have seen her point of view, and to have helped her.

ALICE: You and David think awfully alike don't you?

MARION: Perhaps – I don't know –

ALICE: Oh yes, I'm constantly spotting little similarities in your remarks and general views on things.

MARION (*simply*): I think he has an extraordinarily fine character.

ALICE (*laughing*): Oh my dear do you?

MARION (*a trifle acidly*): Yes, don't you?

ALICE (*re-entering in an attractive negligée*): No, but then you see I've been married to him for six years and you haven't.

MARION: I can't understand you Alice. You have a good-looking, straight, honest husband who adores you, and yet you're not satisfied.

ALICE: Maybe one desires a little more than straightness, honesty, and good looks.

MARION (*crossly*) I hate to hear you talk like that. It's not worthy of you.

ALICE: You mean it's not worthy of David.

MARION: Yes – I do.

ALICE: Poor old Marion, it's beastly of me to tease you and try to shatter your ideals.

MARION: You couldn't, however much you tried.

ALICE: I wonder.

MARION   (*suddenly*): I suppose you're in love with someone else, and
that's why you're sick of David.

ALICE   (*straining her hair back and vigorously rubbing her face with
grease*): No dear I'm not, and even if I were I should never
tell you – it would be sure to leak out during one of your
heart to heart talks with him.

MARION: Don't be catty.

ALICE: I'm not, but one does get so carried away by heart to heart
talks. They're an insidious habit too – David revels in them.
He expounds his theories and views on life. He's an excellent
young man, but he'd be still more excellent with fewer views.

MARION   (*cattily*): Easier to manage perhaps.

ALICE: Oh I find him quite easy to manage thanks – (*smiling*) You
see I understand him so well.

MARION   (*rising*): I think you ought to be ashamed of yourself for not
appreciating him more.

ALICE   (*pulling her down*): Sit down dear and don't be so cross.
You're such an old friend – and you've known us both for
so long, I'm only surprised that you don't see through David
a bit more. I suppose it must be because you're in love with
him.

MARION   (*astounded*): Alice!

ALICE   (*firmly rubbing her forehead*): There seems to be no other
explanation!

MARION: How dare you!!

ALICE: Don't be so silly!! You *know* you are!

MARION: I'm nothing of the sort.

ALICE: Well you needn't look so outraged. There's no earthly harm
in being in love with David, it's quite natural – as you say
– he's very nice-looking!

MARION: You're utterly impossible Alice.

ALICE: Now why? I'm not being in the least catty, or cross, or
anything, I don't love him a bit and I'm perfectly willing that
you should.

MARION   (*stiffly*): Thank you.

ALICE: It's silly to pretend you don't, because it would be quite
obvious to a blind mule – and I'm not quite as stupid as that.

MARION: I'm not so sure. (*She rises.*)

ALICE: Doesn't this cream smell divine? (*She proffers her finger with
a dollop of face cream on it.*)

MARION: Yes perhaps you're right – we'll change the subject.

ALICE: Oh but I don't want to change it altogether – just to branch
off for a moment until you're calmer.

MARION: I'm perfectly calm.

ALICE   (*pulling her down*): Then sit down again. You keep bobbing
up like a Jack-in the box. (*There is silence for a moment
while she massages her chin.*) I love doing this – I think I
must be very sensual.

MARION: Why do you hate David so?

ALICE   (*ceasing to massage*): I don't *hate* him at all – perhaps I
despise him just a teeny bit but –

MARION: But why –?

ALICE: Because he's so 'big' about everything. He loves being 'big'.
He was big about the war – he was big when his sister had
an illegitimate child and came and told him about it. At any
sort or kind of a crisis he rises to to the occasion, and it's
wonderful to watch – for the first time – you feel a thrill
– you say to yourself – 'What a dear he is! What a broad-
minded, understanding, sympathetic old dear!' Then he does
it again over something else – and again and again and again
– until you hear it all clanking like machinery.

MARION: Do you mean to tell me that all his sympathy and
broadmindedness aren't genuine?

ALICE: They're not – really!

MARION: Don't be so absurd.

ALICE   (*seriously*): One day I think I shall do something dreadful
– I'd shatter all his smug complacency somehow – that's the
word that describes it best of all – Smug! Oh if you could
only hear him going on about things – outside things – He
discusses other people's raw aching troubles from his own
elevated standpoint. He spent the whole of breakfast this
morning – forgiving Irene Harrison! I sometimes think that
he regrets the fact that there aren't more worries and upsets
in his own home life. It must be tiresome only to have little
things to be big about, like the coffee being cold, or the hot
water bottle bursting!

MARION: I'm awfully sorry for you Alice.

ALICE: Thank you dear.

MARION   (*sadly*): Perhaps it's having so much money and everything
you want, that makes you lose the real things of life.

ALICE: Oh Marion, for God's sake don't start being 'big' too, or I
shall throw a brush at you!

MARION: All right I won't – but I should like to tell you something.

ALICE: Do dear.

MARION: You were right just now.

ALICE   (*delighted*): You don't mean to say that I've convinced you?
How marvellous!

MARION: No I don't, I mean you were right when you said I loved

David. – I do!

ALICE: Well to quote the popular song 'There you are then'!

MARION (*bitterly*): Don't be flippant about it – it's awful!

ALICE: There I disagree with you. It isn't a bit awful being in love with David, I was once, and I know. He always plays up unless of course you catch him at a particularly bad moment – and I'm sure you never would.

MARION (*with slightly noble defiance*): I've told him that I love him!

ALICE (*sitting back interestedly*): What *did* he say? I'm sure he was *splendid*?

MARION: You can jeer if you like, but he *was* splendid – he showed me quite truly and sincerely that he understood, and – and – he made me very happy –

ALICE (*lightly*): Not too happy I hope dear?

MARION (*furiously*): And you'll never be happy like that as long as you live! Never – never – never!!

ALICE: Don't be vindictive Marion, just because I refuse to have a scene with you.

MARION: You're totally and utterly lacking in any real feeling about things.

ALICE: I'm totally and utterly lacking in any real feeling about David I admit, but that should make it all the more comfortable for you – you'll be able to have your cake and lie on it – or whatever it is!

MARION (*coldly*): That's merely vulgar.

ALICE: It wasn't meant to be. Perhaps David's theories on life have broadened your mind a little too much – you see things that aren't there!

MARION: I'm going now. I don't want to speak to you again for quite a long time.

ALICE: Come to lunch on Friday week and we'll go to 'Loyalties'!

MARION (*turning at door*): I do so hate quarrelling with you Alice, I wish to Heaven you'd really fall in love with someone yourself, then perhaps you'd understand – as he understands!

ALICE (*quietly*): You mean because *he's* in love with *me* still?

MARION (*looking down*): Yes – because he's in love with you.

ALICE (*coldly*): Well you needn't be so Spartan about it – he isn't.

MARION (*trying to repress her eagerness*): What – what do you mean?

ALICE: He's in love with himself.

MARION (*in furious disgust*): Oh!!

(Marion *goes angrily out of the room and slams the door. Alice laughs softly to herself then sighs, she rubs her face vigorously with a towel, powders it, and scrutinises it in the glass. Suddenly an idea strikes her, she thinks intently for a moment then laughs again. Enter* David. *He is in full evening dress)*

ALICE: Hallo – you're dressed early.

DAVID: It's getting on for ten.

ALICE: I'm sorry – I'm not nearly ready yet.

DAVID: It doesn't matter. I've just been across to see Mrs. Benson's kiddie. He's a bit better tonight. (*He lights a cigarette.*) I don't know why, but I can't bear to see a child suffer.

ALICE: How extraordinary! Most of us love it.

DAVID: What are you in a temper about old thing?

ALICE: I'm not in a temper David, perhaps just a little irritable. I wish you'd sit down.

DAVID: All right. (*He sits down.*) Seen the evening paper?

ALICE: No.

DAVID: Irene Harrison's bolted.

ALICE: How typical of her. With Charlie Templeton I suppose.

DAVID: No, that's what I can't make out. It's another man altogether – Ronald something – I'll go and get it– (*He rises.*)

ALICE (*motioning him down again*): No don't David, I'm really too sick of the whole affair to take any more interest.

DAVID: I should have thought you'd be thrilled – knowing her and everything.

ALICE: It's because I know her, that I'm not thrilled, I've no patience with her now and never had.

DAVID: Poor girl, she's been through a pretty rough time.

ALICE: I wonder if you'd be so sympathetic if you were her husband.

DAVID: I'd try to be – I think it's up to a man to try and realise things from all points of view.

ALICE: Perhaps after all, the old way is the best.

DAVID: What old way?

ALICE: Jack Harrison's way.

DAVID: Damned cad!

ALICE (*ruminatively*): Of course he did outrage a club rule – 'Never hit a Woman'.

DAVID: He ought to be shot.

ALICE: Oh don't go on firing off clichés like that –'Damned cad' 'Ought to be shot'. He loved her and trusted her – absolutely.

DAVID: Pleasant way of showing it.

ALICE: She betrayed his trust and failed him all round, therefore he obeyed the first primitive instinct that came to him, and thrashed her – thoroughly – as she richly deserved –

DAVID: Yes, and now she's left him – for good.

ALICE: Which only proves all the more the wisdom of his policy. If he had forgiven her and taken her back – she'd have gone on being unfaithful, and he'd have gone on forgiving and they'd both have been wretched for life. As it is, he's brought things to a head, she's burnt her boats and bolted – he'll be miserable for a few months, then as time goes on he'll gradually get over it and marry somebody else, in a comfortably disillusioned frame of mind.

DAVID: You argue well Alice – I'll give you that.

ALICE: Thank you.

DAVID: But you won't convince me – you see I've really gone into the subject.

ALICE: With Marion?

DAVID (*nonchalantly*): Yes – sometimes with Marion, she's a good talker old Marion.

ALICE: Don't be unkind, she's only a little older than you, and I'm sure she doesn't show it – anyhow at night.

DAVID (*pompously*): I'm always a great believer in talking things over thoroughly – developing one's sense of values.

ALICE: Or completely obliterating it by force of your own sophistry.

DAVID: Everything can be brought to a satisfactory conclusion eventually if you face facts.

ALICE: I think that when the real moments of life come along, one should obey one's instincts and not one's carefully worked out theories – face facts by all means but don't just face the ones you've made yourself.

DAVID (*laughing indulgently*): I'm afraid you're getting a little involved – silly old thing. (*He kisses her.*)

ALICE: You're wonderfully contented, aren't you David?

DAVID: I'm working out my own little philosophy.

ALICE: Splendid! That I suppose is the reason you were so charming and unembarrassed when Marion told you that she was in love with you?

DAVID (*startled*): You know?

ALICE: Yes, she told me just now.

DAVID (*simply and with crushing sincerity*): I shall love you – always – be sure of that my dear.

ALICE: It gives one a warm comfortable feeling doesn't it? Being loved?

DAVID: I don't know – I suppose so –

ALICE: I should like to have been there watching, when she told you – just to see how you really took it.

DAVID (*laughing with conscious modesty*): Well – I –

ALICE: I have a little mental picture of it – correct me if I'm wrong –

DAVID: I say dear, is this quite fair to poor old Marion?

ALICE (*firmly*): Quite. I always believe in facing facts – I'm sure 'poor old Marion' would be the first to appreciate that.

DAVID: It's no use getting angry.

ALICE: I'm not in the least angry – only frightfully interested. I suppose it all took place in the drawing-room?

DAVID: Yes, as a matter of fact it did.

ALICE: I thought so – the atmosphere is excellent for that sort of thing – probably after dinner, one night when I was out?

DAVID   (*uneasily*): Yes.

ALICE: So warm and cosy – I do hope you didn't have all the lights on – just the orange reading-lamp.

DAVID   (*laughing with rather forced roguery*): Yes just the orange reading lamp.

ALICE   (*thoughtfully*): She'd been leading up to it for a long time I expect – talking about you mostly so as to get you into a sufficiently receptive state – then she sprang it on you. There was a silence for a moment I think – You gave her one look – prompted perhaps by the subconscious suspicion that she was playing a joke on you. Then you saw that her eyes were wet, and gleaming with the particular brand of dog-like admiration that all my female friends seem able to assume when you're in the room – and you were re-assured – you put out your hand consolingly and patted hers, and probably said – 'Marion old friend, you shouldn't have told me this – '

DAVID: Look here Alice, you're not being very decent –

ALICE: Sssshh! Don't interrupt! I have a passion for reconstruction like Sherlock Holmes.

DAVID   (*irritable*): Oh –!

ALICE: Then, after a few sentimental remarks from both parties, you said that you 'Understood'; and she asked you to kiss her.

DAVID   (*quickly*): She told you that?

ALICE   (*smiling*): And you kissed her – without hesitation – because you were sorry for her and realised how unhappy she was and –

DAVID: It wasn't fair of her to tell you.

ALICE: She didn't – she told me very little – all this has just been my private conception of the scene – I told you to correct me if I were wrong.

DAVID: Look here Alice. Don't be cross with her, she wasn't betraying her friendship with you – I swear she wasn't. Only you know we *have* talked – she and I – just lately. We've discussed a good many things, her type of mind appeals to me, she's so jolly clear sighted and – and – well we decided a long time ago to be real pals and not try to hide things from one another. That's why she told me, and that's why she told you – she was just – playing straight.

ALICE   (*suddenly – placing her hand on his*): I'm not cross with her but – but – you do love me best – don't you?

DAVID   (*delighted*): Alice!

ALICE: You see I –

DAVID   (*all pride restored*): You silly jealous old darling! I love you better than anyone or anything in the world! (*He kisses her.*)

ALICE: Really and truly?

DAVID   (*a warm glow creeping over him at her persistence*): You know I do – really and truly – now and always! (*He tries to kiss her again but she wards him off.*)

ALICE   (*in a choked voice*): Don't – oh don't –!

DAVID: Why – what's the matter?

ALICE: Don't touch me! (*She buries her face in her hands.*)

DAVID: What's wrong – tell me – what's wrong?

ALICE: I'm – I'm not worthy of you – I –

DAVID   (*startled*): Alice!!

ALICE: I've made my mind up. (*She looks at him bravely.*) I'm not going to deceive you any more.

DAVID: Deceive me?

ALICE: Don't look like that.

DAVID: But Alice ...?

ALICE: David – I haven't been true to you!

DAVID   (*starting back*): What??

ALICE: I haven't been true to you!

DAVID: What do you mean – I – (*Suddenly he laughs.*) Oh I see! This is a little test is it? Just to see whether I'd thrash you or not – like Jack Harrison.

ALICE   (*slowly*): Are you content to go on – considering it a – a little test?

DAVID: Quite old dear, but I'm afraid it hasn't been much of a success.

ALICE: Oh David thank you – thank you!! (*She breaks down and sobs hopelessly.*)

DAVID: Here I say Alice – for heaven's sake don't go on like that – Alice – (*He shakes her shoulder.*) – Alice what on earth's the matter with you?

ALICE   (*in a muffled voice*) Go away – leave me alone.

DAVID: Alice–?

ALICE   (*hysterically*): Go away – go away – go away!!!

DAVID   (*huffily*): I'm sure I don't know what you're going on like this for – just because your little plan for my discomfiture didn't come off –

ALICE   (*sitting up – her cheeks tear stained*): Oh my God!

DAVID: What is it now?

ALICE: Do you still – *really* – believe it was only a test?

DAVID: Believe it? – But – but – it was?

ALICE   (*desperately*): I thought you understood –!

DAVID   (*dramatically*): You mean – you mean – what you said was true?

ALICE   (*trying to control her sobs*): Yes.

DAVID   (*after a long pause*): Alice – who – who was it?

ALICE   (*with bowed head*): Leonard Macyntire.

DAVID: Leonard Macyntire.

ALICE   (*firmly*): Yes.

DAVID   (*bewildered*): But when – where? I've never heard of him.

ALICE: You've seen him several times – but you never suspected.

DAVID: I can't believe it – I –

ALICE: What are you going to do?

DAVID: What is there to do? Do you love him?

ALICE: Not now – not any more. That's all finished.

DAVID: Leonard Macyntire – Leonard Macyntire – I can't place him at all –

ALICE: Well what does it matter whether you can place him or not? The fact remains that I'm an unfaithful wife – I? It sounds funny doesn't it? Oh David–? (*She puts her hand to her head miserably.*)

DAVID   (*pulling himself together*): How long did this go on?

ALICE: Six months.

DAVID: When did you last see him?

ALICE: In November, he came to me to say good-bye. Then he asked me to go away with him.

DAVID: Where to?

ALICE: To India of course.

DAVID: Why didn't you tell me before?

ALICE   (*quietly*): I wish I had – I wish to God I had. You can believe me or not as you like but I've suffered – it's been gnawing at me all these weeks – every morning I woke with that awful leaden feeling of guilt on my heart, crushing me down until I thought I would have gone mad.

DAVID: It's all so unexpected – so incredible – I never thought – I never dreamt –

ALICE: Oh stop – what's the use of all that now? We've got to face it.

DAVID: We'll talk it all over thoroughly – to-morrow.

ALICE: But David –

DAVID   (*magnificently*): Anyhow, whatever we decide – you can rely upon one thing – always. My love for you.

ALICE   (*humbly*): Thank you David.

DAVID: You've often laughed at me, but you see I *can* understand – a little –! (*He takes her hands, but she snatches them away and rises.*)

ALICE   (*cold and despairing*): You mustn't forgive me – you mustn't forgive me – yet! You say you understand, but you never could really understand all that I have done. It seems strange to be telling you all this now in cold blood – but I feel quite numb about it, I suppose because I've made up my mind – absolutely – to tell the truth – whatever happens after. You've been living here in a Fool's Paradise – We've been superficially happy together and you've trusted me – all along. That makes it all so much worse. Oh! If only you'd been suspicious or jealous once or twice, but you weren't, you weren't ever. You trusted me implicitly. And now – to-night – when Marion told me of her love for you, I suddenly realised what a doubly selfish beast I was – to go on deceiving you, lying to you. She loves you truly David, and you could love her in time – I know you could, and she'd be worthy of it, whereas I – I – (*She laughs bitterly.*) I'm not fit to wipe your boots!

DAVID: Stop, stop Alice! I won't have you talking like that.

ALICE   (*wildly*): It's true – it's true!! I've told you of Leonard Macyntire and you were willing to forgive me. What will you say now I wonder? What will you say now when I tell you the whole truth – that he was only one of many – yes, yes don't stop me – let me go on – let me go on to the bitter end – I don't care now – this had to come sometime, why I've had lovers for nearly three years now – d'you hear me? Nearly three years, and you never guessed – don't you see how funny it is the way I've been deceiving you? (*She laughs hysterically.*) What's the use of standing there looking at me like that – I've broken up your life, and my life, and all you [do] is stand there – stand there – looking–!!!!

DAVID: I don't believe it.

ALICE   (*with hopeless conviction*): Yes you do – because it's true!

DAVID   (*covering his eyes with his hand*): Not you! Oh God, not you!!

ALICE: Yes, me. (David *groans and buries his face in his hands.* Alice *watches him, presently he looks up.*)

ALICE: Well?

DAVID   (*brokenly*): Do you want to leave me – for good?

ALICE: There's no other way out.

DAVID   (*after a pause*): Yes, there is.

ALICE: What do you mean?

DAVID: There is, if only you're willing –

ALICE: But – I don't understand–?

DAVID   (*valiantly*): We've been together many years now, and …

ALICE   (*her tone altering slightly*): Well?

DAVID   (*with noble magnanimity*): I want you to try to come back
            to me – I'll leave you now, to think things over. But I should
            like you to understand that I'm here waiting for you if you
            want me – ready and willing to forget and to start all over
            again. We'll gather up our shattered happiness as best we
            can. Good night my dear! (*He is about to go out of the
            room.*)

ALICE   (*quietly*): How dare you go on like that!

DAVID   (*turning*): What?

ALICE: How *dare* you!! Think what I've just told you! That I've been
            living the life of a harlot for the last three years, that I've
            disgraced you for ever and dragged your name in the mud!
            And you go on being 'big' and 'noble' and forgiving me! It's
            nauseating!

DAVID   (*astounded*): Alice!

ALICE: Don't speak to me – don't come near me – you're beneath
            contempt. You've believed all I've told you and never
            once – in the face of such appalling disclosures have you
            ceased to be in the picture! You've been noble, forgiving,
            understanding, and a broken man, in turn. And never really
            sincere for one moment. Love me indeed? You say you love
            me! Do you imagine that if you loved me the tiniest bit that
            you'd behave like that? You were right when you suspected
            me at first, I was testing your wonderful love – just to see.
            You've been calling down the wrath of Heaven on Irene
            Harrison's husband, you've accused him of being a brute,
            and a wife-beater, and a cad. But he loved her – really deep
            down, and that's why he did what he did. All his illusions
            about her shattered at one blow and his trust and adoration
            wrenched out by the roots. He didn't stop to think what an
            opportunity it was for him to be 'big' and 'noble' because
            he was a man – a real man – which is more than you'll ever
            be! I'm sorry to disappoint you David but I'm a perfectly
            virtuous wife. I've never transgressed for an instant –

DAVID   (*with a forced laugh*): I never believed any of the things you
            told me, from the first.

ALICE   (*furiously*): Oh that's a lie! A cheap silly lie, and absolutely
            typical of you!

DAVID   (*with an effort at nonchalance*): I'm afraid you've made
            rather a fool of yourself.

ALICE: I've shown you up miserably, and you know it!

DAVID   (*unctuously*): Not at all my dear – you've merely exposed a hitherto unexpectedly unpleasant side of your character.

ALICE: And what of you? Allowing yourself to be led and taken in by women like Marion. Pals – the type of mind that appeals to you – discussing everything – views on life – oh it's pitiful!!

DAVID   (*nastily*): So all this pretty little scene has been prompted by jealousy of Marion?

ALICE: Jealousy! I might have known you'd put it down to jealousy.

DAVID: Nevertheless I'm right.

ALICE: Why should I be jealous? You're less than nothing to me and have been for years – ever since I first began to see through you. All your high aspirations and ideals, and your wit and humour – shams all of them – silly cheap shams! You've been trying all your life – assisted by a classical education – to throw dust in people's eyes, to make them believe you're intellectual and advanced. The clear modern brain that sees all side of every question and judges impartially. Who knows all about women, a thorough man of the world, and yet decent and clean. So decent and clean! There are hundreds of other men like you – playing up – always playing up – long heart to heart to heart talks – discussions on life – with perfectly commonplace brains clicking like typewriters. You imagine in your absurd conceit that you're really grasping something worth having, just because your endeavours are egged on by women of the Marion type who camouflage their desire for your body behind a transparently effusive admiration of your brain!

DAVID   (*white with anger*): Will you shut up talking like that?

ALICE: No I won't.

DAVID   (*through his teeth*): I'll make you.

ALICE   (*defiantly*): Make me! How!

DAVID: Never mind how. (*He catches her arm and twists it back – she screams and he lets it go.*) Now will you shut up!

ALICE: At last – at last you've done something – you've stopped being 'big'. You're a bully and a coward, but you've stopped being 'big'!

DAVID: I think I'm going to kill you.

ALICE: Not you – not you! Think of the consequences!

DAVID: I'm going to kill you.

ALICE: If you kill me remember one thing. You'll be hanged by the neck until you are dead! And that won't be all – not by any means. With your execution for my murder will die all the

beautiful illusions about your nobility of character which
you have been so busy building up in other people's minds
all your life. And however stoically and bravely you listen
to your death sentence. – 'Without flinching' – 'Leaving the
dock like a soldier' etc: It won't be any use. You'll have fallen
from your self-made pedestal. No really noble husband would
murder his wife just because she was not *unfaithful*! (*There is
a knock at the door. Re-enter* Marion.)

MARION (*halting on the threshold*): Oh! (*She looks anxiously at them
both.*) What's the matter?

DAVID: Marion! Thank God!

ALICE: Yes Marion – Thank God!

MARION: Why? What is it? What's happening?

ALICE: Nothing's happening – nothing ever would happen – but
we're just talking things over – and facing facts – your
favourite sport. Do come and join us.

MARION (*simply*): I came back because I couldn't bear to leave like I
did – both of us having bickered, and said unkind things to
one another.

ALICE: How sweet of you dear. Shall we kiss?

MARION: If you're still going to be beastly, I shall go again.

ALICE: You're never to go again Marion. Never never never!! I've
had a long talk with David which has proved irrefutably how
completely unworthy I am of him –

DAVID (*stepping forward*): Look here Marion –

ALICE: Don't interrupt David, Marion and you were made for each
other – I've been gradually realising it for months past
– Now I *know* it – You both have the same instincts, and you
both read Kipling. I am an outsider – an interloper – I have
nothing in common with either of you. Therefore I am going
to drop out of the picture for ever. David refuses to make it
easy for me. To-night I have tried everything possible, I have
confessed to being a liar and an adulteress in the hopes that
he would cast me out, but No. He wouldn't even consider it.
He has been absolutely unconditionally splendid. The fact
that there wasn't really anything to be splendid about doesn't
matter in the least. He has forgiven me for everything except
my virtue. As he obviously had no intention of divorcing *me*
for infidelity, I tried to make him strike me, so that I could
divorce *him* for cruelty – but No. He wouldn't! He *did* just
twist my arm a teeny bit but not enough even to bruise it.
You see what an appalling position I am in. I'm the one
obstacle in the path of your united happiness. Without me in
the way, you would fall gracefully into one another's arms

and go on being noble together for the rest of your lives. If by any chance either of you succumbed to the temptations of the flesh and were unfaithful, there would always be understanding and forgiveness waiting for you in the home. In fact, understanding and forgiveness would be draped all over the house like those rather florid Christmas decorations that the servants make. It would be ideal, and you would both be happy – really happy. I hereby relinquish to you Marion, all my claims upon David. The house is yours and everything in it, except my clothes – you can send them on to me. And I leave you both in my bedroom as a symbol of the perfect faith I have in your joint integrity. (*She goes to the door.*)

DAVID: Alice – I'm sorry I behaved like a cad just now.

MARION: Alice – can't we all three come to an understanding and be pals together.

ALICE: Never! I prefer to go out into the world – alone! It's rather a big thing to do.

DAVID   (*calling her back*): Alice –?

ALICE: What?

DAVID   (*bewildered*): What do you mean by all this? Where are you going? What are you going to do?

ALICE: As somebody so very truly remarked the other day, the existing Divorce laws, put a premium on perjury and adultery! Therefore I am going to find a lover and live in flaming sin – possibly at Claridges. (*Exit* Alice. *There is a slight pause, then* Marion *goes up to* David *and rests her hand on his shoulder.*)

MARION   (*simply*): David – poor old David. – I'm – I'm desperately sorry that all this should have happened –

DAVID   (*with bowed head*) It's all right old thing – it wasn't your fault –

MARION: She'll come back to you – I'll make her come back to you.

DAVID: Good old Marion– (*He pats her hand.*)

MARION: She's upset and nervy – I've been awfully worried about her lately – she's been looking so pale and seedy. She often goes for me and gibes at me, but underneath she's fond of me. I know she is. We understand each other pretty well, Alice and me.

DAVID: She's a good sort all through – Alice! I don't mind her little tantrums – they amuse me –

MARION: Ah, but that's typical of you – you always penetrate through all the tiresome superficialities – and get to the best of everybody –

DAVID: To my mind, we should all try to make ourselves see things
from every point of view –

The curtain slowly falls ...

I Want To Go Home

by

H.F. Maltby

Preface

I Want To Go Home is a comedy about infidelity, and is thus similar in theme and farcical style to a number of French Grand Guignol sex comedies such as Eugène Héros and Léon Abric's *Chop-Chop!* or René Berton's *Tics!* (Hand and Wilson, 2002, 121–54). But evidently what was the stock-in-trade of the Parisian Grand Guignol, and a light and strategic hiatus in an evening of horror, found itself in a very different position in the British theatre in the context of the 1920s: H.F. Maltby's play was deemed far too risqué for public performance and was banned by the Lord Chamberlain's Office. The censor's verdict probably seems highly draconian but it reveals just how problematic – even in comedy – was any suggestion of indecency and immorality. Evidently, no amount of blue pencil interference could have redeemed the play, which evidently for the censor had a fatal depravity at its very core. While Mary in Gladys Unger's *A Man in Mary's Room* is wholly misjudged, Reginald 'Regums' Field is thoroughly guilty. The censor, of course, gave Unger's play fulsome praise, and thus endorsed the comedy of cross-purposes and misinterpretation: the fact that Field gradually and yet inadvertently reveals his guilt was enough to condemn, not just the character, but the whole of Maltby's play.

I Want To Go Home is a slight play, certainly compared to Maltby's other Grand Guignol offerings, especially *The Person Unknown*. Indeed, it is essentially a protracted 'dirty joke' in which an unfaithful husband mistakes his wife for his mistress while intoxicated. Nonetheless it is a well-crafted and skilfully written work with a number of interesting qualities. The play contains an engagingly comic degree of sexual and class satire with its depiction of a dysfunctional marital relationship predominantly from the perspective of a married, middle-class woman, Mrs Fanny Field. The class satire builds when the maidservant Carrie assists her frigid mistress in her attempts to make herself more sexually appealing to her husband. The play offers great opportunities for comic interpretation in performance with its elements of satire and highly comic dialogic exchanges (including the Fields' 'baby language'). In addition, it is not without a genuine degree of eroticism, especially in Fanny's attempts to seduce her husband.

I Want To Go Home

A Comedy in One Act
by
H.F. Maltby

Mrs Field ... *She*
Carrie ... *Maid (1st Accomplice)*
Mrs Gregory ... *Friend (2nd Accomplice)*
Mr Field ... *Him*

Scene: *Living room of the Fields' Flat, Maida Vale*

THE SCENE *represents a well-furnished sitting room in a London flat. There are two doors. The door on right leads to passage and thence to front door, the one at back to bed room. When the latter door is opened it affords a glimpse of twin beds etc. There is a Chesterfield down stage left.*

As the curtain rises, Mrs Field is discovered seated knitting. She is a woman of about 30 or 35 who might be attractive but for the fact that she has not made the slightest attempt to be so. Her hair is plastered down and her dress suggests the Sunday School teacher. After a slight pause, bell heard off. Mrs Field looks up and listens. After a slight pause, Carrie the maid, enters and announces.

CARRIE: Mrs. Gregory!

(Mrs Field *rises as* Mrs Gregory *enters. The latter is a very attractive woman of about thirty – she is dressed in the height of fashion*)

MRS FIELD: Oh, my dear, it is sweet of you to come in. (Carrie *goes off.*) You have no idea how lonely I was feeling I was simply dreading having to spend the whole evening by myself again. (Mrs Gregory *looks a trifle embarrassed.*) Now let me help you off with your things.

MRS GREGORY: I'm afraid my dear, I'm going to disappoint you.

MRS FIELD:	What do you mean?
MRS GREGORY:	I have only come in for a few minutes – I can't possibly stay longer.
MRS FIELD:	Really?
MRS GREGORY:	Really. I have just received a wire from my husband to say that he is returning from Scotland to-night, his train arrives at Euston at eight o'clock, he would never forgive me if I didn't meet him.
MRS FIELD	(*disappointed*): And that means that you will be going almost at once?
MRS GREGORY:	I'm afraid so. I was going to ring you up, but I knew how disappointed you would be, so I thought I would just drop in for a minute or two.
MRS FIELD:	Thank you, dear.
MRS GREGORY:	Where is your husband?
MRS FIELD	(*pointing to bedroom*): In there, dressing.
MRS GREGORY:	Is he going out again to-night?
MRS FIELD:	He goes out every night – I never see him. Off to business the first thing in the morning – back home at half past six, dresses and then off to his club till midnight. Auction Bridge! Perpetual, everlasting Auction Bridge. I think the man who invented auction bridge ought to be executed.
MRS GREGORY:	Perhaps it was a woman.
MRS FIELD:	What do you mean?
MRS GREGORY:	A woman who invented auction bridge.
MRS FIELD:	Oh, I thought you meant to suggest that –
MRS GREGORY:	Oh no, it isn't Murray's Club that he goes to, is it?
MRS FIELD:	No, the Junior Eccentric.
MRS GREGORY:	Well, that's quite safe then.
MRS FIELD:	I'm sure I don't know what you infer.
MRS GREGORY:	I don't infer anything. (*Clock strikes 11.*) What-ever time is that?
MRS FIELD:	Oh, it is only seven.
MRS GREGORY:	But it struck eleven.
MRS FIELD:	Yes, it is four hours out. I was winding it up this morning, and I must have done something dreadful to it.
MRS GREGORY:	Oh! (*pause*) I say, Fanny, I'm awfully distressed about you.
MRS FIELD:	Why?
MRS GREGORY:	I mean about your home life. I know you are not happy. I wish I could do something for you.
MRS FIELD:	I wish you could do something for Reginald – he is the one who is to blame.
MRS GREGORY:	Yes, yes, I know, dear, I know, but do you think he is

	wholly to blame?
MRS FIELD:	You don't suggest that I –
MRS GREGORY:	A little, dear, a little.
MRS FIELD:	In what way?
MRS GREGORY:	Well, fancy calling him Reginald.
MRS FIELD:	Why not? It's his name.
MRS GREGORY:	I would have thought you would have been on sufficiently good terms with him to have called him 'Reggie'.
MRS FIELD:	I hate abbreviations.
MRS GREGORY:	I'm afraid you don't do so *very* much to make his home life attractive for him – do you?
MRS FIELD:	I'm sure I do. Isn't everything here comfortable? Aren't his meals always well-cooked and punctual?
MRS GREGORY:	Yes, yes, dear – but aren't there other things that a man thinks of?
MRS FIELD:	What other things?
MRS GREGORY:	Well, for instance, you never allow him to have a drink in the house.
MRS FIELD:	Certainly not! I disapprove of drink.
MRS GREGORY:	But he doesn't. Consequently he goes where he knows he can get it – to his club. You won't allow him to smoke in here.
MRS FIELD:	Smoke ruins the curtains.
MRS GREGORY:	He sees that you think more about the curtains than his comfort – so he goes where he can smoke in comfort at his club. And then you –
MRS FIELD:	Me?
MRS GREGORY:	Forgive me, dear, but I'm telling you for your own good. You know you are a pretty woman, but no one would think so to look at you now.
MRS FIELD:	Thank you.
MRS GREGORY:	Don't be cross, Fanny darling. You've got lovely hair – but it is all brushed back from your forehead – why, you mightn't have any hair at all. You've got a beautiful neck – and yet you keep it all covered up. You have beautiful arms – but I bet you never let him see them. You've got lovely –
MRS FIELD:	I don't know if you know it, but you're getting very vulgar, Mabel.
MRS GREGORY:	No, I'm not! It is you who are prudish! Don't you think your husband married you as much for your neck, arms, hair and face as he did for yourself! And having married you he expects to see more of them than – well, other people. He wants to feel that they are his – he wants to

	possess you. Why, I don't believe that you ever allow him to put his arm around your waist or kiss you.
MRS FIELD:	I'm not going to go into these matters.
MRS GREGORY:	You'll have to, my dear, if you want to keep your husband – otherwise he'll go where he can get what he wants.
MRS FIELD:	I suppose you are going to say to his club?
MRS GREGORY:	Well, he's quite safe if he only goes to the Junior Eccentric. (*rises*) Do you think Carrie would get a taxi for me?
MRS FIELD:	Yes, of course. (*rings*)
MRS GREGORY:	I know you simply loathe me for having said all this, dear, but I know I'm right. (*Carrie enters*)
MRS FIELD:	Will you see if you can get a taxi for Mrs Gregory? (*Carrie is about to go*)
MRS GREGORY:	And will you please bring in that bag I left in the hall?
CARRIE:	Yes, mum! (*goes out*)
MRS GREGORY:	I have been thinking about all this for a long time – until I felt I simply had to tell you, and now I have done so. I have taken the liberty of bringing in an outfit for you – so that you can start operations at once.
MRS FIELD:	An outfit? (*Carrie enters with dress bag*)
MRS GREGORY:	Put it on the table, will you please? That's a new maid, isn't it? (*Carrie does so and goes off – Mrs Gregory opens bag*)
MRS FIELD:	Yes, she's only here temporarily. I don't know what she is like yet.
MRS GREGORY:	Oh, really I am surprised at you Fanny! Look at your new maid, she is old enough to be your mother – and yet she knows more about making herself attractive than you do. (*Mrs Field seems struck by this remark. Mrs Gregory takes out two bottles of champagne.*)
MRS FIELD:	What is that?
MRS GREGORY:	Champagne – Malt [*sic*] and Chandon – just see if that won't tempt him to stay in to-night. And here is a case of cigars. They belong to Arthur – but he won't mind. Those are for him – now these are for you – (*takes out small box and opens it*)
MRS FIELD:	What are those?
MRS GREGORY:	Just a few harmless cosmetics.
MRS FIELD:	But you don't suggest that *I* should put them on my face?
MRS GREGORY:	Why not?
MRS FIELD:	But those are what are used by actresses.
MRS GREGORY:	On the *stage* – and by all the best people *off*. And here is a bottle of scent.

MRS FIELD   (*reading label*): Atkinson's 'Chepyre'.

MRS GREGORY: I never yet knew a man who wasn't fascinated by it. Try it on your husband and watch the effect. (*Enter Carrie.*)

CARRIE: The taxi, mum.

MRS GREGORY: Thank you, Carrie. Good day, Fanny darling. *Do! Do! Do!* I'm so anxious that you should be happy and I'm sure it rests with you. (*kisses her*) Don't bother to come out of this beautiful warm room. Good-bye! (*Goes out with Carrie – Mrs Field stands lost in thought. Street door heard to close. She picks up champagne and hesitates, then puts it on corner of sideboard – then She takes out two glasses and puts them on sideboard – then the cigars. Next She goes to mirror and looks at herself, then with an impulse she opens blouse at throat and turns neck back – She seems pleased with effect – She takes out hairpins – Her hair falls down in ringlets – She again seems pleased then she goes to cosmetic box and takes out rouge – hesitates and tries a little on her cheek – seems pleased and tries more. Carrie enters and stands watching her.*)

CARRIE   (*at length*): Oh, mum, I'm so glad!

MRS FIELD   (*turning guiltily*): Carrie!

CARRIE: Oh, mum, I *am* so pleased!

MRS FIELD: About what?

CARRIE: That at last you are trying to make yourself look nice.

MRS FIELD: What do you mean?

CARRIE: Oh, mum, my 'eart as bled for you – straight it 'as! Sitting 'ere all alone and neglected, night after night, while the master 'as gone out gawd knows where.

MRS FIELD: How dare you, Carrie! He goes to his club.

CARRIE: I don't doubt it! But there is clubs and clubs!

MRS FIELD   (*suspiciously*): Mixed clubs, you mean?

CARRIE   (*winking*): Yes, mum.

MRS FIELD   (*annoyed with herself for listening to Carrie*): I'd rather you didn't say anything against your master, please.

CARRIE: I'm not saying against him, mum, I'm a club woman myself.

MRS FIELD: You?

CARRIE: Yes, I'm not too old for a bit of fun. But I don't go to my club like this – bless you, no. I make myself attractive – men don't want women who are not, and if I was married I'd make myself very attractive every night – just to keep my old man at home. (*Pause – Mrs Field is thinking.*) You don't want to be too frightened of that, mum … (*pointing*

	to rouge) Put it on thick!
MRS FIELD:	But I don't know how to use it!
CARRIE:	But I does – will you let me?
MRS FIELD	(*handing box to Carrie*): Don't overdo it, Carrie.
CARRIE:	Don't be afraid of that – there are some things you can't overdo, and this is one of them. (*She dabs it on Mrs Field's face.*) I don't say you wants to spread it as thick as we did when I was a girl – of course I spent my childhood in the Edgeware Road – and the Edgeware Road is thicker than Maida Vale. But men is men all the world over. There was a song they used to sing when I was in my prime 'A little bit of sugar on the top.' And it's just that little bit of sugar on the top that they all wants.
MRS FIELD:	You seem to know a lot about men, Carrie
CARRIE	(*pencilling Mrs Field's eyebrows*): I was considered a hepicure.
MRS FIELD:	And had you many admirers?
CARRIE:	Their name was legions. But I'm not boasting – any girl can get a boy – the job is to get rid of him when you are tired of him.
MRS FIELD:	And I can't keep my husband.
CARRIE:	You will when I've finished with you. You know what your trouble is?
MRS FIELD:	What?
CARRIE:	You ain't flighty!
MRS FIELD:	Flighty?
CARRIE:	Oh, you 'as to be flighty!
MRS FIELD:	But I can't be flighty.
CARRIE:	'Ave you ever tried? It's easy enough – my job is to stop being flighty when I don't want to be. It ain't no good going in for marriage with kid gloves on – it's a skin game – that's what it is. And the biggest curse in marriage is them dressing rooms. You don't 'ear of many divorces among the poor people do you – why? Because they don't 'ave no dressing rooms next to their bedrooms, and husband and wife get to know each other. Some people might think what I'm saying is vulgar – but it's true! (*Steps aside revealing Mrs Field made up like what is usually accepted as a flash chorus girl.*) Now, how's that?
MRS FIELD	(*looking into mirror*): Oh, Carrie, are you sure it isn't too much?
CARRIE:	Not it! Not if you carry it off!
MRS FIELD:	Carry it off?

CARRIE: Well, you've got to dress in keeping with it, as the saying goes.

MRS FIELD: But I haven't anything in keeping with this.

CARRIE: Yes you 'ave. What about that kokomono your old man gave you?

MRS FIELD: What, that flashy, blue thing?

CARRIE: It ain't flashy! It's decolty – just the thing the men like – don't you think 'e gave it you because 'e wanted to see you in it? And yet you never wear it – it's made my mouth water every time I've seen it in the wardrobe. What couldn't I do if I 'ad it? I'd be a proper Margot, I would! I'd put it on if I was you and act flighty.

MRS FIELD: Act flighty!

CARRIE: Yes, same as the girls does at the War Office.

MRS FIELD (*nervously*): But I can't!

CARRIE: Try. You'll be surprised 'ow easy it comes. But you must have plenty of scent – that 'elps.

MRS FIELD: I've got scent.

CARRIE: Eau de Cologne and Lavender water – I know. That ain't no cop – you want something what's voluptious.

MRS FIELD (*pointing to bottle that Mrs Gregory has brought*): Is that more like it?

CARRIE (*looks at bottle – spills a drop on her finger and sniffs*): That'll fetch 'im! That's the stuff to give 'em! (*Mr Field is heard singing off.*)

MRS FIELD: There's the master! What shall I do? I can't let him see me like this!

CARRIE: Don't talk so silly – he'll be tickled to death. I bet 'e won't want to go out to-night when 'e sees you.

MRS FIELD: Oh, don't leave me, Carrie. My courage seems to have gone. I don't feel a bit – er – flighty!

CARRIE (*taking out flask*): Then try a drop of this, old dear! I always keep it by me for emergencies.

MRS FIELD: What is it?

CARRIE: Gin! It's a great comfort to us girls. Don't be afraid of it – take a good swig. (*Mrs Field does so.*) Now how's that? Feel more like it now?

MRS FIELD: It does warm one to it – doesn't it? (*Door latch turns.*) Oh, here he is! (*is very frightened*)

CARRIE: Don't be frightened! Act flighty and 'e's your's for life. (*She goes out as Field enters – he is in evening dress – he hardly bestows a glance on his wife, but goes down to Chesterfield and sits and commences to put on shoes.*)

FIELD: Who was in here just now?

MRS FIELD	(*ill at ease*): Only Carrie.
FIELD:	But before that?
MRS FIELD:	Mrs. Gregory.
FIELD:	Oh, has she gone?
MRS FIELD:	Yes, her husband arrives from Scotland to-night and she is meeting him. (*nervous*)
FIELD:	Oh! (*pause*)

(*Mrs Field makes one or two attempts to 'act flighty' but her courage fails her each time. Business: Field has now got his shoes on – he rises and crosses towards door as if to go out.*)

MRS FIELD	('*acting flighty*'): Going out, darling?
FIELD	(*feeling in his pocket for something and not noticing her*): Yes.
MRS FIELD:	Where?
FIELD:	Oh, the usual place. The club. Don't sit up for me if I'm late – I shall be alright. (*makes as if to go*)
MRS FIELD:	Reggie, darling. Won't you stop with me for a change?
FIELD	(*still without looking at her and with an expression of annoyance*): Afraid I can't. I promised one or two men that I would take a hand at auction and –
MRS FIELD:	Can't they find anyone to take your place, darling?
FIELD:	I can't let them down. I promised old Colonel Barham – he's a funny sort of chap – won't play with anyone but me – some other evening. (*Is going out without having glanced at her.*)
MRS FIELD	(*desperately*): Reggie darling – won't you have a drink before you go? (*He is so surprised at this that he turns and sees her.*)
FIELD:	Eh? Good lord! What have you been doing?
MRS FIELD	(*floating across stage*): Only a little surprise for you, darling. (*puts her arms round his neck and kisses him – leaving some of the lip-salve from her lips on his face*)
FIELD:	Well I'm blowed!
MRS FIELD:	You're not cross with me?
FIELD:	Cross with you – no – but my word – what a change?
MRS FIELD:	A nice change?
FIELD:	Any change is nice from – (*pulls up*)
MRS FIELD	(*floating across stage*): A nice little drop of champagne for hubby! (*lifts up bottle*)
FIELD:	Where did that come from?
MRS FIELD:	Bought purposely for hubby.
FIELD:	You've never done that before.

MRS FIELD   (*skittishly*): I'm going to do lots of things I have never done before. (*puts arms around his neck and kisses him*) Open the champagne, darling – wifey'd like a little drop, too. (*He looks at her in surprise.*)

FIELD: Well, *that* is an improvement anyway. (*suddenly*) You haven't been having some already, have you?

MRS FIELD   (*pulling herself up in old frigid way*): How dare you?

FIELD   (*quickly*): I'm sorry dear – I'm sorry. (*He commences to open bottle – She brings the two glasses on tray and puts them on small table by Chesterfield – He opens bottle and pours out wine – She edges up to him – He hands her a glass and takes one himself – is a bit ill at ease – She clinks glass against his.*)

MRS FIELD: Good health!

FIELD: Er – oh – cheerio! (*Drains glass and puts it down – she is quite close to him – he hesitates – then puts his arm round her waist.*)

MRS FIELD   (*in approved fashion*): Oh, stop it, you mustn't! (*He draws her to him – Her eyes close in a voluptuous manner – He kisses her once or twice – the champagne is spilt – She breaks away and floats away.*) A little more champagne for Reggums! (*He looks quickly at her as she fills his glass.*)

FIELD: Why do you call me Reggums?

MRS FIELD: Why not?

FIELD: Nothing! Only it's a pet name I had when I was at school. (*She hands him glass.*)

MRS FIELD   (*indicating Chesterfield*): Reggums sit down there. (*Pushes him into it and leans over back – face next to his – He puts down glass and suddenly draws her to him over back of Chesterfield.*)

FIELD: Fanny, I – (*Kisses her and she closes eyes – then she breaks away and floats across room saying extravagantly.*)

MRS FIELD: I'm just going to change, Reggums, I won't be a minute. (*She goes up to bedroom – He finishes glass at one gulp and pours himself out another – She has commenced unfastening her dress but comes down.*) A cigar, darling? (*Hands him case – He looks surprised.*)

FIELD: May I smoke in here?

MRS FIELD: Reggums may do anything he likes in here. (*He catches her hand and pulls her to him – She skittishly pulls it away and floats up to bedroom singing – is seen taking off dress – He gives a sigh of satisfaction and drains glass – re-fills and lights cigar.*) Nice cigar?

FIELD: Splendid! But what is the meaning of all this?

MRS FIELD: Shan't tell.

FIELD: Is it somebody's birthday?

MRS FIELD: It is going to be a birthday every day. (*He drains glass and re-fills – She comes down in petticoat and camisole, singing.*)

MRS FIELD: Doesn't Fanny get a drop?

FIELD   (*seeing her*): Of course Fanny gets a drop. (*He is about to pour her out some but she puts her arms round his neck and sips from his glass – He fondles her arms.*) It seems so strange sitting here like this with you.

MRS FIELD: Stranger things are going to happen to-night.

FIELD   (*the wine is getting into his head*): My word, why haven't you always been like this? If you had I wouldn't have had need to have gone so often to my club.

MRS FIELD: Do you want to go now?

FIELD: No, I want to stay with you. I feel I never understood you before.

MRS FIELD: Here's to a better understanding of each other.

FIELD: Here's to a better understanding of each other. (*He empties glass – She tries to refill it but bottle is empty.*)

MRS FIELD: Oh, you greedy! You've finished all the wine. You'll have to open another bottle.

FIELD: Is there another?

MRS FIELD   (*skittishly*): Perhaps. (*Rises to get it – He holds her arm and kisses her before he lets her go – She gets bottle.*) Now you must open it.

FIELD: Oh, I'll open it alright. (*Rises and opens bottle. He pours out wine and chuckles.*) Do you know what I'm thinking of?

MRS FIELD: What?

FIELD: Fancy our having been content with twin beds all these years.

MRS FIELD: Oh, you naughty!

FIELD: No, I'm not!

MRS FIELD: Yes you are. (*slaps him*)

FIELD: No, I'm not. (*slaps her*)

MRS FIELD: Well, anyhow, I'm going to turn over a new leaf.

FIELD   (*raising glass*): Here's to the new leaf.

MRS FIELD: Oh, you do say such things. (*She raises glass and just takes a sip – He drains his.*) Now I'm going to put on my kimona.

FIELD: No, no, don't.

MRS FIELD: Why not?

FIELD:	I like you best like this.
MRS FIELD:	But I'll look nicer when I've got my kimona on.
FIELD:	I don't want you to look any nicer – you're nice enough for me. (*takes her arm*)
MRS FIELD:	Let me go!
FIELD:	I shan't!
MRS FIELD:	You shall. (*Frees herself – dances round the room – he follows her unsteadily – business – she singing and 'carrying on'. He catches her and kisses her – then she escapes and runs into bedroom. He, out of breath, sits and drinks the champagne she has left and pours out another glass. She comes in, in kimona.*) Regums can't catch me.
FIELD:	Yes, he can.
MRS FIELD:	No, he can't. (*He chases her, catches her and kisses her and she escapes. He sits and drinks another glass. She appears with a bottle of scent and freely sprinkles it on herself and then comes and pours it on him.*)
FIELD:	Oh, that scent is lovely.
MRS FIELD:	Regums like it?
FIELD:	It's beautiful!
MRS FIELD	(*holding her face to his*): Boo'ful?
FIELD	(*kissing her*): Boo'ful?
MRS FIELD:	Reggums never smelt it before?
FIELD:	Yes, lots of times. (*She looks surprised.*)
MRS FIELD:	Another little drink for Regums?
FIELD:	Wouldn't do him any harm. (*She pours out glass – He drinks.*) You look beautiful in that kimona. (*He is now quite drunk.*)
MRS FIELD:	Regums gave it to me.
FIELD:	It was a red one I gave you.
MRS FIELD:	No, blue.
FIELD:	Red.
MRS FIELD:	Blue. (*playfully*)
FIELD:	Red.
MRS FIELD:	Blue.
FIELD:	It looked like red the last time.
MRS FIELD:	But I have never worn it before.
FIELD:	Yes, you have. Red kimona and the scent and the champagne – (*drinks*). All beautiful and lovely. (*lies back in Chesterfield*)
MRS FIELD:	Regums tired?
FIELD:	Yes.
MRS FIELD:	Regums want to go to sleep? (*lifts his feet and puts them*

on Chesterfield)

FIELD: Yes, with your arms round me.

MRS FIELD: Like that. *(kneels beside him arms round him and face close to his)*

FIELD: Yes, like that. *(then drowsily)* You're the loveliest woman I've ever met. I keep on telling you that and I'll go on telling you till I die. I could eat you, you're so beautiful. I like to stroke your beautiful hair as it hangs over your beautiful shoulders. I love to kiss you and hug you and – *(Murmurs on and goes to sleep. She looks at him for a second, then she tries to disengage herself.)* Don't go away from me. *(Pause – she tries again and succeeds.)*

MRS FIELD: Nasty tight shoes – he can't be comfortable in them. *(takes them off)*

FIELD: God bless you – you're always good to me.

MRS FIELD: Nasty tight collar – he can't breathe with that on. *(takes it and tie off and undoes the front of his shirt)*

FIELD: I love the touch of your hands round my neck. Tickle me again, I like it. *(business)*

MRS FIELD: Nasty tight waistcoat. *(Undoes waistcoat.)*

FIELD: You're an angel that's what you are. *(She smiles triumphantly as much as to say 'I've won him'. The clock commences to strike 12. He starts up.)* What's that?

MRS FIELD: Only the clock.

FIELD *(when it has finished striking)*: Twelve o'clock!

MRS FIELD *(putting arms round him and snuggling close to him)*: No, it isn't – it's only eight – the striker is wrong.

FIELD: You've tried to tell me that before – but it won't do – it's twelve o'clock. *(sits up and feels for shoes)*

MRS FIELD: What are you doing?

FIELD *(waving her aside)*: Leave me alone. *(gets his shoes and begins to put them on)*

MRS FIELD: You're not going out now?

FIELD: Leave me alone.

MRS FIELD: You're not going to leave me all alone.

FIELD *(who has got shoes on – rises)*: I must.

MRS FIELD *(tearfully)*: But won't you stop with me for just a little while longer.

FIELD: Much as I'd like to it can't be done.

MRS FIELD: Why not?

FIELD: Can't be done. It's too bad of you – it's too bad of you really it is – to tempt me like this. You're a dear little girl and I love you dearly, but as I have told you before, I won't stop all night with you. *(indignantly)* You seem to forget that I'm a respectable married man, Trixie, and I must go home. (*Lurches towards door. Mrs Field looks at him in horror. Curtain cue.*)

MRS FIELD   (*as curtain is falling*): Trixie? Trixie? But my name's Fanny. Here, Reggie, Reggie! (*follows him to door*)

CURTAIN

Appendix 1

London's Grand Guignol 1920–1922

First Series

1 September 1920 at 8 p.m. [subsequently 8.30 daily and 2.30 Thursdays]
How to be Happy, a moral by Pierre Veber (25 performances, ended 25
   September 1920)
G.H.Q. Love, a play by Sewell Collins from the French of Pierre Rehm (110
   performances)
The Hand of Death, a drama by André de Lorde and Alfred Binet (110
   performances)
Oh, Hell!!!, a revuette by Reginald Arkell and Russell Thorndike (110
   performances)

27 September 1920 programme changes to:
G.H.Q. Love
The Medium, by Pierre Mille and C. de Vylars (85 performances)
What Did Her Husband Say?, a comedy by H.F. Maltby (120 performances,
   ended 15 January 1921)
The Hand of Death
Oh, Hell!!!

Second Series

15 December 1920
What Did Her Husband Say?, a comedy by H.F. Maltby (35 performances)
Eight O'clock, a drama by Reginald Berkeley (107 performances)
A Man in Mary's Room, an original comedy by Gladys Unger (107
   performances)
Private Room Number 6, a drama by André de Lorde (107 performances)
The Tragedy of Mr Punch, in a prologue and one act by Reginald Arkell and
   Russell Thorndike (107 performances)

17 January 1921 second series programme changes to:

A Man in Mary's Room

The Shortest Story of All, an episode by George E. Morrison (72 performances)

Private Room Number 6

The Person Unknown, a drama by H.F. Maltby (72 performances)

Eight O'clock

The Tragedy of Mr Punch

Third Series

28 March 1921

Gaspers, an episode by Sewell Collins (104 performances)

The Love Child, a play by Frederick Fenn and Richard Pryce (104 performances)

Seven Blind Men, a drama from the French of Lucien Descaves (104 performances)

Dead Man's Pool, a play by Victor and T.C. Bridges (104 performances)

The Kill, a drama by Maurice Level (adapted by W.H. Harris) (104 performances)

The Chemist, a comedy from the French of Max Maurey (adapted by Blanche Weiner) (104 performances)

Fourth Series

29 June 1921

Latitude 15° South, a drama of the sea by Victor MacClure (117 performances)

The Vigil, a drama by André de Lorde (117 performances)

Rounding the Triangle, an original comedy by E. Crawshay-Williams (117 performances)

The Old Women, from the French of André de Lorde adapted by Christopher Holland (117 performances)

Shepherd's Pie, a comedy from the French of Léon Frapié and Georges Fabri adapted by Sewell Collins (117 performances)

Fifth Series

12 October 1921

Haricot Beans, a farce from the French of MM Pierre Chaine and Robert de Beauplan adapted by Sewell Collins (119 performances)

The Unseen, a drama from the French of J.J. Renaud adapted by Lewis Casson (119 performances)

The Old Story, a comedy from the French of C.H. Hirsch adapted by Hugh McLellan (4 performances)

Fear, a play by André de Lorde (119 performances)

Crime, a drama from the French of Maurice Level adapted by Lewis Casson
      (119 performances)
E. & O. E., an original play by E. Crawshay-Williams (119 performances)

2 December programme changes to:
Haricot Beans
The Unseen
Fear
Crime
E. & O. E.

Sixth Series

25 January 1922
Amends, by E. Crawshay-Williams (72 performances)
Changing Guard, a fantasy by W.G. Nott-Bower (72 performances)
De Mortuis, a play by Stanley Logan (72 performances)
The Regiment, a drama from the French of Robert Francheville adapted by
      Lewis Casson (72 performances)
Cupboard Love, a comedy by E. Crawshay-Williams (72 performances)

Seventh Series

3 April 1922
Amelia's Suitors or Colonel Chutney's First Defeat, a farce of 'The Good Old
      Days' by H.F. Maltby (63 performances)
Progress, a drama by St John Ervine (63 performances)
The Nutcracker Suite, a play by E. Crawshay-Williams (63 performances)
Colombine, a fantasy by Reginald Arkell (63 performances)
At the Telephone, a drama by André de Lorde and Charles Foley (63
      performances) (This script was previously produced at the Wyndham's
      Theatre under the title of *Heard at the Telephone*, 1 March 1912)

Eighth Series

31 May 1922
A Happy New Year, a merry thought from the French of Gustave du Clos
      adapted by Seymour Hicks (29 performances)
The Sisters' Tragedy, a play by Richard Hughes (29 performances)
To Be Continued, a comedy by M. Jean Bastia adapted by Sewell Collins (29
      performances)
The Hand of Death, a drama by André de Lorde and Alfred Binet (29
      performances)
The Better Half, a comedy by Noel Coward (29 performances)

Appendix 2

The Complete Repertoire of London's Grand Guignol 1920–1922

Amelia's Suitors or Colonel Chutney's First Defeat, a farce of 'The Good Old Days' by H.F. Maltby

Amends, by E. Crawshay-Williams

At the Telephone, a drama by André de Lorde and Charles Foley

Better Half, The, a comedy by Noel Coward

Changing Guard, a fantasy by W.G. Nott-Bower

Chemist, The, a comedy from the French of Max Maurey (adapted by Blanche Weiner)

Colombine, a fantasy by Reginald Arkell

Crime, a drama from the French of Maurice Level adapted by Lewis Casson

Cupboard Love, a comedy by E. Crawshay-Williams

De Mortuis, a play by Stanley Logan

Dead Man's Pool, a play by Victor and T.C. Bridges

E. & O. E., an original play by E. Crawshay-Williams

Eight O'clock, a drama by Reginald Berkeley

Fear, a play by André de Lorde

Gaspers, an episode by Sewell Collins

G.H.Q. Love, a play by Sewell Collins from the French of Pierre Rehm

Hand of Death, The, a drama by André de Lorde and Alfred Binet

Happy New Year, A, a merry thought from the French of Gustave du Clos adapted by Seymour Hicks

Haricot Beans, a farce from the French of MM Pierre Chaine and Robert de Beauplan adapted by Sewell Collins

How to be Happy, a moral by Pierre Veber

Kill, The, a drama by Maurice Level (adapted by W. H. Harris)

Latitude 15° South, a drama of the sea by Victor MacClure

Love Child, The, a play by Frederick Fenn and Richard Pryce

Man in Mary's Room, A, an original comedy by Gladys Unger

Medium, The, by Pierre Mille and C. de Vylars

Nutcracker Suite, The, a play by E. Crawshay-Williams

Oh, Hell!!!, a revuette by Reginald Arkell and Russell Thorndike

Old Story, The, a comedy from the French of C. H. Hirsch adapted by Hugh McLellan

Old Women, The, from the French of André de Lorde adapted by Christopher Holland

Person Unknown, The, a drama by H. F. Maltby

Private Room Number 6, a drama by André de Lorde

Progress, a drama by St John Ervine

Regiment, The, a drama from the French of Robert Francheville adapted by Lewis Casson

Rounding the Triangle, an original comedy by E. Crawshay-Williams

Seven Blind Men, a drama from the French of Lucien Descaves

Shepherd's Pie, a comedy from the French of Léon Frapié and Georges Fabri adapted by Sewell Collins

Shortest Story of All, The, an episode by George E. Morrison

Sisters' Tragedy, The, a play by Richard Hughes

To Be Continued, a comedy by M. Jean Bastia adapted by Sewell Collins

Tragedy of Mr Punch, The, in a prologue and one act by Reginald Arkell and Russell Thorndike

Unseen, The, a drama from the French of J.J. Renaud adapted by Lewis Casson

Vigil, The, a drama by André de Lorde

What Did Her Husband Say?, a comedy by H.F. Maltby

Appendix 3

Extract from *Oh, Hell!!! A 'Revuette'*

by Reginald Arkell and Russell Thorndike

MANAGER (*manager/owner of a film studio*): I say, is he very hot? I don't want to crack my lens.

CINDERS: He's not so bad. I'll give the Devil his due.

MANAGER: You know, he'd be all right without her.

MINISTER (*of War – a female*): Her? Who's her?

CINDERS: The missus!

MINISTER: Is the Devil married?

CINDERS: He was!, but she was too 'ot for this place, so she ran away and went on the stage.

MANAGER: Where is she now?

CINDERS: That Jose Levy got hold of her for his Little 'Orrible Theatre.

MINISTER: What's her name?

CINDERS: Dorothy Minto.

MANAGER: Can she act? (*Enter* Dorothy Minto.)

MINTO: What do yer mean? (*To* Cinders) Give these two bits of cheese a couple of free seats. Come 'ere, George Bealby! We'll learn 'em! Can we act? (*She goes off.* Cinders *places two chairs –* Charon *with 'Little Theatre' cap comes out of door and places a placard 'Stage Door' – Enter* Bealby *in coat and hat.*)

BEALBY: Evening, Jock! Anything for me?

CHARON: Nothing for you, Mr. Bealby.

BEALBY: Miss Minto in yet?

CHARON: Not yet, sir.

BEALBY: She's running it rather fine.

CHARON: They've called 'Overture and Beginners'! (Bealby *Exits quickly – Noise of taxi – Enter* Miss Minto.)

MINTO: Hello Jock! What's the house like? Any letters? (Charon *hands her a large pile.*)

CHARON: You've no time to read 'em now, overture's on.

MINTO: Oh Shooks! They'll have to wait. (*Exit.* Charon *moves 'Stage Door' placard.*)

CINDERS   (*having placed two chairs*): Stalls this way! Tickets! Keep that half! (Minister *and* Manager *sit.*) Programme? (Manager *takes programme and hands note.*) Haven't change!

MANAGER: Oh, it's all right! It's only a fiver! (*Exit* Cinders.)

MINISTER: What's the play called?

MANAGER: Can't see! It's smothered in blood! (Cinders *puts on 'House Full' board.*)

MINISTER: What a nasty smell of death!

MANAGER: No, it's only my cigar!

CINDERS   (*enters with wood*) Sh! They're going to begin. (*bangs stage three times*) Oh! Are you there?

MANAGER: I'm not sure. It's so dark.

THE PLAY

(*Enter* Bealby *followed by* Minto)

MINTO: Why are you so strange to-night, Daddy?

BEALBY: Strange?

MINTO: I noticed it at dinner. You scarcely touched your Glaxo. You're not jealous because I'm going to marry Edgar?

BEALBY: No, no! But time is short and my experiment –

MINTO: Your experiment? Oh, tell me about it, Daddy? Look, I'll sit here, with you beside me, just as we used to in the dear old days at Brixton.

MANAGER: Horrible!

MINISTER: Well, don't look at them.

MINTO: There! Now you can tell me. I know I'm only a silly little thing, but I will try to understand. I make experiments too!

BEALBY: You make experiments, child?

MINTO: Yes! I mixed the salad to-night.

BEALBY: Salad? Salad? Was there lettuce in the salad?

MINTO: Of course, of course! There's always lettuce in a salad.

MANAGER: Oh, I can't stand this!

MINISTER: Oh well, shut your eyes and think of something else.

BEALBY: Yes. There's always lettuce in a salad.

MINTO: Why, how strange you are to-night, Daddy!

BEALBY: But how rarely we see a human being eating salad like a rabbit.

MINTO: But does that matter?

BEALBY: Of course it matters! We have always subscribed to the Brown Sequard Theory with regard to the mastication of lettuce. Brown Sequard, you remember, maintained that the curious formation of the human lower jaw was responsible for this. No, no! My theory is quite different. It is the brain which is responsible and not the lower jaw. Given a human being with the brain of a rabbit, and that human being will eat lettuce like a rabbit.

MINTO: But the opportunities of testing must be so very rare.

BEALBY: Exactly! Do you love me very dearly?

MINTO: You know I do. Ever since Grannie died.

BEALBY: Then pass me the corkscrew.

MINTO: Yes, Daddy! What are you going to do?

BEALBY: Try my new theory. I'm going to pull out your brain with this corkscrew and substitute the brain of a rabbit. (Manager *wails*.)

MINISTER: Shut up!

MINTO: No, no! You must be mad!

BEALBY: I shall try! I shall try! (*comic business of fight*)

MANAGER: He's strangling her with the bell rope. (*He operates.*)

BEALBY: Empty. She hasn't got a brain. (Manager *faints*.)

MINISTER: What's the matter?

MANAGER: I've fainted!

MINISTER: No, no. It's syncope! Pass me the electrodes. (*business with camera – six o'clock strikes*)

CINDERS: It's six o'clock! You can see the Devil now.

MANAGER: Six o'clock!

MINISTER: What's the matter?

MANAGER: Another syncope! I'm terribly syncopated this evening!

CINDERS: Mr. Nicolas, you're wanted!

(Curtain *as before with* Devil's *entrance*)

Bibliography

Barker, Clive, 'Theatre and Society: the Edwardian legacy, the First World War and the inter-war years', in Barker and Gale (eds), *British Theatre between the Wars, 1918–1939* (Cambridge: Cambridge University Press, 2000)

Barker, Clive and Maggie Gale (eds), *British Theatre between the Wars, 1918–1939* (Cambridge: Cambridge University Press, 2000)

Boal, Augusto, *The Rainbow of Desire: The Boal Method of Theatre and Therapy* (London: Routledge, 1995)

Casson, John, *Lewis and Sybil: A Memoir* (London: Collins, 1972)

Clarke, Peter, *Hope and Glory: Britain 1900–2000* (2nd edn) (Harmondsworth: Penguin, 2004)

Conrad, Joseph, *Collected Letters of Joseph Conrad Volume 7* (edited by Laurence Davies and J. H. Stape) (Cambridge: Cambridge University Press, 2002)

Conrad, Joseph, *Notes on Life and Letters* (London: Dent, 1921)

Conrad, Joseph, *Three Plays* (London: Methuen, 1934)

Coward, Noël, *Autobiography* (London: Methuen, 1986)

Crawshay-Williams, Eliot, *Five Grand Guignol Plays* (London: Samuel French, 1924)

Curtis, James, *James Whale: A New World of Gods and Monsters* (Minneapolis: Minnesota University Press, 2003)

Deák, Frantisek, 'The Grand Guignol', *The Drama Review* (March 1974), pp. 34–52

Devlin, Diana, *A Speaking Part: Lewis Casson and the Theatre of his Time* (London: Hodder & Stoughton, 1982)

Ervine, St. John, *The Organised Theatre: A Plea in Civics* (London: George Allen & Unwin, 1924)

——, *The Theatre in My Time* (London: Rich & Cowan, 1933)

Findlater, Richard, *Banned! A Review of Theatrical Censorship in Britain* (London: MacGibbon and Kee, 1967)

Galsworthy, John, 'Introduction', *Laughing Anne and One Day More* (London: Castle, 1924)

Goldstein, Robert Justin, *Political Censorship of the Arts and the Press in Nineteenth-Century Europe* (New York: St Martin's Press, 1989)

Gordon, Mel, *The Grand Guignol: Theatre of Fear and Terror* (New York: Amok Press, 1988; rev. edn New York: Da Capo Press, 1997)

Grams, Jr., Martin, *Inner Sanctum Mysteries: Behind the Creaking Door* (Churchville, MD: OTR Publishing, 2002)

Hand, Richard J. 'Conrad and the Reviewers: *The Secret Agent* on Stage', *The Conradian* (vol. 26, no. 2, 2001) pp. 1–67

Hand, Richard J. 'Proliferating Horrors: Survival Horror and the *Resident Evil* franchise" in Hantke (ed.), *Horror Film: Marketing and Creating Fear* (Jackson: University of Mississippi Press, 2004)

Hand, Richard J. *Terror on the Air: Horror Radio in America, 1931–52* (Jefferson: McFarland, 2006)

Hand, Richard J. *The Theatre of Joseph Conrad: Reconstructed Fictions* (London: Palgrave, 2005)

Hand, Richard J. and Michael Wilson, 'The Grand-Guignol: Aspects of Theory and Practice', *Theatre Research International* (vol. 25, no. 3, 2000) pp. 266–75

——, *Grand-Guignol: The French Theatre of Horror* (Exeter: University of Exeter Press, 2002)

Harding, James, *Gerald du Maurier: The Last Actor-Manager* (London: Hodder & Stoughton, 1989)

Hardy, Thomas, *The Collected Letters of Thomas Hardy Volume Five: 1914–1919*, edited by R. Little Purdy, and M. Millgate (Oxford: Clarendon Press, 1985)

Homrighous, Mary, 'The Grand Guignol', unpublished Ph.D dissertation, Northwestern University, 1963

Hughes, Richard, *Plays* (London: Phoenix Library, 1928)

James, Henry, *Henry James Letters IV: 1895–1916*, edited by Leon Edel (Cambridge, MA: Harvard University Press, 1984)

Johnston, John, *The Lord Chamberlain's Blue Pencil* (London: Hodder & Stoughton, 1990)

McPherson, Mervyn (ed.), *The Grand Guignol Review 1921* (London: 1921)

Maltby, H. F., *Ring Up The Curtain* (London: Hutchinson, 1950)

Mowat, Charles Loch, *Britain Between the Wars 1918–40* (London: Methuen, 1955)

Nicholson, Steve, *The Censorship of British Drama, Vol. I, 1900–1968* (Exeter: University of Exeter Press, 2003)

Nicoll, Allardyce, *English Drama 1900–30: The Beginnings of the Modern Period* (Cambridge: Cambridge University Press, 1973)

Parker, John, *Who's Who in Theatre* (publisher unknown: 1924)

Partington, Wilfred, 'Joseph Conrad Behind the Scenes', *The Conradian* (vol. 25, no. 2, 2000), pp. 177–84

Pellizzi, Camillo, *English Drama: The Last Great Phase*, translated by Rowan

Williams (London: Macmillan, 1935)

Pierron, Agnès, *Le Grand Guignol: le théâtre des peurs de la belle époque* (Paris: Robert Laffont, 1995)

Poel, William, *What is Wrong with the Stage* (London: George Allen & Unwin, 1920)

Shellard, Dominic and Steve Nicholson (with Miriam Handley), *The Lord Chamberlain Regrets ...: A History of British Theatre Censorship* (London: The British Library, 2004)

Smith, Andrew, *Victorian Demons: Medicine, Masculinity and the Gothic at the fin de siècle* (Manchester: Manchester University Press, 2004)

Sprigge, Elizabeth, *Sybil Thorndike Casson* (London: Victor Gollancz, 1971)

Stevenson, John, *British Society, 1914–45* (Harmondsworth: Penguin, 1984)

Stokes, John, 'Body Parts: the success of the thriller in the inter-war years' in C. Barker and M. Gale (eds), *British Theatre between the Wars, 1918–1939* (Cambridge: Cambridge University Press, 2000)

Thomson, Peter, *On Actors and Acting* (Exeter: University of Exeter Press, 2000)

Thorndike, Russell, *Sybil Thorndike* (London: Thornton Butterworth, 1950)

Trewin, J. C., *Sybil Thorndike* (London: Rockliff, 1955)

——, *The Gay Twenties: A Decade of the Theatre* (London: MacDonald, 1958)

Wheatley, Alison E., 'Laughing Anne: an Almost Unbearable Spectacle', *Conradiana* (vol. 34, nos 1–2, 2002), pp. 63–76

Index

Index entries in **bold italic** type relate to illustrations or their related captions